CSI

TOLD

YOU

LIES

Meshel Laurie is a comedian and radio and television personality. She has been the host of ABC's *Stand Up!*, the co-host of Ten's *This Week Live* and a regular guest on shows such as *Rove Live*, *The Glass House*, *Can of Worms*, *Spicks and Specks*, *Good News Week*, *The Circle* and *Adam Hills: In Gordon Street Tonight*. She is the author of *The Fence-Painting Fortnight of Destiny*, *Buddhism for the Unbelievably Busy*, *Buddhism for Break-ups* and *Bad Buddhist*, and co-hosts the podcast *Australian True Crime* with Emily Webb.

MESHEL LAURIE

CSI TOLD YOU LIES

Giving victims a voice
through forensics

EBURY
PRESS

EBURY PRESS

UK | USA | Canada | Ireland | Australia
India | New Zealand | South Africa | China

Penguin
Random House
Australia

Ebury Press is part of the Penguin Random House group of companies
whose addresses can be found at global.penguinrandomhouse.com.

First published by Ebury in 2021

Cover images by Ioannis Tsotras/Getty Images (skull) and
oleksii arseniuk/Getty Images (forensic rulers)

Cover design by James Rendall © Penguin Random House Australia Pty Ltd

Typeset in 12/18 pt Sabon by Midland Typesetters, Australia

Printed and bound in Australia by Griffin Press, part of Ovato,
an accredited ISO AS/NZS 14001 Environmental Management
Systems printer

A catalogue record for this
book is available from the
National Library of Australia

ISBN 978 1 76089 800 7

penguin.com.au

MIX
Paper from
responsible sources
FSC® C009448

This book is dedicated to:

Hae Min Lee, Mary Ann Nichols, Annie Chapman, Elizabeth Stride, Catherine Eddowes, Mary Jane Kelly, Laura Folbigg, Caleb Folbigg, Patrick Folbigg, Sarah Folbigg, Azaria Chamberlain, Jaidyn Leskie, Lauren Barry, Nichole Collins, Helga Wagnegg, David Hookes, Julie Ramage, Jai Farquharson, Tyler Farquharson, Bailey Farquharson, Kim Meredith, Mo Maslin, Evie Maslin, Otis Maslin, Nick Norris, Helen McMahon, Renita Brunton, Margaret Maher, Mersina Halvagis, Kathleen Downes, Nicole Patterson, Eurydice Dixon, Aya Maasarwe, Elizabeth Stevens, Deborah Fream and Natalie Russell.

CONTENTS

INTRODUCTION

'So, why true crime?'

I'm still astounded that anyone finds my foray into true crime odd. I was never asked 'Why daytime television?' or 'Why breakfast radio?', or about anything else I've done over the course of my career, with such a sense of incredulity. Actually, I lie. 'So, why Buddhism?' was big for a while, because I've written a few books on that topic too.

What can I say? I guess I have broad tastes and I like to keep busy.

I started podcasting around 2006 with the guys I was doing a radio show with, and then, in 2014, I decided to start a podcast of my own so that I could interview people for longer than the three minutes our FM radio station allowed. I called it *The Nitty Gritty Committee*.

When I interviewed local true crime author Emily Webb in September 2016, podcasting was still very low-key, although there had already been two significant developments that had changed the course of the medium forever. The first was the Apple podcast app, which had just appeared on our iPhones one day whether we liked it or not, and the second was a certain true crime podcast from 2014.

Traditional media increasingly contends that consumers have shrinking attention spans (hence the three-minute radio interviews). That may be, but we also have ever-expanding commutes, whether we use cars or public transport, which makes the repetitive, old-school radio formula of time, temp, and traffic reports pretty uninspiring. We've also been conditioned over these many years to abhor a vacuum cleaner. Personally, I can't conceive of cleaning the house unless I've chosen an entertainment option up to the task of distracting me. The selection will often take far longer than the chore itself, but I'm not going in without one.

We have an insatiable appetite for entertainment, but more than that, we now want to experience exactly the content we feel like experiencing in the format that suits the activity we're pairing it with and the environment we're in. For those of us who enjoy documentaries and longform journalism but don't have a lot of time to sit still and watch or read something, the podcast was an absolute life-changer. No peak-hour commute, waiting room, solo trip or boring chore has ever been the same.

*

In 2014 journalist Sarah Koenig introduced the world to Hae Min Lee in the weekly podcast *Serial*. Hae was a senior at Woodlawn High School in Baltimore in 1999. Like many of her friends, including her former boyfriend Adnan Syed, Hae kept secrets from her strict immigrant parents as she tried to navigate life as an American teenager, all of which made for compelling fodder when Koenig came to investigate Adnan's conviction for Hae's murder.

Week after week, *Serial* unfolded in meticulous detail. It was at times a story of typical (if cringeworthy) teenage drama and intrigue. We felt the flush of first love in Hae's swooning diary entries detailing her devotion to Adnan. We admired the convoluted ingenuity they employed to speak nightly on the home phone without Hae's mother ever knowing, despite the many obstacles she'd placed in their way.

In the end, though, none of it mattered for the two young people at the heart of the story. Neither of them could be protected by their parents from the evils of the world, and neither would graduate high school alongside their classmates. Hae would be discovered in a shallow grave in Baltimore's Leakin Park, a notoriously popular site for the dumping of bodies, and Adnan would spend the rest of his life in the prison system for leaving her there.

For her part, Sarah Koenig did much more than just recount this tragic story. She presented many disturbing failings in the investigation, the case against Syed and the defence provided for him by his attorney, Cristina Gutierrez, who was subsequently disbarred following complaints from multiple clients.

Rather than pander to an imagined audience of goldfish-brained listeners who couldn't possibly sit still and focus for more than a couple of minutes, Koenig and her team dived deep on the details and demanded that we keep up.

Serial has been downloaded roughly 175 million times (and counting). It has spawned several spin-off documentary series and books, and the world still seems split down the middle as to the guilt or innocence of Adnan Syed.

As for the attention span of the audience, the passion and clarity with which every aspect of evidence and testimony continues to be debated by fans of the podcast is truly peak internet, not to mention the hours invested in understanding cell-tower 'ping' technology as it stood in 1999. To google 'the Nisha call', 'the Best Buy payphone' or 'Jay Wilds' is to plunge oneself down a rabbit hole for experienced players only. Beginners' questions will not be tolerated.

Serial changed the media landscape in many ways, but the choosing of a true crime story was surely no accident for Koenig's seasoned team. When considering this audacious project, they no doubt hedged their bets on the naturally engaging nature of the true crime genre. Why is it so engaging? Because at the end of the day it's about the explosive emotion that lurks within us all. We fear it and we're fascinated by it.

Someone wrapped their hands around Hae Min Lee's neck and strangled her to death within minutes of engaging with her that day. An 18-year-old schoolgirl. She could only have arrived at their meeting minutes before the attack. Did they plan it? Is that why they asked her to meet them? Or was it an argument that quickly spiralled out of control? What could possibly have precipitated such violence? Whomever is responsible, these questions still remain.

'That could never be me,' we say, and yet inside we wonder if it could. We hear these stories about other people, some of whom we can convince ourselves are so very unlike us but some of whom really are not, and we wonder, what would it take?

Victim or perpetrator, what would it take for me to end up in that position? Would it take rage, jealousy, fear, shame, alcohol, drugs? A combination? Plus time? How much time? Would it take a campaign on the part of someone else? Could I snap? Could my ex? And how could the systems designed to protect us let us down? These are the questions that drive the visceral engagement between good true crime and its devoted audience.

There was no sign that a true crime podcast boom was on the horizon as I interviewed Emily Webb about her books *Murder in Suburbia* and *Angels of Death*. But I was so drawn to her, and to her sympathetic approach to her work, that when we finished recording, I asked if she'd be interested in doing a dedicated true crime podcast with me. She leapt at the idea and in March 2017 we launched our podcast, *Australian True Crime*.

I know that I speak for both of us when I say that the biggest impact of our early entry into the true crime genre is that the ensuing explosion in similar podcasts brought with it a level of scrutiny that neither of us had anticipated. Some of it has been easy enough to ignore, particularly for me because I've been a comedian, television and radio broadcaster for more than twenty years. You would hope I've developed a certain level of immunity to criticism by now! But some of the scrutiny has raised genuinely interesting and timely questions about the way we tell stories about crime, punishment and victimhood. Perhaps the most important question is who the stories belong to. The second most important question: what is the purpose of telling them?

In the past, the focus has been squarely on perpetrators of crime. In her excellent book, *The Five*, Hallie Rubenhold seeks to tell the stories of the five known victims of Jack the Ripper. While that still-unidentified murderer remains the subject of a multimillion-dollar industry fuelled by books, movies and merchandise, the five women he murdered are described as drunk prostitutes, and that is all.

The victims of the Whitechapel serial killer were women hamstrung by the circumstances of their birth. Widowed, fleeing domestic violence, debilitatingly impoverished. They were mothers and daughters with devastating stories of courage and survival. The way they each met their end – slashed and disembowelled by their attacker in 1888 – is enraging when seen through Rubenhold's lens. That is the power of true crime storytelling when it's done well.

There is a lot of cynicism directed at true crime story-telling and I'm constantly asked to explain (although by implication, defend) my interest in the genre. Women make up the largest percentage of the true crime audience, and I'm often asked (most frequently by men) to explain that attraction.

Although the statistics are repeated with slim varia-tion around the world, I'll stick to my own backyard and remind you that while Australian men are more likely to be victims of violent crime than women, they are also far more likely to commit it. Roughly 80 per cent of violent crime in Australia is committed by men.[1]

As I write, the media is dutifully reporting the 'signifi-cant drop in violent crime during the pandemic lockdowns' throughout Australia in 2020. 'The figures show national drinking and assault rates have dropped,' says *The Age*,[2] and 'crime decline raises question mark over state prison plans.'[3]

Meanwhile, data collated by the Australian Bureau of Statistics indicates that the rate of sexual assaults reported in Australia rose by 2 per cent in 2020, which was the eighth consecutive annual rise and the highest increase for this offence recorded in a single year.[4] Add to that the increase in family violence incidents attended by Victorian police (up 7 per cent on 2019 levels during some months) and you start to get the feeling that not much has changed since 1888.[5]

Violent assaults against men have dropped, that's what the headlines should say.

With thanks to Our Watch, the independent not-for-profit organisation established to drive real cultural change for Australian women and children, we know that one in three Australian women (34.2 per cent) have experienced physical and/or sexual violence perpetrated by a man since the age of fifteen. Australian women are nearly three times more likely than men to experience violence from an intimate partner. And almost ten women a day are hospitalised for assault injuries perpetrated by a spouse or domestic partner.[6]

Those are the facts and figures. The somewhat less tangible, more nebulous and more insidious aspect of our culture is the intrinsic acceptance of feminine victimhood.

From birth we're warned about our weakness. We're informed we are prey. We're told what kinds of clothes and behaviour make us more vulnerable, and what times of day are more dangerous for us to be outside. We learn that drinks and drugs make fools of us and beasts of men, even nice ones, and how to negotiate with them when we can't outrun them.

We accept the inherent danger of being left 'alone' in either a crowd or a deserted place. By the time we're old enough to go out unchaperoned, we've been so conditioned to accept responsibility for whatever happens to us that we're beyond questioning why we should have to feel unsafe at all. I mean, when you think about it, who are these monsters we're in danger of running into anyway?

Presumably they're the same men we're interacting with during daylight hours. Our neighbours, our workmates, the boys we sat next to at school, their brothers, our brother's friends, our father's friends and so on. By extension, then, our friends should be fearing our brothers and our fathers. As we mature, we are warning our daughters about our friends' sons and they about our sons. Does that seem acceptable to you?

It seems we accept that an Australian woman will be murdered by her current or former partner this week, and another one next week, and another the week after that. We must be accepting of it, because it's been happening on average for years.

'Who is next week's woman?' I often wonder. She's out there. Is it you? Is it me? Is it someone we know?

Forewarned is forearmed, right? So perhaps the more we know about how these things happen, how the final act plays out, the more capable we might be if our moment comes. The more likely we will be to make a different decision. To zig where we might have zagged. To live.

Next week's woman is someone who is loved by many, no doubt about it, and those people's lives will be shattered by her violent death. Her parents, her children, her siblings and friends will be left behind with the trauma for the rest of their lives.

For the first responders – the police and paramedics – and later the lawyers and jurors, the aftermath will be life-changing. As it will be for the forensic pathologists who conduct her post-mortem examination.

I was contacted in 2018 by the legendary media maven Deb Withers. I wouldn't dare place a number near the span of her media career, but I will say that having worked as a journalist, publicist, television producer and even media manager for the St Kilda Football Club, there's nothing Deb hasn't done (or seen) in Australian showbiz. Upon returning her call, I discovered we could add media consultant for the Victorian Institute of Forensic Medicine (VIFM) to the list.

Deb had a gig for me, if I was interested. She was producing a web series called *Afterlife* for the Institute and she wondered if I was interested in co-hosting it with actress Catherine McClements. It would involve interviewing the forensic pathologists who carry out the autopsies for the coroner. Well, I was absolutely thrilled. I didn't tell her that I regularly logged on to the Victorian Coroners Court website to read the latest inquest findings for my own interest and education, but I leapt at the chance and a wonderful relationship was born.

One of the many outcomes of that phone call that I could never have predicted, though, is that forever more I will include the small team of forensic pathologists in my thoughts whenever I hear the terrible news of a tragic death in my city. When I wake up to the news that a young woman's body has been found in a park or some such circumstance – an all-too-common occurrence, sadly – I wonder who is on call at the mortuary. When I hear of a small child dying in horrendous circumstances, I feel for whomever will be working on the small body at that very moment.

We all know this is part of the story, but we're used to hearing about it much later, during the court process, and so we often don't place it where it belongs. I never did, but I do now. These people, these crucial links in the chain who are so vital in giving the dead a voice in the judicial system, are perhaps the least visible. My potentially disturbing habit of reading inquest findings informs me that the same handful of experts are called to give evidence in the biggest trials in the country and yet, unlike the highest-profile homicide detectives with whom they work closely for decades, we never see them on the television or read their autobiographies.

They are there, though, at the coalface, every bit as invested and affected as any other first responder – in fact, on many occasions, Australian forensic pathologists will attend crime scenes and conduct initial examinations of remains in situ.

Why don't we know about these people? A couple of good reasons come to mind. One is that their work is very hard to think about, especially when they're actually doing it. Having spoken to families who have lost loved ones to violent crime in order to obtain permission to include their stories in this book, I've naturally had to broach the difficult topic of the post-mortem. During that conversation I've asked family members if they knew where and when the procedure took place. Almost without exception, they did not. Most assumed their loved one had left the scene much earlier than they in fact had, and that they'd been transported in the ambulance to a hospital. It's difficult to imagine the hospital not being the obvious destination for an ambulance, isn't it?

The actual post-mortem procedure itself is exhaustive and 'thorough', to put it mildly. It won't be described in detail in these pages, because it's one of those things that, once known, cannot be unknown, and the only way to ascertain if you'll be thrown into an existential crisis by the knowledge is to learn it. I'd rather not take the risk.

Anecdotally, it seems to be the case that healthy human minds either have an aptitude for scenarios such as autopsies and crime scenes or they don't. Crime-fighting dreams have been known to begin and end during a routine training observation in the mortuary. Without a doubt, the effects of long-term exposure can have negative mental health outcomes in some but not all, and again, it seems as though there's only one way of knowing which way it will go for any individual. Fascinatingly, it's a risk many are willing to take.

When I talk about the people I've met at VIFM, which I find myself doing often, many people ask me a version of this question: 'Why would anyone choose to do something like that for a living?' It's my hope to shed some light on why people might choose to do such a thing, why I treasure every opportunity I have to spend time there myself, and why it feels like such a privilege to know more about the work that's done there.

1

PROF

'*CSI* demonstrates no appreciation of uncertainty, which . . . is the milieu in which my craft is practised. How can you be sure that that baby died as a result of shaking? How many times was that person punched? Was he alive when he sustained those injuries? To take some of the current examples crossing my desk.'[1]

So wrote Professor Stephen Cordner in 2007 at the peak of the TV show *CSI*'s popularity. Why would a busy professor like Stephen take the time to write a grumpy article about a TV show? And why does every forensics practitioner I've spoken to, and there have been many, inevitably raise the spectre of the *CSI* television franchise?

It's called 'the *CSI* Effect',[2] and it has real ramifications in our court system. The best example is the time-of-death plot twist. We couch detectives can generally rely on our fictitious forensics expert to peel off his rubber gloves after examining a fat maggot or a lividity pattern and tell us the *exact* time the victim died. Then we can rule the husband in or out, and if we're lucky our work is done with time to spare for a sexy subplot.

Unfortunately, it doesn't work that way in real life. So, when an actual forensics expert tells a jury they believe the victim died probably somewhere within a six-hour window, some jury members are so disappointed they discount the evidence entirely. 'He mustn't be a very good forensics guy if he can't read the maggots properly,' they reason.

According to a study by Arizona State University,[3] people who watched *CSI* were less likely to believe the forensic science presented to them in court and more likely to substitute the experts' testimonial evidence with their own research and expertise, which they'd gained from watching television.

Surely that would please show creator Anthony E. Zuiker, who once bragged the show was 'educational' and that 'all of the science is accurate'.[4] His claim prompted Tom Mauriello, a forensic consultant and lecturer from the department of criminology at George Washington University, to conduct an independent audit. He estimated that 40 per cent of the scientific procedures depicted on *CSI* did not exist at all.[5]

Professor Stephen Cordner is not a grumpy guy by nature. Far from it. He's a gentle, unassuming sexagenarian who favours fawn-coloured suits and holds his glasses in one hand all day unless he's reading. He's a born educator. One of my favourite things in the world is when I ask him a technical question and, waving his glasses at me, he says, 'Well, that's an excellent question, Meshel!' He makes me feel like I'm really going to ace this PhD in forensic science and criminology – which is ridiculous, because it doesn't exist, but he's very empowering.

Stephen is the embodiment of the culture of VIFM, where he is affectionately known as 'Prof'. In Stephen's lifetime, and under his steerage, the 'Dickensian shambles' of the former coroners court and mortuary in Melbourne has been replaced by an internationally recognised forensic facility that regularly loans out its experts to the rest of the world. And there's no egocentric fervour about it. Not within Stephen and not within VIFM.

To understand the extraordinary things the people of VIFM have done and continue to do, we must begin with Stephen, which he would dispute with every ounce of his being. But it is his leadership – an alchemy of expertise, authority and that elusive, unteachable ingredient, charisma – that drives the entire organisation.

Stephen's charisma is the humble kind. The kind that inspires by example, because there's always so much to be done. When I ask what drew him to forensic medicine, he tells me about his father, a country GP.

'He could fix fractures, he could do appendixes and hernias. The life of a country GP in those days was very practical. All the sorts of things that occupy Emergency departments these days were done by the local GP. He was very astute clinically; he could react quickly – all the attributes you need to be a great GP, and they were not attributes of mine. So I realised I had to find a place that was a bit more suited to my temperament and my skills, which weren't necessarily the same sorts of practical skills.'

No doubt Stephen's father, Dr Donald Cordner, cast a long shadow indeed. Not only did he save lives during the week, but on the weekends, he fitted in a bit of footy. He was one of four brothers who played in the Victorian Football League (VFL) for the Melbourne Demons, was a member of the 1941 and 1948 Premiership teams (he captained the side in '48 and '49) and was awarded the Brownlow Medal in 1946. He was President of the Melbourne Cricket Club from 1985 until 1992 and helped secure the agreement that meant the fabled MCG would be shared between cricket and the footy. He also oversaw the building of the MCG's Great Southern Stand.

If none of those details mean anything to you, just know this: Dr Donald Cordner is responsible for institutions and traditions of such immense cultural and spiritual significance in his community that many would swear they've existed since the dawn of time. The triangulation of Australian Rules football, the Great Southern Stand and the MCG are touchstones for literally millions in times of misery and uncertainty, such as the Melbourne winter. They are also part of the welcoming melting pot that makes the proudly multicultural city of Melbourne so great. No matter your language, your income, your gender, your sexuality, your age, you can always strike up a conversation anywhere in Melbourne about football, and everyone's welcome at the G.

Stephen's dad was one of the giants of the VFL, and he could also do an emergency appendectomy in his country surgery. So I can see how Stephen felt like his dad was a hard act to follow. Intriguingly, neither Cordner seemed to consider the idea of Stephen pursuing a life outside of medicine. Rather, Stephen expressed an interest in forensics and felt he had the right disposition for it.

'The first dead body I ever saw was outside my father's surgery. I would've been thirteen or fourteen. He was lying in the back of a car. I can't remember how but I knew he was dead . . . I can remember not being too fussed by it, which has always been my attitude, that once somebody's dead they're past any suffering. One can feel that about a dead body and still feel very upset in various ways when I see people in pain or suffering or gratuitously injuring somebody else.'

When Stephen expressed an interest in forensics, which was at that time a rather low-rent discipline, his father did his best to encourage him.

'Forensic pathology in those days tended to be a bit of a part-time thing in Australia. There were a couple of people who were full-time. One in Sydney, one in Brisbane, but the one in Melbourne at that time was actually a GP. We're talking about the sixties and seventies.

'Up until the mid-sixties, Melbourne had been pretty strong in forensic science. Keith Bowden was the head forensic to the coroner. He was very good. Wrote a textbook and everything.[6] That was a huge achievement because he was in appalling circumstances and conditions, but he was really interested in his subject, so he was a well-regarded pathologist. But in the mid-sixties there was a huge abortion crisis in Melbourne involving police corruption and backyard abortions. It became a very complicated environment medically and he got caught up in that.'

In 1970, Inspector Jack Ford, the chief of the homicide squad; Superintendent Jack Mathews, the head of the traffic branch; and a former detective constable, Martin Jacobson, were charged, convicted and sentenced to lengthy jail terms in Pentridge for running a backyard abortion racket in suburban Melbourne during a period in which abortion was banned in Victoria. At its peak, it is said the conspiracy involved up to thirty doctors and many non-doctors performing illegal abortions around Melbourne and paying thousands of dollars a week in bribes to police.

(Incidentally, one of the most prolific practitioners of Melbourne's so-called backyard abortions during this period was a lady by the name of Belle Moran. We'll discover as we make our way through these chapters together that Melbourne's crime culture moves around like a thick batter being constantly folded back into itself, and all the same raisins seem to float to the top again and again. Belle Moran begat Lewis and Des Moran, who made careers of theft and drug trafficking. Lewis and his wife Judy begat Jason and Mark Moran, whose decade-long war with Carl Williams over Melbourne's drug trade cost dozens of lives, including all of theirs.)

Dr Bowden, the talented forensics expert at the Melbourne mortuary, was unhappy with what he believed to be a corrupt environment and left.

'Dr Bowden was a patient of my father by the early seventies,' says Stephen. 'When I was starting to form an interest in forensic medicine, Dad took me along to see this chap, thinking he might have some advice about what I should be doing and how I should be going about it.

'So I went along and Dad said, "This is my son, he's a medical student and he wants to be a forensic doctor. So what do you reckon?" And this fellow said, and I can remember as clear as day, he was a man of few words, he said, "DON'T!" I can remember being sort of shocked by that.'

Shocked but not deterred, young Stephen Cordner was about to meet his mentor, the wonderfully named Professor Vern Plueckhahn.

Professor Plueckhahn, who grew up on a farm without running water or electricity and studied for his science degree part-time because he couldn't afford to do it any other way, took his position as the first pathologist at Geelong Hospital and turned it into an incalculable legacy.

21

He didn't even know that the mortuary at Geelong Hospital was a coronial mortuary when he accepted the job. What that meant was that he had to perform autopsies and report to the coroner in matters of unnatural deaths, which he'd never done before and wasn't trained to do. So, with no training available to him, he taught himself forensic pathology. He started that job in 1954, and by the time Stephen became his student in the early 1970s, Plueckhahn was regarded as one of Australia's leading forensic pathologists and he was developing a reputation for spotting and nurturing talent.

Stephen soon graduated and started looking for his first job. 'I wrote letters to all the forensic departments in Britain – I think there were about five – and I got answers from about three, including Guy's Hospital [in London] who, sight unseen, said, "You've got a job."'

'I thought it was sight unseen but Professor Dick Lowell of Melbourne University's School of Medicine had written them a letter about me too, so that helped. Things were no better over there in terms of facilities. The work would be going around different London mortuaries every morning and doing autopsies. And these mortuaries, I mean, if Melbourne was bad, these mortuaries were . . . these were literally from the nineteenth century. They were freezing cold, they were, generally speaking, dirty, and that's because it was very difficult to keep these places clean. But also, it was just the whole atmosphere of nobody really caring and that type of thing.

'I can remember the first autopsy I did in London and it's stuck with me for years. It was a man, I suppose he was in his late sixties, who thought he had cancer and over the last six months of his life had lost a huge amount of weight. Every time he ate something he would vomit it up.

'I think he'd had one visit to a GP, who'd said to him, "You look like you might have some blockage down there because you're vomiting things up as soon as you eat them, we should investigate that," but he never went back to the GP. He just assumed that he had cancer and basically wasted and faded away over the next six months.

'At autopsy I found that he had a rusty nail— now, I don't know whether you know any anatomy, but when you swallow, you swallow down into your stomach, and the stomach empties into the small intestine, and it empties through a hole called the pylorus. Well, this nail was jammed across the pylorus, so food couldn't get past.

'It turned out he was a bit of a home handyman and six months earlier he'd been doing something that involved having nails in his mouth. It's hard to imagine swallowing a nail without knowing, or maybe he did know he swallowed it but didn't connect it to the later problems, I don't know, but it cost him his life. A simple X-ray would have saved him.

'And I can remember early on doing an autopsy on a 45-year-old man who'd died suddenly, he was playing soccer or tennis or something, and he had a very large heart due to a genetic form of heart disease called obstructive cardiomyopathy. We knew that was genetic, so we were in the process of trying to see if any members of his family had the same condition when his father appeared in the mortuary, dead. He died at his son's funeral of the same condition.

'I always tell myself, "I suppose it's unlikely that even if we'd been able to track him down and talk with before his son's funeral it would've made any difference." There wasn't a lot of treatment available in those days but there are cases like that that stick in your mind.

'After about five years in London, I reckoned I couldn't keep doing it if I stayed there. Then I got the call about the job in Melbourne.'

The job in Melbourne was to be the first director of the brand-new coroners court and forensic facility, the Victorian Institute of Forensic Medicine. There's a bit more to that story, but we'll circle back.

Stephen has a way of making unimaginable things sound almost natural somehow. He is seemingly always without doubt and at peace with what he's doing and why he's doing it. Nothing he does is black and white; everything Stephen Cordner does is about the grey area, but he's even at peace with that. I get the impression that once he has chosen his ethical position, he's able to push on with the work without the emotional accoutrements that encumber some of his colleagues.

He once told a journalist, 'A number of people in my field have had problems with depression and alcohol.

My analysis of that is that they never really appreciated the value of what it is they do, and therefore became affected by the mechanics of what they do.

'There is no drama, I suppose, in uncertainty, in shades of difference; but for me, getting those shades of difference clear in my own mind, and then trying to convey them to a court, is one of the challenges and attractions of the work.'[7]

One of the areas that can be greyest for other people, if not for Stephen, is that of sharing the VIFM resources with doctors from around the world. The first time I heard Professor Cordner speak was in 2018, when he delivered an inspiring lecture about the many clinicians from around the world who'd visited VIFM for months at a time to learn about the techniques Stephen and his colleagues were using. Those clinicians then took that knowledge back to their own laboratories. It was proper give-a-man-a-fishing-rod-and-he'll-never-go-hungry stuff. Right up my alley.

Just a couple of months later I sat in my car on a rainy morning listening to Stephen defend that same program on talkback radio, in the wake of the alleged involvement of one of VIFM's former guests, Dr Salah al-Tubaigy, in a shocking crime.

Described as the Head of Saudi Arabia's Forensic Medicine Commission, Dr Tubaigy had been sponsored by the Saudi government for a three-month training placement at VIFM in 2015, with a specific focus on studying the use of the CT scanner. In his role as the Head of Saudi

Arabia's Forensic Medicine Commission, Dr Tubaigy was responsible for responding to potential fatalities at the Hajj, the annual event in which Muslim pilgrims descend upon the holy city of Mecca in Saudi Arabia. The Hajj must be carried out at least once in a lifetime, and with the increased prosperity in Muslim countries in the latter half of the last century, numbers attending the Hajj began increasing exponentially. With more people came safety issues, and stampedes and camping-ground fires have led to thousands of fatalities since the early nineties.

Many of VIFM's senior pathologists have worked in Disaster Victim Identification (DVI) teams after some of the world's largest tragedies, including the 2004 Boxing Day tsunami, so Dr Tubaigy's interest in learning from them made sense. By all accounts, his tenure at VIFM was largely unremarkable. He completed his three months and was neither seen nor heard from by anyone at VIFM again – until three years later, in late 2018, when he was linked to the assassination and dismemberment of journalist Jamal Khashoggi.

Khashoggi was a high-profile Saudi journalist whose family connections and social media presence, including more than two million Twitter followers, made him one of the most influential men in the Middle East. On 2 October 2018, Khashoggi arrived at the Saudi Arabian consulate in Istanbul, Turkey. He wanted to marry his Turkish fiancée, Hatice Cengiz, and he'd been told that he needed to obtain a Saudi divorce certificate first. Khashoggi entered the

Saudi consulate at 1.14 pm, while Cengiz waited for him outside in the car. He never returned.

Sometimes in life we're offered proof that fact is stranger than fiction. In this case, we were offered proof that fact is more like an old Bruce Willis movie than we could ever have imagined. It turns out that the Saudi consulate in Istanbul was thoroughly bugged, so within days the Turkish government started leaking the details of what happened to Khashoggi while his fiancée waited outside, a terrible fate that involved one Dr Salah al-Tubaigy.

'Minutes before [Khashoggi] entered the building,' *Al Jazeera* reported, 'one of the members of the hit team asked if the "sacrificial animal" had arrived.'[8]

The *New York Times* continued the story: 'Mr Khashoggi was dead within minutes, beheaded, dismembered, his fingers severed, and within two hours the killers were gone, according to details from audio recordings described by a senior Turkish official.'[9]

'I know how to cut very well,' the Saudi forensic doctor, Tubaigy, added, according to ABC News.[10] 'I have never worked on a warm body, though, but I'll also manage that easily. I normally put on my earphones and listen to music when I cut cadavers. In the meantime, I sip on my coffee and smoke. After I dismember it, you will wrap the parts into plastic bags, put them in suitcases and take them out.'

And finally . . .

'A Saudi doctor [Tubaigy] implicated in the suspected assassination and dismemberment of dissident journalist Jamal Khashoggi trained for three months with the Victorian Institute of Forensic Medicine,' the *Australian* informed us.[11]

When I told Stephen how upset I was at his having to defend himself on the radio that morning, he was, as always, at peace. 'Since 1990, we've had visiting forensic doctors, from many other countries including Sri Lanka, Israel, the Middle East, African countries . . . it is one of the things that I'm proudest of.'

But later he does tell me that, 'It gets really interesting, because there are some countries around the world that are autocratic dictatorships, very unpleasant on political and security arrangements for their citizens, and they have forensic doctors. Now, we have never said, "We're not going to have people from these countries but we are going to have people from those countries."'

'It's not like Dr Tubaigy learned how to dismember bodies at VIFM,' I say, trying to be helpful, but Stephen delivers a gentle reminder as to why I should probably leave references to experts.

'There is nothing he would have learned from us that would have had any bearing on his involvement in . . . But also, I mean, countries like Saudi Arabia being what they are and misinformation being what it is, who knows the absolute truth of who was involved and what they did.'

I try for a more conservative angle. 'Would it surprise you if the head doctor in charge of safety at the Hajj was also part of the Saudi security apparatus?'

'I can easily conceive of that,' he answers. 'But who knows what sort of hold the authorities have over a person. And once he's, sort of, out there, he might be sucked in by forces beyond his control. The authorities in countries like that, being what they are . . . as soon as they've got any hold on you, they can swiftly turn that into a total hold on you, and swiftly turn that into having you do things that you would not ever have expected you could be doing, and would horrify the rest of us.

'What happened to Mr Khashoggi is one of the possible outcomes but, personally, I don't think that example is really any cause for us to change our approach to training overseas doctors.

'Take, for example, our colleagues who are forensic doctors in Indonesia. They are all employed by police. And we know as a matter of public record that those doctors attend executions. Now, if you take a certain view about the rightness or wrongness of executions, and I'm getting a bit out of my depth, but I think the World Medical Association basically says it's wrong for doctors to participate in any way in executions . . .'

(Bless him for empowering me again – yes, the World Medical Association officially adopted a resolution in 2018 prohibiting physician participation in capital punishment.)

'So those doctors are breaching a sort of basic ethic of world medicine but Indonesia and quite a few countries around the world are not members of the World Medical Association so those doctors could say, "We're not bound by that and we don't necessarily believe in execution, we just want to make sure it works and is as painless as possible for the victim."

'Should we not have those doctors for training?' he continues. 'If we had those doctors colluding in some way with capital punishment should we actually say, "We're not going to have you because we don't believe that what you're doing is right?"

'You'll remember there was an Australian by the name of Van Tuong Nguyen who was executed in Singapore in 2005 for drug offences. At that point, the Institute [VIFM] had a memorandum of understanding with the Singapore Health Sciences Authority, and I got on extremely well with the person in charge of it. So the Institute's senior staff thought we should collectively write to our friends and colleagues in Singapore and say we don't like capital punishment and we just thought we would like you to know that.

'Anyway, we wrote a letter to our opposite numbers in Singapore in a fraternal spirit, and I rang my opposite number up there, and I said, "We're just about to send you this letter."

'And he said, "No, don't! Don't send me such a letter, because I will have to send it up the line and it will cause trouble for me."

'And I said, "It shouldn't be too much trouble . . ."

'We get a letter back from our colleagues, after Van Tuong Nguyen's been executed, saying, "Thank you for your letter, we have no compunction about capital punishment, we think it's particularly important for drug crimes because they are such a pernicious thing."

'So they defended capital punishment, which, of course, they had to do. So yeah, doing things with people overseas isn't always plain sailing. It can cause trouble and the Tubaigy situation certainly caused us some reflection.'

Reflection is an interesting word to use. Reflection requires time. It can't be done under pressure. And it involves a fair degree of autonomy. As a body dependent on government funding, I'm curious about how much time VIFM has to reflect on something like a Tubaigy affair before someone else steps in to reflect for them.

'It seems like the ABC gets a call from a federal minister every time they air a *Four Corners* episode they don't like,' is my reasoning. 'Did you get a phone call after Tubaigy?'

'No,' says Stephen. 'And, actually, we are so lucky. I have never in my entire life had any experience of anyone in authority trying to influence us, air opinions about cases or interfere with our operations or what we do.'

I'm taken with Stephen's word choice again, but before I have a chance to even clarify in my own mind why I'm snared on his use of the word 'lucky', he contextualises it.

'I can remember a story of a doctor from Iran. I met him in London when I was working there and he had come over for six months. He had been in London some years before and got a relatively modest qualification called the Diploma of Medical Jurisprudence from the centuries-old Society of Apothecaries. Anyway, he had lost the certificate of his diploma. Well, he hadn't lost it, it had been burned in a house fire.

'When eventually I got to know him well enough to ask him about the house fire and what had happened, it turned out that the house had been burned down by the authorities as a result of his work. He related an occasion when he was in the mortuary. Soldiers brought in the body of a shot man and stood around a mortuary table with their guns on him and told him that, of course, the cause of death was heart attack, and he would write a certificate to that effect, wouldn't he? What would you do in that situation?'

'I'd do whatever I was told, I guess,' I answer.

'Exactly right, and that's what I'd do, that's what anyone would do, and that's what he did and he said if he didn't do that they would have shot him. What would have happened is that first of all a few days later his dogs would have been killed and left on the porch. If he still didn't do what he was asked to do, one of his family would be bashed up and eventually one of his family would go missing. Then that family member would have been killed and so it would go on.'

The 'luck' Stephen speaks of is nothing short of his winning the birth lottery. Some people are born to helpful parents in safe countries and some people are not. Some people in the first category spend their entire lives unaware of their massive win, while others spend their lives trying to earn it. Some people never get the chance to choose.

*

On the afternoon of 27 February 1999 Kathleen Folbigg carried her daughter Laura inside from the car and put her to bed. The toddler had had a big day, playing in the children's room at the local gym while her mum worked out before calling in to visit her dad at his work. She'd been a bit clingy and grizzly in the previous couple of days, but that's kids. Maybe she was coming down with a cold, or maybe it was growing pains. Although she'd had three other babies, Laura was Kathleen's first toddler.

When she checked on Laura and found her unresponsive, Kathleen knew what to do. She ran her into the kitchen, laid her daughter out on the bench and started CPR. She also called for an ambulance, which was there in two minutes. The ambulance officers reported that Laura wasn't breathing when they arrived, and they were unable to find a pulse; however, they were able to detect a weak heartbeat with the ECG heart monitor.

They rushed the child to hospital but she was pronounced dead shortly after arrival. Kathleen's husband Craig met her at the hospital and they cried together. How could this possibly have happened to them again? Two babies lost to SIDS already, and one to a seizure, and now Laura, who, at eighteen months, they'd thought was past the danger point. God help them, they had actually been starting to relax a bit with Laura but here they were again with doctors telling them their child was dead and no one knew why.

Then Craig found his wife's diaries.

Four years later, Kathleen Folbigg was convicted of murdering Laura Elizabeth Folbigg and her siblings, Caleb Gibson (born 1 February 1989, died 20 February 1989), Patrick Allen (born 3 June 1990, died 18 February 1991) and Sarah Kathleen (born 14 October 1992, died 29 August 1993).

Kathleen was labelled Australia's most hated woman and sentenced to thirty years in jail. It remains an open-and-shut case in the minds of the overwhelming majority of the population, probably not because of the *CSI* effect but more because of Ockham's razor, the principal stated by thirteenth-century philosopher William of Ockham that the simplest explanation is usually the correct one.

Folbigg's own diaries were the most damning evidence against her. Once presented to police by her grieving husband Craig, they formed the basis for the case against her, and they still do.

> I cherish Laura more, I miss her [Sarah] yes but am not sad that Laura is here & she isn't. Is that a bad way to think, don't know. I think I am more patient with Laura. I take the time to figure what is rong [sic] now instead of just snapping my cog . . . Wouldn't of [sic] handled another like Sarah. She's saved her life by being different.[12]

Folbigg maintains that her diary entries reflect the self-blame that afflicted her as a result of her children's deaths. Her defence team produced expert witnesses who testified that the reaction was common in parents who've experienced the death of a child. But with four dead children it was always going to be a hard sell.

Kathleen's diary entries in the lead-up to her fourth child's death came in for particular scrutiny. 'With Sarah, all I wanted was her to shut up, and one day she did,' she wrote in November 1997, adding in January 1998 that Sarah 'left, with a bit of help'.

She wrote about Laura being 'a fairly good-natured baby', which 'saved her from the fate of her siblings'.

'I think she was warned,' Folbigg wrote about Laura in December 1997.

By the end of February 1999, Laura was dead.

In 2013, Kathleen Folbigg's legal team commissioned Professor Stephen Cordner to examine the forensic evidence presented at the original trial and provide them with an extensive report of his findings. It was part of their campaign to get a retrial for Kathleen. Stephen's report made headlines around the world and was a major piece of evidence presented to a 2019 enquiry into Kathleen's conviction.

'The first baby died at nineteen days and the cause of death was given as SIDS,' says Stephen now. 'The second baby, at about the age of two or three months, suffered an acute life-threatening event of some form. No diagnosis [was] ever made, but it was such a severe event that the baby was left with severe brain damage, which meant the baby had awful seizures on a very regular basis and was found dead at about the age of six months. Any babies with seizures, there's a possibility of having a seizure and dying or just dying of the severity of the brain damage.

'The third baby was SIDS. And then the fourth child was found dead having probably had a little bit of a sniffle, being alive and again found dead, but at the autopsy there was myocarditis, which is inflammation of the heart. Now, that is a well-recognised cause of death. It isn't common but it isn't uncommon either.

'The cause of death, however, was given in that fourth case as undetermined because of the three previous deaths, meaning that the pathologist couldn't be sure that this fourth death wasn't the same kind as the previous three. And the other possibility is smothering.'

'How could the pathologist take the previous three deaths into account?' I ask. 'Surely those deaths are irrelevant to the autopsy of the fourth.'

'Well, that's a very good question, Meshel! Because, of course, that is potentially very biasing, yes! It's a really interesting question and nobody can really give you an honest answer how they would treat that fourth death if they didn't know anything about the other three deaths.'

Kathleen Folbigg was tried for the deaths of all four of her children together, rather than tried separately for murdering each child. Had she been granted four separate trials, Laura's myocarditis, which Stephen found was 'unexceptionally' her cause of death, may have played a bigger factor in all four verdicts.

Stephen also confirmed there were no visible signs of smothering on any of the four children. So, ultimately, it seems there is no evidence at all that Kathleen Folbigg killed any of her four children, apart from the vibe.

In September 2019 Justice Reginald Blanch found the enquiry reinforced Kathleen Folbigg's guilt and dismissed her request for a retrial.

'My bottom line here, Meshel, is that drawing conclusions about what was meant in her diary entries has led to Mrs Folbigg being locked up for thirty years. She's only halfway through it now and her chances of getting out earlier are probably slim. So she got locked up on that sort of basis, versus the evidence.

'You know that we had a similar case in Victoria, which I am so pleased that, I believe, the Victorian system got it right.'

Carol Matthey also lost four children between 1998 and 2003. The VIFM pathologists found that two of her children died of SIDS, one died of a rare infection and one died the day after an accidental fall.

'She was charged,' says Stephen, 'but she was never proceeded against. The fact is that most jurisdictions around the world have one or two cases like these where there's multiple infant deaths in one family and their criminal justice systems have laboured terribly over them and haven't really known how to deal with them.

'Britain's had two or three convictions of mothers over deaths of multiple infants and eventually they were overturned. Of course, the circumstances are slightly different in each case. It's a rare occurrence but it sort of happens all over the place.'

'VIFM was built on a rare occurrence that people found hard to believe and led to a mother being wrongly convicted,' I remind Professor Cordner.

He looks very pleased with me indeed as he points his glasses at me and says one word: Chamberlain.

'Yes, that was a very significant part of the context within which VIFM came into existence.'

On 29 October 1982, Lindy Chamberlain was convicted of the murder of her baby Azaria. Lindy and her husband Michael maintained that the baby had been taken from their tent by a dingo during a family camping trip to Uluru in 1980. The infant's remains were never recovered.

'Mrs Chamberlain's barrister was John Phillips,' Stephen continues, 'who became the Director of Public Prosecutions in Victoria and then became the Institute's first chairman. After his experience with the Chamberlains he was really keen that the defence could get access to some decent forensic expertise and so that's always been in the DNA of the institute.

'And Vern Plueckhahn, who provided the emotional energy, if you like, for the Institute to come about, was John Phillips's main forensic pathology adviser. Even though there was no body [in the Chamberlain case] there needed to be a lot of understanding about death and different forms of it and what might have happened.

'And Vern, to his undying credit, right from day one he understood the truth of this case – he always knew that it was a dingo that had done it, and he and John Phillips were about the only two people in Australia who believed that at one point. And here we are in 2020 and it's an established fact! The biggest trial in the history of Australia, short of Ned Kelly's trial, perhaps, and she was wrongly convicted!'

Stephen is positively giddy with it.

'It is just unbelievable. So, it just goes to show how careful we have to be, just on a day-to-day basis, to make sure we don't get things wrong because fact is sometimes stranger than fiction.'

Spoken like a true scientist.

As gentle and serene as Stephen is today, there's no denying he's waged a relentless war for social justice on an international scale. He has borne witness to mass graves in Iraq, Burma, Kosovo and Serbia and served on the International Committee of the Red Cross in Geneva. He consulted on the Khmer Rouge trials in Cambodia, and deployed to Liberia at the peak of its Ebola outbreak to advise on dead-body management. Yet one of the most important ways he's fought for social justice is through a commitment to teaching and empowering local authorities so that they can continue the work long after he and other visitors are gone.

It's always clear that the beating heart of every VIFM achievement is its purpose. What's the purpose of having the best people in the world? To create opportunities for them to share their skills where they're most needed. What's the purpose of sending the best people to the worst disasters in the world? To inspire them to use the facilities at their disposal to create better systems.

Dr Cordner's bio makes me wonder if he's relaxed in spite of what he knows of human nature, or because of it. As a consultant in forensic pathology to the International Committee of the Red Cross, Stephen advised on attempts to identify the countless dead in Saddam Hussein's mass graves. An estimated 300,000 Iraqis disappeared during Hussein's presidency. That's above and beyond those who died in war. Three hundred thousand people lost to the tyranny of arbitrary arrest, imprisonment and execution. Families without answers, living on rumours for decades. When help came at last, in the form of international teams to excavate the graves and identify the dead, violence erupted in Iraq again, and off and on it's been ever since.

In 2014 Stephen was summoned to Liberia, which was, at the time, the scene of an unimaginable horror: an outbreak of an unpredictable new disease.

'The main advertisement you see when you are in Monrovia (the Liberian capital) is a billboard that says, "Ebola is Real",' Stephen reported upon his return to Australia in 2014. 'Because a large section of the population was not convinced that Ebola was real.'[13]

I remember reading about the unwillingness of some members of the West African public to embrace the advice of the scientific community during the Ebola outbreak back in 2014. Needless to say, I was somewhat incredulous at the time and I'm now somewhat less so. At times it seems as though the sheer depth and breadth of Prof's experience affords him buoyancy no matter how turbulent the sea.

'Well, I mean HIV is a pandemic without a cure, and we've learned to live with it,' he says in as relaxed a tone as you can imagine. 'And always there are background diseases that are ever-present, so they're endemic. Like a lot of my colleagues, I've caught tuberculosis from an autopsy.'

It's getting rather late in the day by this stage of my Zoom call with Prof. The afternoon sun is streaming through the window of his home office, a cosy book-lined space with timber accents. I imagine some lovely warm dinner smells are beginning to waft through his office door, although our COVID-era Zoom meetings mean I'll never know for sure. We'd definitely both started to kick back – until he launched into his tuberculosis story.

'That was in England. Certainly in England, many of the forensic pathologists had had TB, which they'd caught in the mortuary. I caught it from a person who'd had pelvic TB so it wasn't immediately obvious. Although I did notice it eventually but I didn't think I was at risk of catching it.'

It's around this point that I become slightly more tense.

'You catch it,' continues Stephen, stretching back in his leather chair, 'because when you cut into the TB lesion itself, the organism itself, it . . . what's the word? It doesn't spray . . . but it can easily sort of, um, create a few droplets that might spread into the air . . .'

Am I feeling a bit woozy?

'. . . or the organism itself, which is quite a hardy little thing, may not even need moisture to spread. It might just sort of click out of the tuberculous lesion'—he has a great chuckle at this—'and of course it depends on how careful one is with their technique. But I'm pleased to say we had to change virtually nothing operationally at the Institute for COVID. We'd been operating this way for years.'

And with that, Prof is off for his tea. Thank goodness.

2

THE FLINDERS
STREET EXTENSION

I know it doesn't look like much, but the image on the first page of the picture section of the old Flinders Street Extension, the former home of the Victorian Coroners Court and mortuary, is something of a holy grail for me. I'm a pretty good googler but I'm certain that you won't find an image of the Flinders Street Extension anywhere online. This is because it wasn't the kind of place in which people tended to take happy snaps, and also because the authorities who demolished it would no doubt prefer it was forgotten.

For many years, Stephen Cordner's old mentor Professor Plueckhahn had passionately wanted to see the Flinders Street Extension demolished and replaced with a more modern, independent forensic organisation.

'The facilities in Melbourne were a total shambles,' Stephen says. 'Dr Plueckhahn told the government, "These conditions are so awful, that not only is it a disgrace to the public, but it is also the case that nobody who's got half a brain is going to work there because it's so unattractive. No medical student can get properly taught or trained there, let alone any future pathologist, so the whole thing is just a vicious downward spiral to injustice."'

In retrospect, you'll be hard pressed to find anyone to disagree, but at the time Dr Plueckhahn had his work cut out for him because, as far as the state government was concerned, the old system wasn't broken, so why fix it? Plueckhahn would have to provide a pretty extraordinary example of the importance of investing in forensic science to realise his dream of better, more reliable forensic services – and he eventually did, with the Lindy Chamberlain case. Thanks to Plueckhahn's tireless work advocating for the importance of investing in forensic services, VIFM was established in 1985. But, in the meantime, there was the Flinders Street Extension.

It was retired homicide detective Ron Iddles who first uttered the name of the Flinders Street Extension to me. It all started when I asked Ron if he remembered his first autopsy.

'My very first post-mortem was when I was at the police academy,' Ron said with complete certainty, in the way detectives do when giving evidence. 'It would've been 1973. We were all put on a bus and taken into the coroners court, which, in those days, was in Flinders Street, and it was something that you just had to do. We all went into a room, there was no viewing room, and the body was on a stainless-steel table right in front of you, and you just had to watch it. That was the first time I'd actually ever seen a dead body, and the process of seeing it cut up there was pretty daunting.

'I knew I wanted to be a homicide detective, that was why I'd joined the police force, so I knew this was going to be part of my career, but back then, things were pretty basic.

'The equipment was very basic. When you do the full post-mortem, you have to take the top of the skull off, and they had a sort of a buzz-saw that went round, but then he used just a normal tradesman's hammer with a chisel to prise it open, so not all the tools were proper medical. I think there was two or three out of our group of about twenty-eight that had to leave the room. The other thing was, say, fifteen feet away was a small room, and that's where they ate their lunch.'

Ron told me all this while we were waiting around for filming to begin on a separate project, and I decided to whip out my phone and record his post-mortem memories. He was sixty-four at the time and had no notes, no warning of the conversation, but while we spoke he never hesitated or searched his memory for details. He seemed to have intellectual access to every name, date, address and witness statement he ever encountered over his forty-three years in policing. Maybe it's bluff but it's bloody convincing.

'The first autopsy I requested was an eighteen-year-old, Thomas Cooper, who'd been shot with a twenty-two rifle in the car with his girlfriend. It was 1980. Again, the post-mortem was done in the mortuary at the Flinders Street Extension and it didn't have facilities to X-ray. Because he'd been shot, and you want to have a look at the trajectory of the bullet and see if there's fragments and all that, we wanted one, so we had to then escort the body, we had to get the government undertaker to take the body from Flinders Street Extension to Prince Henry's Hospital on St Kilda Road, go up to X-ray on the seventeenth floor where the body was X-rayed. So that might take an hour and a half, then you do the return trip.

'James McNamara was the pathologist at the time. At times we were in the mortuary with him, and he would put the X-ray up, and either Brian McCarthy, my old boss, or I would say, "Well, you've put the X-ray up upside down."'

History will also show that Dr James McNamara was widely known around the traps as 'Mac the Knife', a fact Ron is far too classy to divulge to me. Many others I spoke to did mention the nickname, though, and told similar stories about Mac's work.

'We never gowned up,' Ron says. 'So, you went in, the body was on a mortuary trolley, you stood beside the pathologist, and you watched it and you talked. You did get a good understanding of what the cause of death was, because you're basically there. On one occasion, Sid Graham had been killed up at Yarra Junction . . .'

Ron also had a habit of expecting me to know who he was talking about at all times, as though I had been in the job right alongside him for forty-three years. I found it so enormously flattering that I never interrupted to ask him for any further details. I just nodded knowingly and waited until I got a chance to google it and catch myself up.

When Ron excused himself to 'spend a penny', I discovered that Sid Graham was a bank robber, active around Melbourne in the 1970s and early 1980s.

Back to Ron.

'McNamara did the post-mortem and he said, "He's been hit in the back of the head with a block of wood or something, he's got blunt force trauma to the back of the head."

'We really didn't accept that, and a day later the armed robbery squad picked up some information that there were crooks saying, "Well, they're dickheads, 'cause they think he's been hit in the back of the head and we shot him."

'So, we went back there and Brian McCarthy put some rubber gloves on, I put some rubber gloves on, we put our fingers in there and we found pellets inside the brain. Then what Brian decided to do was to get some plasticine and he filled the skull up with plasticine, and all the broken parts of the skull, he put back together around it, right? What we were left with was a hole that showed he'd been shot with a shotgun. Now, that wasn't the job of an investigator, that should've been the job of the pathologist, but that's how it was back then. That was 1982.'

It didn't take long for Ron and Brian's enquiries to lead them to a couple of the victim's bank-robbing associates, Lee Patrick Torney and Grant Curran, who'd committed a stick-up at the State Bank in Hawthorn with Sid Graham just days before his death. They soon charged Torney with Graham's murder.

Ron wasn't the only one with colourful memories of the Flinders Street Extension. Many of the people I spoke to felt unable to reflect on VIFM without referring to its predecessor. This rather small building was the chief forensic facility for the state not very long ago. Could things really have been so different so recently? Apparently, yes.

Professor Stephen Cordner first encountered it as a young medical student in the 1970s. As an example of the sheer inhumanity of the place, Prof immediately nominates the 'delivery bay'. Indeed, it seems unfathomable that when the building was being designed and built, this system was deemed either appropriate or at least inconsequential.

'You could see the deceased being moved from hearses or ambulances into the mortuary – From. The. STREET!' he exclaims, leaning forwards in his chair towards me. (In the photograph, you can see the exposed driveway to the loading bay running down the right-hand side of the building. It's probably one of the many reasons for the lack of published photographs.)

'You'd just look down the laneway and see bodies

being transferred one way or the other. It was Dickensian, really.'

As you know, Stephen is familiar with Dickensian mortuaries. He trained in Britain.

'If you want to find out a bit more about it you should speak to David Stevens,' Prof says, chuckling. 'He'll talk to you all day about it.'

In his memoir *Man's Search for Meaning*, Austrian neurologist and Holocaust survivor Viktor Frankl wrote that humour had helped him survive his imprisonment in concentration camps. He called it one of the 'soul's weapons to transcend despair'. Humour, he said, more than anything else, 'can afford an aloofness and an ability to rise above any situation'.[1]

That's the weird thing about the old building: as much as everyone is absolutely appalled by it in hindsight, there's a kind of cringing affection for it too. Anyone who's been around long enough to have experienced it is definitely part of a club. And, from my perspective, it's what makes the old extension such an important part of the story. It is a perfect example of the esoteric environs inhabited by this group. This is the kind of place that forges certain relationships between people, relationships the rest of us can't help but envy, even as we fear the circumstances that created them. Do any of us want to go to war? Of course not. But do we long for the famous camaraderie of the trenches? Endlessly. And in the same way an in-joke with a lover makes us feel like we're blissfully alone in a crowded room, gallows humour amid the profundity of death reassures us we are not alone and are still among the living.

'Are you talking to Rolly?' someone asked me once with the ubiquitous chortle. 'He would've been around in the Flinders Street days.'

'Rolly' was legendary homicide detective Rowland Legg an 18-year homicide squad veteran who led the investigations into the murders of Moe toddler Jaidyn Leskie, the Bega schoolgirls Lauren Barry and Nichole Collins and Carlton Crew drug dealer Jason Moran and his rather unsuccessful bodyguard Pasquale Barbaro, infamously gunned down in a van full of children at a Saturday morning Auskick game, to name but a few. And I did indeed speak to Rolly.

'I remember when they were still doing it, with the trainees, that they came in to see an autopsy at the new mortuary, behind the glass . . . I remember a group of them all filing in behind us one day when we were making our notes.'

Rowland Legg is trying to stifle a laugh at the memory of the fresh-faced young coppers. I've no doubt he sees every one of them in perfect photo-realness too.

'And the first thing I thought of when they came in, was . . . well, first, the value of them being there [laughs], but second, the fact that they had it pretty easy, compared with when I went through my training.

'Of course, at that stage, the Flinders Street Extension

was still operating. We had to go in for an autopsy for a murder victim one day and all the trolleys were set up, one beside the other being worked on, bodies being worked on in different ways. There was one fellow who'd put himself on a railway track. So, he was a lot taller than the others'—he laughs—'being in two pieces.

'The actual coroner's courtroom was in the same building. And, of course, it was an old building. And although there were two doors between the main court area, or the administrative area of the coroners court, and the mortuary out the back, there was basically . . . I don't know how to describe it – an alcove, I suppose, and then the next door just went straight into this autopsy room. So there was . . . the unpleasant odours are totally noticeable from one area to the other.

'There'd always be this aerosol spray of deodoriser around the courthouse part. Particularly if there was a decomposed body out in the mortuary room, there'd be someone wandering round with this aerosol spray.

'There was one freezer room for recents and another freezer room for older ones. These days, of course, they're in, like you see on TV, in sliding drawers so to speak, but back then they were all just uncovered on trolleys. Sometimes they'd be one on top of the other. It was a house of horrors. That's what it was.

'You know, one of the things that always goes through my mind, with Flinders Street, from the very first time I went there, it went through my mind, "I hope myself, or any of my family and friends are never on one of these trolleys in this building."

'The police surgeon and the coroner and Dr Mac, I mean, you know how many pathologists are involved now, and how many coroners are involved but back then, they were one-man-bands. It's just amazing when you think back.

'Dr Mac was a good guy and very capable, but we had a good . . . we had an argument. I think he wasn't well at the time because he suffered from TB. He was insisting that we were on the wrong track suggesting this bloke had been knifed numerous times in the back and an argument developed.

'Our senior person on the crew decided he wanted the ribs looked at, but Dr Mac wouldn't entertain it, so what ended up happening was that we took the ribcage out ourselves, into the driveway down the side, and cleaned it up with the hose. We were able to match up a couple of notches on the ribs that looked like knife nicks but in the process of the cleaning we caused a bit of a smell.

'They were building that World Trade Centre next door at the time and I recall that some of the builders claimed the stench got inside the building and they actually went on strike. They said it didn't dissipate, you know? Blow away? Would've been August 1979. It's a long time ago now but it was an interesting day.

'This might sound strange, but we would occasionally get together with the coronial staff for barbeques. In the seventies, beside the building on the CBD side, there was an old abandoned building, and sometimes we'd have a barbeque in this abandoned building. And it was always a bit disconcerting, because the technical people, who would assist the pathologist, they'd be in white overalls, clean ones, the ones they wore at the autopsies, with their white rubber boots. And they would bring out the burgers and the sausages in these white buckets . . .

'Look, it was different times, but there's always some black humour, some restricted black humour, and it has to be allowed because that would really keep you going. And I think it's probably the same with anybody in an unpleasant sort of occupation.

'And there was a bit of trepidation there of course, when I first went in there. I really had no experience of blood or dead bodies or anything before that but it was just part of the training then and it should be now. That's what I was saying earlier about the value of it, and that goes for whether you'll end up in the homicide squad or not.'

It is much lamented among the older generations that the attending of an autopsy as part of Victoria Police's basic training is no longer a compulsory requirement.

'It was a very vital part of the training, I thought,' adds Rolly.

He seems to remember at this point that he has in fact retired and is no longer shackled by the tight yoke of the police media unit. This office is usually run by an immaculately turned-out female officer with a few stints in the squads herself. What she says goes, and what she usually says to media requests is 'No'.

I can understand why, of course. The media is very quick to criticise the police no matter what they do, so why give us any ammunition at all? No news is good news, as they say. It does create a bit of a build-up in a bloke like Rowland Legg, though. He has played a major part in some very high-profile cases in which the performance of investigators has been much discussed, but he's had to keep it zipped. He has also seen some management styles that were . . . controversial, shall we say, and some decisions that led to a very bruising Royal Commission, and yet Rolly hasn't uttered a word. He's got some stuff to get off his chest about the value of police trainees attending autopsies, though, and he'll be buggered if he isn't going to say it.

'The price was paid on occasion after they dropped the requirement to attend the autopsy because some of the people [uniformed police] were not doing what they should've done at the scene. They didn't like the fact that the body might be decomposing or might be in some kind of state they didn't like looking at. By the time we turned up – well, it caused issues.

'But when you're passionate about something, and you're really interested – and I always wanted to be a detective, ideally in the homicide squad – well, I suppose lots of things in life have an unpleasant side to them. If you really want to do something, and it's all you want to do, and you're given an opportunity to do it, it steels you more. You develop a mindset. You know it's not pleasant, but you just sort of remove the appearance of it all from your mind, I suppose, and focus on what you're supposed to be focused on. What way did the bullet go through here or what have you. But anyway, my mother ended up there.'

Rowland wasn't chuckling anymore and for reasons best known to himself, he said this after roughly two hours of chatting about his career.

'Sorry, Rolly,' I had to ask, 'where did your mum end up?'

My head was swimming by that stage with so many dates and names and locations. I was desperately trying to catch up with him. Which one of them was he thinking back to with reference to his dear old mum?

'Flinders Street Extension,' he said with a weary sigh.

I was stunned. It's fair to say I hadn't been expecting that.

'She was killed in 1985,' he continues, as though delivering another yarn from an old police diary. 'She stepped off a tram and was collected by a truck. I was subsequently down at the inquest and, sure enough, someone was spraying air-freshener on the day of the inquest again. Yeah, you might say it brought back the memories.'

After months of messages, I finally connected with David Stevens, the man Professor Cordner insisted I needed to speak to. It was well after hours on a Thursday night and I quickly discovered that rather than being uninterested, David is just a very busy man. He was still at work, he sounded exhausted, and I'm pretty sure he was rifling around in other people's desks in search of snacks as we talked.

He's now the Operations Manager of Tobin Brothers Funerals in Melbourne. When I tell him I'm frankly shocked at how busy he is, as I'd imagined that to be the sort of job that afforded a person some reasonable hours, he laughs heartily. He assures me he's still very much at the coalface of death, with all its unpredictability.

David's first postgraduate job, back in 1981, was Clerk of Courts for the Victorian coroner, which meant his office was located in the Flinders Street Extension.

'My first day in the mortuary, Ian Griffiths was the coroner, he literally grabbed me by the earlobe and said, "Come with me. Have you ever seen a dead body before?"

'He said some words to me which probably best go unrepeated and then he said, "Just, whatever you do, don't throw up on a body," and I was marched into the mortuary with thirty deceased all open and ready for their autopsy examinations. I sort of looked around this room and thought, "Yeah, okay, that's interesting, I can deal with that, it doesn't cause me any problems," and I learned to breathe through my mouth, not through my nose . . .

'The foyer of the court was bordered on one side with the identification office, and then on the other side of the court directly opposite them was the clerk's office, my office. Then at the top of the T, if you like that description, was the courts where the inquests were held, and then immediately behind the court was the ID room where the bodies were and then immediately adjacent to that was the autopsy area.'

He drew up a handy floorplan for me later.

'So literally sitting at our desk, you could smell the odours coming from the mortuary. If you had a person who had been deceased for some time, then, you know, that odour was a particularly unpleasant odour.

'Scattered around the foyer of the court area there were these gas cylinders that would intermittently spit out this pink sweet-smelling mist that would mingle with the unpleasantness of a decomposed body. So walking down Spencer Street and turning right into Flinders Street from the train, particularly at the height of summer with that stillness of the air that you get in Melbourne in spring and summer, you'd turn the corner and look across and you'd see this pink mist snaking its way out of the front doors and you'd know what the day was going to hold for you.

'And in among all that, you could probably hear the saw in the mortuary room because they didn't use sophisticated equipment like they do today. They used a circular saw, and it made a lot of noise, believe me. It was horrible. The worst part about it was that it wasn't just us working there, it was families coming in and going through inquests or just identifying loved ones. They had to wait in that foyer area too.'

Yes, families had to walk in off the street and wait in that environment with the smells and the noises of the mortuary gnawing away at them like ... well, you get the picture.

'More than once I would hear a bloodcurdling scream come from the ID room because of the emotions of Mum or Dad or whoever. We had an instance of a lady who actually collapsed from a heart condition and that was my first emergency situation. Luckily there was an ambulance there and one of the officers was able to come and do the proper CPR and she survived. But that was over the death of her daughter, if I remember correctly, and that's all happening in among everything else.'

Today, inquests are unusual and unlikely to blight the lives of most people, but in the days of the old extension they were much more common.

'Of course, all non-natural deaths were inquests in those days,' says David, 'so all of the motor car accidents were inquests, all of the suicides, all of the people falling off their ladders trimming their trees or whatever. Today you don't have inquests into all those non-natural deaths but back then you'd have twelve families in by one o'clock most days. Then you'd have the more complicated cases taking one or two days.'

That's a lot of ordinary, bereaved families finding themselves in that confronting environment three or four months after the sudden death of a loved one, mostly to hear how the coroner believed some system or other may or may not have contributed to the death. What I mean by that is that regularly there was no person at fault, per se, and so for most families it must've felt like an awful waste of time and tears.

But these inquests were very important. They were the kinds of enquiries that led to seatbelts and bicycle helmets becoming mandatory, to speed limits and blood alcohol limits being lowered. Our lives have become safer because of them. That's the purpose of these kinds of inquests and, to a lesser extent, they're still carried out today.

Of course, there are also inquests into deaths where it seems as though a person or persons may well be responsible for someone else's death.

'Edwin John Eastwood, the Faraday school kidnapper, was there with me one day,' says David, remembering one of the colourful characters who was plonked on a chair in his office by police. The police often left people with him simply because they had nowhere else to put them while they waited to appear before the coroner.

Eastwood was well known for the Faraday kidnapping. On 6 October 1972, Mary Gibbs was the sole teacher at tiny Faraday Primary, only 70 kilometres up the highway from Melbourne but a world away. It had been a long day for Miss Gibbs and her six students, when two masked men burst into her tiny schoolhouse waving a sawn-off shotgun. One of them, in a perverse attempt at humour, said, 'School's over for today, kids!'

The men were unemployed Melbourne plasterers Edwin John Eastwood and Robert Clyde Boland, who'd hatched a very specific plan to abduct a teacher and students from a small rural school in order to extort a ransom of one million dollars from the Department of Education.

After leaving their prepared note, they drove their hostages to a remote location and locked them inside a stolen van. The teacher and kids were left there, in the dark, all night long.

Mary Gibbs had no way of knowing if Eastwood and Boland were just outside the van but she eventually decided to kick out the back door.

'I must admit,' she told a reporter later, 'I hadn't thought of escaping until dawn and the children were all desperate to do you-know-what!'[2]

She walked the children out onto the road, where they were found by rabbit hunters, who delivered them to safety.

Miss Gibbs gave police excellent descriptions of the men, both of whom had criminal records already, and they were arrested within days. She was awarded the George Medal for bravery and remains one of only three women ever to have won the honour.

Eastwood was sentenced to fifteen years and Boland to sixteen, possibly because he was ten years older and the judge was under the impression that Boland was the instigator of the crime. Unbelievably, five years after the Faraday kidnapping, Eastwood escaped from Geelong Prison and committed an almost identical kidnapping at the tiny one-teacher school in Wooreen, 150 kilometres south-east of Melbourne. Fortunately, no one was killed during the Wooreen kidnapping either.

The reason Eastwood found himself enjoying the sights and sounds (and possibly smells) of David Stevens's office in the Flinders Street Extension was that in 1981 he strangled a fellow inmate, rapist Glen Davies, in the exercise yard of Pentridge Prison and was charged with murder.

Having Eastwood plonked down in front of him was particularly startling for David, because the kidnappings had been huge news stories. The Faraday kidnapping occurred during a particularly trying period of David's high school career and he empathised with the children on the front page of the paper who'd survived their brush with those dull-eyed brutes. Dreading his morning bus commute, he hoped he'd be so lucky. The second kidnapping, a deadset tabloid sensation, took place during David's first year of university, by which time he'd resolved to make legal matters his life's work.

Now Eastwood had appeared in front of David again, only this time it was in the flesh and, as is so often the case, it sounds as though the brute of the tabloids was pretty underwhelming in the end.

'He seemed pretty docile, I have to say,' David says. 'Not at all the "evil criminal" his crimes would suggest.

Interesting enough to talk to, I suppose, but sort of quiet. I also had the main witness in that case in my office on another occasion. He was another matter. Really one of God's gifts. Greg Brazel.'

The coroner found in Eastwood's favour during that inquest and he was acquitted on the grounds of self-defence. He had been stabbed ten times during the fracas, which helped his case, but so too did Brazel's evidence.

Brazel is still incarcerated and has been described as 'one of Victoria's most violent and manipulative inmates'.[3] When he entered prison, he was a serial killer, arsonist and armed robber, but he's actually managed to add to his resume since then. Among his achievements while in prison: he took a staff member hostage in 1991; he conned an elderly woman into depositing $30,000 into a TAB account in 2003; and in 2006 he was caught collecting personal information about senior prison staff.

Brazel has successfully sued Corrections Victoria more than once for failing to protect him after violent attacks by other inmates. But, despite all of this, he has competition when it comes to the most terrifying person young David Stevens was left to babysit in his office at the old extension.

'I remember sitting down talking to Dennis Allen when he was there for an inquest. He was there for many inquests, of course,' says David, without a hint of showmanship.

Dennis Allen was the eldest and most feared of the

notorious Pettingill clan, named after the matriarch, Kath Pettingill. Dennis grew up thinking Kath was his sister, and that his parents were his grandmother Gladys and her husband Harry. Neither would hear a word against the boy, even though he put Harry in hospital more than once.

By the time he reached his mid-teens, Dennis and his younger brothers were developing a reputation as street brawlers and petty thieves. Eventually he earned a sentence in the notorious Turana Boys Home, which was in reality a factory mass-producing angry men, such as Chopper Read, Christopher Dale Flannery (aka 'Mr Rent-a-Kill') and most of the Pettingill boys.

Dennis was doing his first stretch in Pentridge Prison at the age of eighteen when he learned his true heritage in a letter from Kath. It began, 'Dennis, I'm not your sister. I'm your mother and I love you.'[4]

The revelation seems to have triggered something in Dennis, and the guilt forever tethered Kath to his defence and servitude. He was turned from a petty thief and street brawler into an amphetamine-driven fear machine, terrorising friend and foe alike. Not even family felt safe around him. His cruelty and inhumanity knew no shame or restriction. He was driven to new pinnacles of violence with an almost inspired creativity.

Dennis made a fortune from drug dealing and invested in a little corner of Richmond called Cremorne, which is now home to advertising agencies and bespoke recording studios. In the 1980s it was a madman's fiefdom, nestled in a bow of the Yarra River. Dennis bought house after house around the historic Cherry Tree Hotel, which had already been a favourite watering hole of criminals for a hundred years by then.

Most of Dennis's houses were used as brothels; he dealt drugs out of them, kept some as safe houses for associates and lived between several, including one in which he kept a young woman hostage for a number of years. She witnessed Dennis murder three people and eventually bore him a son. He allowed her to take the baby to visit her mother and she never returned. By that point his health and his mind were failing him thanks to his heavy drug use. Dennis was dead of chronic heart disease at thirty-five.

Dennis was never convicted of a single murder; however, police believe he committed eleven and he bragged of thirteen. One of his suspected victims was thirty-year-old Helga Wagnegg, who was last seen alive at his house and was later fished out of the Yarra River. Helga was a drug addict who'd been a sex worker for some time and was suspected of informing to police. It's been alleged over the years that Dennis gave Helga a 'hot shot', a deal of pure heroin, as opposed to the gear commonly sold on the street, which is always cut with something else. People don't hand out hot shots to be generous, they hand them out to kill. It's said that after Helga had overdosed, a bucket of water was retrieved from the nearby river and poured down her throat before her body was carried back down and thrown in, to make it look like she'd drowned.

Six months later, and the night before the coroner was to begin an inquest into Helga Wagnegg's death, a bomb was hurled at the front doors of the Flinders Street Extension. 'I remember getting a call at home from the superintendent of police saying the coroners court's just been bombed, is there a significant inquest on tomorrow, and I said, "Oh well, there's the inquest into Helga Wagnegg's death,"' says David with a chuckle. 'And as soon as I mentioned that he basically hung up the phone. He said something about making further enquiries elsewhere and that was that.'

It's widely accepted that Dennis Allen's 21-year-old nephew Jamie bombed the Victorian Coroners Court that night. He wasn't the natural-born killer some of his uncles were and his nerves got the better of him. He apparently threw the bomb too early and caused only minor damage to the Flinders Street Extension.

Jamie died five days later of a heroin overdose, and the Pettingill family, among other highlights, became the inspiration for the 2010 film *Animal Kingdom*. Jacki Weaver played the character based on Kath and it launched her career in Hollywood. Kath was not impressed and was quoted talking about the film, although former tabloid journalist and Kath Pettingill biographer and confidant Adrian Tame recently admitted that it was in fact he who invented Kath's infamous quotes, with her blessing. Repeated breathlessly and endlessly ever since, they are as follows.

'We're both short and blonde, but that's where the similarities end. She's supposed to have read books about me and studied me for the part, but it doesn't come off.'

In the coup de grace, Tame's Kath takes particular issue with Weaver kissing her sons on their mouths. 'If I'd done that to any of my boys, I'd have copped a smack in the mouth, not a kiss.'[5]

In fact, Kath Pettingill, who bore the brunt of Dennis's violence on many occasions, has been in peaceful retirement in a small coastal Victorian town for many years. She participates in bingo and knitting blankets for premmie babies and is fiercely protected by the locals if any strangers come around asking after her. It wouldn't make for a very interesting movie, I'm afraid, but there you are.

There was another explosion at the Flinders Street Extension not long after the Helga Wagnegg inquest, but it was rather less suspicious.

'The still blew up upstairs,' confides David. 'I think they were distilling ether or something and it blew up. It actually blew an air-conditioning unit out of a window and onto the footpath down below. It could've hurt someone.

'We'd already had the bomb from Dennis and co. and so it was, you know, a bit touchy. The funny thing from my memory was walking away from the court and there was lots of the journos and stuff, and I got approached by a young Tracy Grimshaw in the middle of the street. She knew that I worked there, and she wanted to do an interview with me. Everyone thought it was another bomb and

THE FLINDERS STREET EXTENSION

we couldn't tell them it was a still. Then we had a commit-tal hearing for a deceased called Sid Graham.'

It's a small old world, isn't it?

'The perpetrators were Torney and Curran and they hated each other because one of them had sort of gone belly-up with the coppers and let fly with all of the details. That didn't sit well with Mr Torney, who was a particu-larly vicious individual.'

(Actually, as you may remember, Detectives Ron Iddles and Brian McCarthy were only able to charge Torney with the murder.)

'They had him chained up to the left of the court in Huey Adams's office, and I would have been ten feet away from him, I suppose. Curran was in the body of the court in front of me at the clerk's desk, and the magistrate was behind me and Torney was to the left of me in this little room. Curran and Torney couldn't see each other.

'Torney had the leash between his legs around his waist and through his groin and his bum, and if he moved the leash just pulled. He'd be incapacitated.

'Anyway, and I was sitting there, just wet behind the ears, innocent young man not making too much of being near the ne'er-do-wells of the world, and I just drifted off and started staring at Mr Torney. You know, I'm just sitting there, and I just looked across and I'm sort of looking at him, and he jumps out of his seat, and excuse my language, but he comes charging towards me, dragging the policeman behind him and he's screaming, "What are you fucking looking at, cunt?" This is during an inquest and committal!

'And the magistrate got up and said, "I'm sorry, excuse me." It was Kevin Mason, and we quickly adjourned the court, and I was beside myself with panic. [Torney] was literally ten feet away. He ended up being released many years later and I had it in the back of my mind for years that he was going to come after me, you know, that he knew who I was. I was sort of relieved to read he ended up in a mineshaft.'

Torney was an associate of the Williams family – as in, underworld heavy-weight Carl Williams and his father George. It's rumoured that Torney carried out several hits on Carl's behalf while on parole in the late 1990s.

Despite his many dangerous connections and activities, Torney was murdered in 2005 by a gentle giant, known as 'Bushy', for his love of the land. Torney had entrusted the management of his marijuana crop to Bushy but, by all accounts, Torney's years of bullying had rendered Bushy quite terrified of him. Torney had moved into Bushy's home and made him feel so uncomfortable that Bushy had taken to sleeping in a cave rather than in his own house whenever Torney was around.

It seems that Torney pushed his luck, and eventually one night the gentle tree-hugger snapped. He took to Torney's skull with a shovel and threw his body down an abandoned mineshaft.

'I always saw him as bad and evil,' Ron Iddles said

of Torney some twenty-five years after arresting him for Sid Graham's murder. 'He was somebody I probably was scared of.'

Obviously, the Flinders Street Extension wasn't the kind of environment that left a young man 'wet behind the ears' for long. For David Stevens, the turning point was a day that Australians still know simply as Ash Wednesday.

'Ash Wednesday' refers to the terrible bushfire event that occurred on 16 February 1983. Over a twelve-hour period across Victoria and South Australia, 180 separate fires raged. With forty-seven fatalities, they were, until the Black Saturday bushfires in 2009, the deadliest fires in Australia's recorded history.

'After Ash Wednesday, they sent two police officers down from Russell Street to do the DVI,' says David, incredulous. 'Russell Street' was the headquarters of Victoria Police until 1995, and DVI is short for Disaster Victim Identification. I'll allow David to explain why sending inexperienced officers from HQ for such a mission was ridiculous.

'Without putting too fine a point on it, they left very quickly, having walked into the mortuary, and seeing approximately thirty or so of the deceased from Ash Wednesday. Straight back to Russell Street.

'It was horrific. That was my first involvement with physically handling a body. It was something that I'd had a little bit of a phobia about because it wasn't my job. So I jumped into that role then, and I did the whole DVI for all of the autopsies. I started at six and I finished at about midnight. Basically, my role was just to stand with each pathologist as the day progressed and take any property from the deceased that the pathologists would find, a watch or whatever it might be.

'It was very basic; it was nowhere near as advanced and sophisticated as what it was by Black Saturday, and I remember having not been there for very long – it must've been about twelve months, I suppose, at the time – and thinking, "What the hell am I doing here? This is bizarre."

'But it was a very special time in my life, I have to say. It was something that, when I look back on it, I was young and I was faced with all of these different issues to deal with, and mingling with the homicide squad, with people like Ron Iddles and Rowland Legg, I mean, I still feel very fortunate. It was a really special place, you know. We had the most wonderful barbeques, would you believe, Meshel?'

'I believe I would, David, yes.'

The Flinders Street Extension was demolished in 1989.

3

THE DAVID HOOKES MATTER

Detective Senior Sergeant Charlie Bezzina's phone rang just after midnight on 19 January 2004, waking the household momentarily until his wife Josephine and his teenage kids remembered that he was on call. The trill of the phone simply meant there was a job on and, with a bit of luck, he'd be back sometime the following day. It's the lifestyle of the homicide detective's family. Jobs rarely come in during the daylight hours, and traditional family holidays such as Christmas and Easter are the busiest times of the year.

Grown children of homicide detectives often talk about those phone calls in the middle of the night. They smile begrudgingly at the memories of their father's mumbled conversations in the darkness, the shuffling sounds of him pulling on his dark suit and shiny shoes, followed by the thwack of a stiff necktie. Then the front door, the car door, the garage door and away, for weeks at a time if it was a bad one. They never knew what might happen when they went to bed and he was on call.

When Charlie received that particular call, the young constable on the other end nervously informed him that the job was a big one. No one was dead (yet), but there was a bloke in a pretty bad way. There was another bloke in custody and a hell of a lot of onlookers, but neighbourhood rubbernecks would soon be the least of their worries.

Moments later, as Charlie headed east through Melbourne's quiet Sunday night streets, he steeled himself for a job that was going to have an extra element of pressure, whether the injured man survived or not. He slid past the city and around Port Phillip Bay to the eclectic strip of St Kilda, where he knew the scene awaiting him outside the Beaconsfield Hotel was about to be big news or enormous news, depending on the prognosis of the injured man.

The local coppers had already ascertained that the man had been involved in some kind of physical altercation with the hotel's bouncers. They'd arrested one of them, 22-year-old Zdravko Mićević, and charged him with assault. He was accused by witnesses of 'king-hitting' the injured man.

Mićević had no idea who the man was, nor did he recognise any other members of the group who'd been drinking in the pub together that night, but witnesses recognised several of them as members of the Victorian and South Australian cricket teams. The injured man was

David Hookes, the legendary Australian cricketer, coach and commentator.

Hookes was forty-eight years old, and he'd spent the day at the venerable Melbourne Cricket Ground coaching his Victorian cricket team, the Bushrangers, to a narrow victory over the South Australian Redbacks in a one-day ING Cup match. The Redbacks included his great mate, batsman Darren 'Boof' Lehmann, who was happy to catch up for a post-match beer despite the loss.

They ended up heading out with a group of around twenty people, made up of members of both cricket teams, friends and girlfriends. As luck would have it, they found a nice pub in St Kilda that was playing the one-day international between Australia and India in Brisbane on a big screen. They settled in for the night at the Beaconsfield Hotel, right opposite the beach, and it must have felt like the perfect end to an exceptionally good day for David Hookes.

Hookes had been exceptional for as long as he or anyone else could remember. He was described as having enjoyed 'a spectacular career in Adelaide schoolboy cricket',[1] which demonstrates more than his prodigious talent. It speaks also to the hyperbolic fervour that surrounds young Australian men who are gifted with talent in one of the nation's favourite sports.

The dichotomy is that the very exceptionalism that sets these young men apart from almost everyone else they know in childhood delivers them into a life in which nothing less than complete conformity will do. These days our sports stars are pressured to avoid controversy at all costs. 'Upstanding young role model' is the norm to which they must conform. You're more likely to find a hair straightener in a young man's away bag than a carton of Winfield Reds, sledging is bullying, and tasteful designer duds are the uniform entering and leaving training. Some might say if they could forgo personalities altogether, that would be the perfect scenario.

You don't have to cast your Google image search too far back, though, for proof that it wasn't always thus. The cricketing world young David Hookes walked into in the mid-1970s was a decidedly more colourful environment. Players of his generation would become at least as famous for their drinking records as for their on-field achievements, and nobody had a problem with that.

David Hookes was very much a man of his generation, moulded by his time, his place and his talent. In 1977, at twenty-one years of age, Hookes hit England captain Tony Greig for five successive fours in the Melbourne Centenary Test, and that night he was the most exciting young player in international cricket. He expected (and probably hoped for) Greig to be mad, but instead the elder statesman came looking for him after the match with a beer. Greig had been commissioned by media magnate Kerry Packer to headhunt players for the rebel cricket competition Packer was planning to run on his television network.

Several months later, in a blaze of publicity, Hookes was named among the players who'd signed up for what would become known as World Series Cricket and, as usual, he was in exceptional company. All the world's biggest players had joined because Packer was offering sums of money hitherto unheard of in the gentleman's game.

The announcement threw international cricket into disarray and a quagmire of legal action and uncertainty. It served as a major distraction. Then, the following year, Hookes suffered a broken jaw at the crease in Sydney. Some say his batting never recovered its relaxed confidence. The power behind the faultless forward momentum he'd enjoyed since his schoolboy cricket days subtly flamed out within twelve months of that star turn against Tony Greig at the MCG.

Although he surfed waves of brilliance over the following dozen years, he never again achieved the consistency that had been the hallmark of his early career. He did, however, grow increasingly confident when it came to public commentary.

Sensing his willingness to provide provocative headlines about everything from the game's greatest traditions to the form of individual players, the media was keen to supply him with opportunities to speak.

He was eventually lured into professional broadcasting on radio and became loved and loathed as an 'outspoken commentator' who 'ruffled feathers' on Melbourne's stalwart AM talkback station 3AW.

Hookes's escapades remained mainly on the back pages until 2003, when he leapt to the defence of a promising young bowler with equal talent for finding trouble, by the name of Shane Keith Warne. Warnie was being accused of sexual harassment via text message (can you imagine?) by Helen Cohen, a South African woman who claimed he'd bombarded her with unwanted messages.

David Hookes gave listeners his read on the situation, which was that it was unfair to judge Warne, who normally handled himself well, because 'some dopey, hairy-backed sheila has dobbed him in on the other side of the world'.[2]

He later apologised 'for causing any offence'[3] but by then he'd been elevated to heights of mainstream outrage that in this day and age would have him cancelled by the Twitterati. Everyone suddenly knew who he was, for better or for worse.

Of course, it's nonsense to suggest that that one statement captured the full length and breadth of David Hookes's character. It's much more accurate to say that, from that time on, many more people *thought* they knew who David Hookes was, and that distinction will become very important later, at least in the mind of one experienced investigator.

As the mythology of Shane Warne's love-life germinated that summer, there must have been some chuckles among those in the know at Hookes's passionate defence and the subsequent media storm and his chastened apology. Hookes's own romantic life was as complicated as ever. His second marriage was on the rocks thanks to his chronic unfaithfulness. Around September or October

2003, he moved out of the family home he'd shared with wife Robyn and her two children.

There seemed to be one girlfriend in particular, Christine Padfield, who was with David Hookes on the night in question at the Beaconsfield Hotel in St Kilda. She worked as a marketing manager for Cricket Victoria and was dubbed the 'mystery blonde'[4] in the following days after being seen driving Hookes's car.

That night at the Beaconsfield, as closing time drew near, at around 11.30 pm, it wasn't Hookes's girlfriend he was standing with in the glassed-in smoking area of the Beaconsfield Hotel, but Sue-Anne Hunter, who was the girlfriend of the young Victorian bowler Michael Lewis. Lewis and Hunter had argued and while a grumpy Lewis waited outside in the car, Hookes counselled Sue-Anne.

The bar staff flicked on the lights and called last drinks, and the security team, made up of four young bouncers, began walking the floor encouraging the patrons to drink up and leave the hotel.

It's at this point that witness accounts begin to diverge rather wildly.

According to most of the Hookes party, they quietly set about finishing their drinks and preparing to leave. Hookes, they said, told Mićević they'd be on their way as soon as Sue-Anne Hunter finished her 'chardy'.

According to Tania Plumpton, who was in the Hookes party, Mićević responded by saying, 'Tell the bitch to skol her drink.'

Hunter agreed, saying David replied with something like, 'That's no way to speak to a lady, you shouldn't tell a lady to skol a drink.' However, Padfield later said that, while David did take umbrage at the bouncer's demand that Hunter 'skol' her drink, Mićević never called anyone a 'bitch'.

Hookes's party can offer no further motive for what happened next, which was Mićević grasping Hookes and physically dragging him from the premises.

According to the bar staff, however, David Hookes took exception from the moment he was asked to finish up. His attitude towards the bouncers, particularly Mićević, was described as 'disdainful'. They said when Hookes was asked to leave he replied, 'Fuck you! You heard me, fuck you! How many times do I have to repeat myself? Fuck you!'[5]

South Australian coach Wayne Phillips was later asked in court if Hookes had said to staff, 'Don't you know who I am?' and whether he had said he would complain about his treatment on his radio show the following day.

'I assumed that was the tack he was taking,' was Phillips's reply.[6]

Bar staff reported that Hookes threatened to use his influence to have Mićević sacked and the pub closed down. Bar worker Lucas Cacioli said the group of cricketers was swearing and arguing aggressively with bouncers who were trying to move them on. He also said David Hookes appeared to be 'the leader of the group'.[7]

Bar staff said this was the catalyst for Hookes's physical

ejection from the Beaconsfield Hotel by Zdravko Mićević, in a headlock or a bear hug or some kind of combination of the two. They testified that a woman jumped on Mićević's back as he dragged Hookes outside. 'Some of the ladies were trying to get at [Mićević], trying to rip at him,' fellow bouncer William Niumata said.[8]

Once the fracas moved outside and onto the footpath, a new cohort of witnesses entered the fray, thanks to ongoing tensions about noise restrictions with local residents.

(The Beaconsfield Hotel looks about as pubby as a pub can look and has stood its ground since 1840. I'll never understand how the late-night noise of drunk people talking loudly and whistling for taxis comes as such a shock to people after they move in next door to a pub!)

Anyway, directly across Cowderoy Street from the Beaconsfield is a three-storey apartment block with balconies protruding towards the shoreline across the street, and the hotel. It was a warm Sunday night, and several of the apartment residents were enjoying the sea air through open balcony doors and windows as the yelling, swearing and screaming of the headlocked, piggy-backed ejection burst through the old pub doors and onto the footpath outside.

A number of residents leapt to their balconies, which provided an unfettered view of the melee. They were very used to observing and detailing late-night events around the pub so as to complain about them, so Charlie Bezzina found them to be particularly attentive witnesses. With that said, though, the differing recollections of the night became a study in the unreliability of human memory.

We tend to believe our memories are photographic and trust them implicitly, especially when it comes to scenes we consider important. We find it hard to accept that our minds could allow us to reimagine events, to leave details out, move them around or even create entirely new ones.

Our legal system has long held that the eyewitness account is among the hardest pieces of evidence to refute in court, regardless of the overwhelming evidence of its fallibility. As far back as 1885, published studies were suggesting that in human beings quizzed just one hour after witnessing a controlled scenario 50 per cent detail loss and significant memory distortion were the norm.[9]

Professor Giuliana Mazzoni has spent her life researching the nature of human memory, including studying people who once had 'vivid autobiographical memories of events and people but no longer believe they happened'. She's distilled the truth of memory down to this: 'Remembering is not like playing a video in your mind – it is a highly reconstructive process that depends on knowledge, self-image, needs and goals.'[10]

She also writes rigorously on hindsight bias, which is the rethinking of a memory after new information is provided. That's what's happening when you say something like, 'Actually, now that you mention it . . .'

Obviously, there were people involved in the Hookes case who had reasons to wilfully rearrange the truth to suit their own ends, but a little modern memory theory makes reading the witness statements all the more fascinating, in my view. There were a lot of bystanders with nothing to gain or lose, who all stood and watched the same scene unfold at quite close quarters but recalled significant details quite differently.

As Anthony Perks wandered out onto his balcony, he clearly heard a woman say, 'David, leave it alone.'[11]

By then, the Hookes party was in Cowderoy Street, where their cars were parked. Christine Padfield went ahead to get her car in the hope of getting Hookes away, and another woman was heard threatening to sue over her broken glasses.

Jonathon Porter, the South Australian cricket team's physiotherapist, reported that the group was followed by two bouncers who were 'completely focused on David'.

'They were yelling at him, "Come back here, we don't want to hit you, we just want to talk." Someone else then said, "We're fifty metres away from the bar – go away, leave us alone."'[12]

As the residents of Cowderoy Street looked on from their vantage points, the conflict became physical again. One neighbour, Roman Longer, called triple zero to report a fight. He told the operator a group of women appeared to be calming the situation down, 'trying to get people to be sensible'.[13]

Craig Ravells said he saw arms swinging and a man who seemed to be trying to pull loose from the crowd, as if he were being held. He heard a woman screaming, 'Let him go!'[14]

Anthony Perks said he saw between ten and fifteen people scuffling and wrestling, and men trying to get other men into headlocks.[15]

Bouncer William Niumata said that, in those minutes, some pushing and shoving escalated into wrestling. Another bouncer, Demitris Demetriou, admitted to becoming scared. He said Hookes got in his face and swore at him.[16]

Another resident, Joseph Robilotta, said he saw Darren Lehmann put in a headlock by the bouncers, before being choked and thrown to the ground.[17]

Eventually, according to Anthony Perks up on the balcony, one man broke away from the wrestling, arguing crowd and headed towards a car, but that man was followed by another 'quick moving' man.[18]

Victorian all-rounder Shaun Graf remembered Christine Padfield pulling up in the car and David trying to get in, but he said the bouncers stopped him. 'I turned around and saw one of the bouncers had tried to pull him to the ground. He lifted his hands up and said, "Hey, I'm out of your pub, I'm out of your pub."'[19]

Paul Chow, who witnessed the action from his town-house, said Hookes's arms were by his side when he was standing in the road.[20]

When the quick man caught up with the first man, the first man turned around and was punched with what Anthony Perks described as 'a big hit'.[21]

Eerily, every witness account comes back into alignment at this point.

'And then he punched him.'

'And that's when he got hit.'

'. . . punched him in the face.'

They all describe the stiff rigidity of David Hookes's body as he fell, straight back onto Cowderoy Street.

'Like a tree.'

'Like a plank.'

'David was completely out.' [22]

All agree, too, about the sickening sound of his head hitting the ground.

'It was a horrible sound,' said Anthony Perks. 'The sound I heard when his head hit the ground left no doubt in my mind that this person was going to die.'[23]

Physiotherapist Jonathon Porter didn't see the fall, but he heard it. He pushed through the crowd and found Hookes lying flat on his back, unresponsive and bleeding from the nose and mouth. His pulse was already faint. Within minutes he stopped breathing and Porter commenced CPR with the assistance of a nurse at the scene. Hookes was in full arrest when paramedics arrived, and they defibrillated him four times before deciding he was stable enough to travel to the nearby Alfred Hospital.

David's wife Robyn was still his next of kin and she received the terrible knock at the door in the middle of the night. She rushed to Alfred Hospital to be by David's side, where Darren Lehmann and another cricketer, Darren Berry, were waiting.

'One minute we were all there, Hookesy, myself, Wayne Phillips having a drink and forty-five minutes later Darren Lehmann and I were sat next to him with tubes hanging out of his head,' said Berry some years later. 'I thought he'd just been knocked out and four hours later I'm sitting there with Hookesy, Robyn and Boof and the doctor comes in and says he can't do anything for him.'[24]

Charlie Bezzina, meanwhile, had commenced his investigation, interviewing witnesses and everyone involved in the incident, including Zdravko Mićević.

Mićević was, in Charlie's words, 'devastated' and he co-operated from the outset. Charlie is quite famously empathetic, but he saw this as a clear case of one-punch manslaughter and he intended to get a conviction. He'd need to rewrite the law books to do it, though, because it had never been done before.

In order to successfully prove manslaughter, he needed to show that an offender understood at the time he was committing the act that it was both dangerous and unlawful. We've now had years of publicly funded education campaigns informing us that 'one punch can kill' but back in 2004 it wasn't a common or legally held belief. At the time, it was accepted that killing someone with a single punch was an accident that simply couldn't be anticipated.

Charlie had investigated half-a-dozen 'one-punch' deaths by bouncers and security staff during his career to that point and he saw a very clear distinction in these cases that he believed he could exploit. Like many bouncers working around Melbourne's hotspots at the time, Zdravko Mićević was a highly trained fighter. Like David Hookes, he showed immense talent as a teenager and at fourteen was the runner-up at the Australian Amateur Boxing Championships.

Charlie's point was that Mićević's years of training made him an expert in the potential damage that one of his punches could do to another person. Therefore, whenever he chose to use even one of his punches outside of his sport, he had to know he was risking killing someone.

Charlie took his thesis to the Director of Public Prosecutions, Paul Coghlan. It's the DPP who'll ultimately decide whether or not to charge a person with a crime, depending on the brief of evidence the police can put together, so before he committed a lot of time to the attempt, Charlie wanted to get a gauge of what his chances might be. Coghlan liked it, and he supported the plan to make the killing of another human being with a single punch manslaughter in the state of Victoria.

At the Alfred Hospital, Robyn Hookes had a decision to make too. Their separation was still very raw, and she found herself dealing with homicide detectives and a confusing story about a violent pub brawl with bouncers; there was a new girlfriend wanting to be allowed into the hospital room, friends and family all around the world waking up to media reports and the dawning realisation that there would be no miracle recovery.

'He had one blow to the head, and within twenty-four hours I had to make the decision,' she said later.[25]

She had, in effect, to make two decisions on that Monday. The first was when to allow the respirator that was keeping David breathing to be turned off. Although he appeared virtually uninjured to the layperson's eye, the brain haemorrhage he'd sustained when his head hit the ground the night before meant that he would never again regain consciousness. In harsher terms, he was brain dead.

The second decision she had to make was whether to allow him to be taken into surgery first, so that his wish to become an organ donor could be realised.

Many Australians are under the misguided impression that ticking a box when updating a driver's licence or registering on a website is enough to ensure their organs will be donated after death. In actual fact, it's still up to the next of kin to give permission in what is generally the hardest moment for them to consider doing so.

'How could you possibly just say yes to giving someone's organs away when you are so desperately trying to hang onto them?' she asked later. 'David to me was warm, he was breathing, what appeared to me as normal. How do I say "Yes, take him to theatre, take out all his organs and tissue," and then I know that, after that theatre process, he is going to be dead?'[26]

When it came to actually giving doctors permission to take David away, she probably wouldn't have agreed had he not been so strident about his wishes.

It's no doubt a rare and great relief for the Donor Tissue Bank people when a family is as prepared for the conversation as the Hookes family was, but for Charlie Bezzina, it presented a complication. He needed an autopsy.

I'm fortunate enough to have spent a bit of time with Charlie, and I make it my business to see him in action on the speaking circuit and to tune in whenever he's on television and radio. There's one phrase he uses more than any other when describing how he achieved various outcomes throughout the course of his career: 'you build a rapport'.

Whether he's talking about victims, offenders, witnesses, other investigators, or anyone at all, Charlie always advises building a rapport. And it's something he seems to do effortlessly. As another great former detective, Gary Jubelin, once told me, 'My observation of the way he's gone about his business, and something that struck me about Charlie, is that he does have genuine empathy, and empathy leads to making that human connection.'

As committed as Robyn Hookes was on that day to following through with David's organ donation wishes, Charlie knew that there would be another day sometime in the future when she'd be equally emotionally attached to representing his interests in court. Charlie's job was to ensure he did everything he could to give her and the rest of David Hookes's family the best chance of success down the track, even if she couldn't possibly think about it yet.

So what to do?

Somehow – and no one, not even Charlie, seems to remember quite how – Charlie Bezzina managed to negotiate with all the relevant parties that afternoon to achieve the outcome he needed. He convinced the Hookes family to agree to a partial autopsy taking place during the organ removal process. The Donor Tissue Bank agreed to allow it and the Director of Public Prosecutions gave the whole process the nod too. Then it was time to get VIFM involved.

Just like the homicide squad, the pathologists at VIFM have a roster system whereby someone is always on call. On that particular Monday the pathologist on call was Dr Michael Burke and, wouldn't you know it, he and Detective Senior Sergeant Bezzina happened to share a great rapport.

'He's a great man,' says Burke immediately. 'He's very calming. He has a way of making you feel like everything's under control and there's nothing to worry about. And he's meticulous.'

Compliments don't come much more effusive than 'meticulous' from a forensic pathologist.

'Charlie used to come into the autopsy room. He used to get changed into the scrubs and in he'd come. And he's quite a presence,' Burke says, chuckling, 'especially when you're junior. Have Charlie next to you, boy! He had a presence to him.

'His forensic knowledge was pretty good, surprisingly good. You know we talk about lacerated injuries from the application of blunt force; if someone hits you on the head with a cricket bat, it squashes your scalp between the bone and the wood, and it splits the skin. You might get a bit of debris in there that you look for. Whereas if someone's cut with something sharp, a Stanley knife or something like that, it leaves very clean edges. Charlie always used the correct terms. He'd be asking about a lacerated injury; he'd be asking about direction if it's undermined in a different way . . . he'd keep you on your toes.'

Michael Burke is quite a presence too, although he's also unwaveringly modest and much happier when singing the praises of colleagues or chatting about interesting forensic facts than talking about anything that might reflect well on him. He's mortified by the mention of the Goodreads reviews for his book, *Forensic Medical Investigation of Motor Vehicle Accidents*, and practically begs me to stop talking about them (they're all good, and he'll never read them).

He distracts me with his passion for the topic. 'They're probably the hardest cases we have . . . Everyone thinks homicide cases are difficult but they're usually reasonably straightforward. A person who's found on the side of the road? They could've been hit by a car, they could've been hit by a car while standing, they might've had too much to drink and gone to sleep on the road, they could've been assaulted and left on the road, they could've been dumped from a car after being assaulted elsewhere. Very difficult.'

I guide the conversation back to the Hookes matter by wondering if Burke feels increased pressure when working on high-profile cases.

'I think everyone does. For that case, there's people all over the world who've got access to my report and they've gone over every word. You try just to do your job, but I think you'd be lying if you said you weren't aware of it.'

Despite assuring me he probably has 'nothing of interest to add' to the David Hookes story, he takes me immediately to a scenario I hadn't even considered.

'I remember arriving at the ICU. I remember that very clearly. It was uncomfortable because everyone knew who we were. Everyone else who's there is trying to help the patient. Everyone is trying to help him recover and get better. That's not why I'm there.'

Given that David Hookes's organs obviously needed to remain intact for donation and there wasn't going to be any dissection involved, I wondered why the team performing the organ removal couldn't take the samples Dr Burke needed.

'We're the ones who have to go to court and explain ourselves . . . and people who've been assaulted, they have a certain look about them. If you've had blunt-force trauma you might have injuries around your mouth, around your nose, that sort of thing. Someone might've grabbed you around the neck . . .

'They're things you'd think would be important to those clinicians, and they probably are, but they're more interested in number one, keeping people alive, and when the person's brain dead, or heading that way, they're interested in making sure their organs are suitable for transplantation. Whereas what I do is to come in from a different angle. We see things a bit differently.

'And our attitudes have changed a lot in the last few years. We were a bit nervous back then about the possibility of a case of assault and homicide going into theatre and having organs retrieved, and then we do the autopsy . . . we were concerned about there being injuries we couldn't explain but I think we've all realised that it's not going to introduce artefacts that'll give us trouble in court. I've never heard of anyone, any of my colleagues, having problems in court.

'But it's not a common occurrence and people tend to get a bit nervous whenever things are outside their normal practice.'

At 5 pm on Monday, 19 January 2004, David Hookes was declared dead. Up to ten seriously ill people benefited from his organs, inspiring his widow Robyn to establish the David Hookes Foundation to raise awareness around organ donation.

When interviewed by police, Zdravko Mićević claimed self-defence. He said that during the scuffle Hookes punched him twice in the stomach and managed to grip him in such a way that scared Mićević and made him feel vulnerable. 'I was worried of getting pulled down to the ground and I threw a punch back,' he said.[27]

'We had about thirty-five-odd witnesses, and not one, not one witness sees that,' remembers Charlie.

Memory distortion notwithstanding, you'd have to consider yourself very unlucky for thirty-five witnesses to have missed or failed to mention those two punches. But that was Mićević's position and he stuck to it.

What was never in doubt as far as Charlie was concerned was the sincere distress and remorse of Zdravko Mićević. Having had no prior contact with police, Mićević was bailed and allowed to return to the home he shared with his parents and siblings in working-class St Albans. Friends and family came to show their support, as did the family priest, and former boxing opponents called radio stations to say he was not only a good fighter, but a good sport and a good bloke.

'I feel sorry for the parents,' neighbour Vince Camilleri told a door-knocking reporter, 'they're such nice people, they don't deserve this.'

'There's no doubt it was a tragedy for both families,' says Charlie.

Roughly a month after the incident, the Mićević family moved. The death threats hadn't stopped coming. If anything, there were more frightening letters and phone calls every day. A month or so after that a passer-by called triple zero to report the house was on fire.

'Every letter says, "We're going to kill you, we're going to kill your family,"' said neighbour Lily Fry the next day, but 'one of the letters had threatened to burn the house down with the family in it.'

Mićević's lawyer Brian Rolfe lamented that it was 'beyond imagination' that he might receive a fair trial. [28]

It was August 2005 before the matter finally made it to the Victorian Supreme Court. Ever practical, Charlie and the DPP had decided to charge Mićević with assault as well as manslaughter, figuring they'd accept assault if they couldn't get manslaughter over the line.

The trial was a media circus of epic proportions, with a number of high-profile witnesses like Darren Lehmann called to give evidence and pushed hard by Terry Forrest, QC, acting for Zdravko Mićević.

Forrest asked Lehmann if his was a 'sanitised version of what happened'. 'Have you cleaned it up in order to protect the reputations of the people involved?'

'No,' was Lehmann's response. [29]

There was much interest too in the appearance of Christine Padfield, who had accompanied David Hookes on the night.

Three months before the trial got underway, Padfield appeared on an episode of the flagship ABC program *Australian Story* and spoke of her heartache at being 'shut out' of the last moments of Hookes's life.

'Not long after we had turned up at the hospital, Robyn arrived probably about five minutes after us. So it was hard. It was hard not being able to go and see him and be there for him because the family wouldn't allow it.'

Christine went on to say, 'I had a call from Cricket Victoria just to say that the family had decided to turn off the life-support system and that it would be on the news that night.

'It was hard not to be able to go back and get my things from his place, but unfortunately other people had gone to his place and decided that all the things that weren't David's would just be thrown away.'

David's half-brother Terry Cranage had some views about the David Hookes Foundation as well. 'The one thing that made me very sad was what I would call the commercialisation of David's organs being donated,' said Terry. 'The fact that Robyn has started this organisation, the David Hookes Foundation – I think obviously it's a great cause. At the same time, she's maintained a very public notion that her and David were happily married when in fact they were separated.'[30]

Understandably the program raised a few eyebrows, but the outpouring of anger from other women claiming to be in intimate relationships with David Hookes at the time of his death turned the usually sedate Monday night program into a media sensation.

'I too was David's lover for fifteen years and probably not the only one,' read one post.

'A very dear friend of mine was having a relationship with Mr David Hookes for many years, approx eight years in fact, right up until his sudden and tragic death,' added another.

Derryn Hinch, who was also on Melbourne radio station 3AW at the time, claimed to know two other women who were in relationships with Hookes. One of them emailed him: 'I wasn't aware of a so-called Melbourne girlfriend. David and I had been seeing each other for some six years . . . Now I feel like I was just used, lied to, led on and whatever else you can think of.'

Upon reflection, Ms Padfield posted the following response: 'At no point in time was I that naïve in thinking that David was not seeing any other women as we had not made a dedicated commitment to each other.'[31]

It wasn't ideal from the perspective of the prosecution. Already attempting to rewrite the law books, they had to counter the perception that their victim was a famously argumentative man, if not downright arrogant and entitled.

At trial, Zdravko Mićević's story started to cut through. He told the court that he and the other two bouncers were outnumbered, which was clearly true, and that he was trying to protect himself in a violent and volatile situation. Slowly and skilfully, his legal team chipped away at the stereotype of the aggressive bouncer, revealing instead a young man who, in the minds of many, had never been in trouble in his life, who nobody had a bad word for, and who was just doing his job. At the same time, they built a picture of a group of arrogant sportsmen led by an alpha male who believed himself exceptional in every circumstance, even during closing time at the pub.

Dr Michael Burke's evidence was as straightforward as one would expect. He testified that the amount of alcohol David Hookes drank on the night may have affected his ability to break the fall that caused his death. He found that the blood alcohol content of between 0.14 and 0.162 may also have affected Hookes's breathing and heartbeat and lessened his chances of survival.

According to Dr Burke, the autopsy showed significant injury to Hookes's skull caused by his head hitting the road, resulting in a brain haemorrhage. He found bruising behind the ears and neck as a result of the bleeding.

Burke described the punch that landed on Hookes's left cheek as 'mild to moderate'. While there was some facial bruising, there was no damage to his teeth, which would be expected from a stronger blow. There were small cuts on his lips that may have been caused by the resuscitation attempts.

After a thirteen-day trial and four days of deliberations, the jury acquitted Zdravko Mićević of all charges in the death of David Hookes.

'The jury accepted it wasn't a dangerous act,' says Charlie Bezzina in retrospect. 'The defence was that no one expects to kill someone with one blow.

'Sure, I can understand the manslaughter, but the common assault? See, this is the thing with juries, and we never know what goes on in a jury room, but he's the only one saying it was self-defence. We've got thirty-five witnesses looking at one incident and not one of them is supporting him in what he's said, and they acquit him?

'I believe the jury thought David Hookes would have antagonised Zdravko because of his reputation. The evidence didn't show that but I believe they read that into it and acquitted Zdravko on everything.'

On the steps of the Victorian Supreme Court after the verdict, Zdravko Mićević, who was by then twenty-three years old, told reporters, 'I feel like a million dollars, to tell you the truth.' He also offered his condolences to the Hookes family.[32]

According to Charlie that was no empty gesture. Zdravko and his father met with Charlie within weeks of the acquittal. There were no hard feelings between them because they'd built a rapport. There was a reason for the visit, though: Zdravko wished to meet with the Hookes family, in person, to offer his condolences and apologise. Charlie agreed to pass the message on but advised that the family was still 'too raw' for such a meeting.

In the years following the Hookes matter the Victorian government ran a concerted campaign to rebrand the 'king-hit' as a 'coward-punch'. In 2014 the Napthine government introduced the Coward's Punch Manslaughter amendment into legislation. It mandated a ten-year minimum sentence for anyone found guilty of causing death by a punch to a victim's head or neck, or in circumstances of gang violence.

It's hard to draw comfort from an event like the David Hookes matter. Charlie Bezzina still smarts at the memory of the 'not guilty' verdict even as he praises the young man it spared a prison sentence. David Hookes gave life back to untold numbers of people not only though his own commitment to organ donation but through the attention he drew to it. That's cold comfort to those he left behind, though. Scores of people saw and heard the sickening smack that killed him that night and many have suffered life-altering stress as a consequence. And the forensic pathologist in the middle – the man who made it possible for the aims of the family, the homicide squad, the hospital trauma team, the organ donation team and the organ recipients to all be achieved – remembers little aside from the looks on the faces of people when they realised who he was when he arrived.

4

FLOODS
AND FLAMES

'Oh god, girl, you need your roots done!'

So says Associate Professor Richard Bassed as I appear via Zoom on his computer screen. I couldn't deny it. We were twelve weeks into what would become a fifteen-week COVID-19 lockdown and I, like everyone else in Melbourne, was looking shabby. For his part, Professor Bassed was not only uncharacteristically dishevelled but was also nursing a very amorous hairless cat in a colourful pullover. But, by that point, Zoom had made us all immune to each other's private proclivities. No insight into another person's domicile provoked the slightest intrigue anymore.

Nor was I provoked by the comment about my hair. After months of regrowth, my roots were awaiting a date with a bowl of industrial-grade bleach. In Richard Bassed I have a kindred spirit and I took the comment in the vein in which it was intended. We two cheeky outliers, who've always enjoyed our witty, flirtatious encounters, had been reduced to a pair of fluffy wrecks Zooming from our spare rooms. He was commiserating with me rather than insulting me.

Richard made me laugh about that and other things, and distracted me for ages. 'I knew you'd do this,' I said. 'I knew you'd make this fun and then I'd have to be the one to bring up the tsunami and Black Saturday.'

Despite being one of the most senior members of the VIFM team, Richard comes across as one of the most relaxed and approachable forensic specialists, but it's a bit of a deception. The truth is, he guards difficult memories with a Swiss Army knife of charm-based deflection mechanisms. Every so often, though, one of the memories punches through and then he tends to look you right in the eyes to see if you'll stay with him.

When Richard's memories punch through, they punch hard. He doesn't speak in clinical jargon or search for gentle language to soften things. He says it how he feels it and when he looks you in the eyes it's not a challenging look but a look of helplessness, as if he's asking what you thought was going to happen when you invited his memories out.

Richard is a farm boy, which is perhaps why death in its purest sense doesn't trouble him. For as long as he can remember, he's known that creatures die and that, even in perfect health, they are but meat and bones. He has a keen sense too that there are natural and decent reasons for creatures to die. There are also indecent and unnatural reasons and when he comes face to face with those he is appalled, sometimes to the point of heartache.

Not all of his colleagues have an emotional reaction to the circumstances that deliver other human beings to them. Some of them don't engage with those circumstances beyond a passing acknowledgement. Anecdotally, the amount of emotion forensic specialists expend on the job doesn't seem to predict the impact of the work on them or the longevity of their career. As with homicide detectives, it seems you never can tell who will turn up day after day for forty years without a problem, and who'll be pushed too far one day and snap. Some believe it's the ability to fully emotionally process each job that enables them to keep moving through them, while others believe their firm boundaries are the key to their success.

Richard Bassed has certainly worked through some of the most harrowing scenes imaginable and appears to have survived to tell the tale. I have wondered, though, to his amusement, how much of that is down to the fact that he's married to a psychiatrist.

On top of being deployed to do challenging work by virtue of his expertise, he's also been known to volunteer for the messiest jobs. When the homicide squad located a dead drug dealer down a sewer drain some two weeks after his demise, it was Richard who ended up going in to retrieve him. It's way beyond his professional remit, but he was the only one on the scene who could stomach it and he likes it when everyone just mucks in to get something done. 'That's the way it should always be,' he says more than once about these kinds of situations. It's what he likes about the big jobs. 'Like' isn't the best word to use when describing victim identification after a massive disaster but it's the only one that comes close in the English language. The Germans probably have a perfect word that's fourteen letters long, but the point is that Richard is happiest when human beings are pulling together and flouting the conventions of rank and respectability.

Eventually he acquiesces to the task at hand and shifts gears for the conversation we need to have. He knows where he has to get to, and it's a long way beneath his normal, outward-facing, social self, so he enters into a kind of process. He starts letting some of those memories filter through. He's clearly verbalising scenes he's seeing in his mind's eye. There's little context, and each vignette seems unrelated to the one before and the one after, as far as I can make out, but they are somehow strung together in a stream of consciousness for him. They are sketches that flicker through his mind when he focuses on the idea of 'cases that have disturbed me'.

I vaguely remember raising the question of why some cases are more disturbing than others for him, but he seems to have latched onto it and is now using it as a mantra.

'I had to watch a video the other day of a guy getting king-hit. Just horrible. He was stiff before he hit the ground. That disturbed me. There was a young guy who murdered his mate. Years ago. He made a diagram about how he was going to do it. So I walked into the mortuary and there was the body and next to it was the bit of paper with the drawing. "Cut here, cut here, cut here . . ." The deliberate thinking behind it. The premeditation. That disturbs me.'

He seems to be taking himself down through levels. It's like some kind of self-hypnosis.

'Old people who want to die and can't. They've just had enough. They're sick, whatever, their pain medications aren't working, and they can't bloody die. Like this old guy who dug his own pacemaker wires out of his chest with a knife, wired them into a power cord, plugged it in and turned it on. In his late eighties. Just had enough. It's just such a horrible, disrespectful way for someone to have to end their life.'

Down, down . . .

'Suicides are hard. Especially the young ones who probably don't even know what they're doing. It brings to mind the memory of two young girls, fourteen and fifteen, probably in the same year of school. They were found hanging up in the bush somewhere and they'd written all over their legs in texta, "This'll show you, I'll get you back, Jason, for being mean to me," and they bloody hanged themselves.

'I recovered the wife in the Ramage case, remember the nice, rich family from Canterbury? Husband killed his wife, took her out and buried her in a forest? Few years ago? Just a perfectly happy couple and one day the husband gets up and murders his wife, and no one knows why. Those sorts of things bother me.'

Down, down . . .

'I had to identify the three kids who were dragged out of the dam after their father pretended to have a coughing fit . . . He got convicted, didn't he?'

He did. He was Robert Farquharson, and he was convicted of murdering his three sons Jai (ten), Tyler (seven) and Bailey (two) on Father's Day in 2005. He was supposed to be returning them to their mother after an access weekend, but instead drove off the Princes Highway at Winchelsea in south-west Victoria and into a dam. He then left the boys in the car and swam ashore. Farquharson flagged down Shane Atkinson and Tony McClelland on the side of the dark highway and told them immediately that he'd 'killed the kids', and when they tried to go and look for them, he insisted, 'It's too late, they're already gone.'

Instead, they said he was fixated on getting to his ex-wife Cindy Gambino's house to tell the news to her and her new partner Stephen Moules in person. Atkinson and McClelland later testified that Farquharson wouldn't even allow them to call the police or any other emergency services. His only interest was in telling the children's mother, face to face, that their children were dead.

Farquharson was found guilty on three counts of murder on 22 July 2010. At sentencing, Justice Lex Lasry said, '. . . when you left the vehicle you did so with the knowledge and intent that your three children would be drowned and they were. For them it must have been a terrifying death . . .

'Ms Gambino was not able to be present when her victim impact statement was presented to the court due to illness and those kinds of difficulties are likely to remain with her for the rest of her life. Mr Stephen Moules went to the dam on the night of 4 September 2005 and spent significant time in the water searching for these children . . .

'I have no hesitation in coming to the conclusion that the appropriate sentence for you in relation to each of these three counts is life imprisonment . . . Therefore, for the murder of Jai Farquharson you will be sentenced to life imprisonment, for the murder of Tyler Farquharson you will be sentenced to life imprisonment and for the murder of Bailey Farquharson you will be sentenced to life imprisonment.'[1]

The memory of Cindy Gambino's three lost sons creates a very clear thread and Richard starts listing the names of child victims he's tended to. As he does, their faces flash before my eyes too because these stories are seared into the memories of everyone of a certain age in a certain community. They are the children we never forget. Sometimes laws are changed because of the terrible things that happened to them, sometimes people write books and make movies about them, but they are locked forever in childhood and in fleeting, freckle-faced images taken before we knew their names.

Someone has to care for them after the terrible thing has happened, although it's not something most of us want to think about. We know that when it comes to seeking justice against the perpetrators, the work undertaken by Richard and his colleagues is vital in securing convictions in court, but we don't like to think about those processes. Now that I have been afforded some insight into the processes performed at VIFM, and more importantly into the culture of the place, I actually found it comforting and also moving.

I became aware of a profoundly intimate relationship between the pathologists and the families of the dead that I suspect most of the families remain unaware of, simply by virtue of the fact that they'd rather not think about where their loved one was during those hours. I remember speaking to a lovely man about the possibility of including the story of his father's murder in this book. In the end it wasn't possible because there was an unresolved inquest pending, but he and the rest of his family were very generous with their reflections on the experience, which was particularly shocking as it was the result of a completely random attack. The first inkling he had that there was any trouble at all was when he encountered a police roadblock on his way to the family business. He didn't know his father was lying dead on the road up ahead.

Over the course of several meetings, this man and I circled closer to the subject matter of this book, which is to say, I tried to find a way to tell him I wanted to write about the person who'd conducted his father's autopsy. Can you imagine? Finally, I broached the topic this way: I asked what, if anything, he knew about where the ambulance took his dad that day. He said he actually had no idea. The hospital, maybe? I asked him if he wanted to know.

It's so easy to say that a person 'isn't there anymore' in a dead body unless it happens to be the body of a person you love. Especially if the person has been torn from that body suddenly and recklessly. A lovely woman called June Meredith told me once about the agonising hours she sat in her lounge room in Albury, knowing the police were processing the crime scene around her daughter Kim's body in a car park downtown. 'I said to the detective, Belinda Neil, "How long did she sit there for, and why couldn't I just go and hold her hand?"

'Why couldn't I just go there and sit there? Not touch any evidence or anything, but just go there and sit there . . . and care for her?'

It's hard to convey the depth of the powerlessness experienced by families in the wake of a suspicious, unexplained or violent death. The man whose father had been killed in the street by a stranger was upset about the upcoming inquest because although it had nothing to do with his father and everything to do with the perpetrator, and whether or not he should have been living in the community at the time of the attack, the family still had to participate in the proceedings. It was several years since the murder and they still felt powerless, even when it came to putting it behind them.

So when I asked this man if he wanted to know about who was caring for his father during those first confusing hours when he and the rest of the family were finding out what had happened, and why his father hadn't returned from his walk, it was in the context of this powerlessness. It was part of a broader conversation about all the infuriating unknowns and dehumanising officialdom. He said yes, he did want to know more about the people who brought his father back inside and protected him after that terrible thing happened out in the street. It was good to remember his father had been cared for.

Many victims' families form a close bond with the detectives who work their cases. A kind of intimacy is created when strangers are brought together for the sole purpose of surviving something brutal together. Knowing what I know now, I often think of the forensic pathologists as the invisible members of those relationships, from the family's point of view at least. Most families will never know that the unseen thread that binds them for the rest of their lives to those detectives extends a little further. Just behind the detectives there's another small group of men and women, a little shyer, a little less commanding, perhaps, but no less involved in the fight to survive the brutality of it all.

So Dr Richard Bassed sits in his spare room this day and names a dozen or so children whose deaths have rendered them intimately bound to him for life. Eventually he falls silent and I believe he's reached the place where he needs to be to talk about two of the bleakest environments I can imagine ever setting foot in. Two places he called 'home' for months on end.

Over the second weekend of February 2009, Richard was holidaying in the historic gold rush town of Heathcote in northern Victoria with his three eldest children when Premier John Brumby issued a warning about the weather conditions expected for Saturday, 7 February.

'It's just as bad a day as you can imagine,' he said of the record-breaking temperatures, expected to peak at 46 degrees Celsius in Melbourne, 'and on top of that, the state is tinder-dry. People need to exercise real common sense tomorrow,' he pleaded, before declaring that, in terms of fire conditions, it would be 'the worst day in the history of the state'.[2]

Along with the high temperatures, winds of up to 125 kilometres per hour completed the so-called 'perfect storm' of fire danger. At 11.50 am on that Saturday morning, the winds took out power lines in the Kinglake/Whittlesea area, igniting a fire. The winds fanned the flames towards the nearby pine plantation, where they rapidly grew in intensity.

The first time VIFM Office Manager Dr Jodie Leditschke called Richard Bassed was mid-afternoon. 'There's fires everywhere,' he remembers her saying. 'There's five people dead. I'll keep you posted, we don't know what's going on.'

He continues: 'Then by Saturday night, "There's twenty people dead . . . I'll keep you posted but you'd better come back to work."

'So Sunday morning I piled the kids in the car, drove back through Wallan, and when you drive over that hill, Pretty Sally Hill, and you look to the left, the whole mountain was just a wall of fire. The road was covered in smoke and there were fire engines everywhere.

'I was on the phone to Jodie. She was saying, "We think there's at least fifty people dead, when are you going to get here?"

'The kids were a bit scared. They were fifteen, thirteen and nine at that stage. They knew I had something to do with it. They knew I was involved at a certain level. They didn't know exactly what I did, but they knew I'd been to the tsunami so I guess the fifteen-year-old had a pretty good idea of what I did.'

What Richard Bassed does, at least when it comes to disaster scenarios like the Black Saturday bushfires of 2009 or the Boxing Day tsunami of 2004, is identify the dead. Specifically, he specialises in identifying the dead via dental records. He's an odontologist. As he puts it, 'They don't call me in unless there isn't much else left.'

It's hard to believe a fifteen-year-old girl doesn't know what her father was doing in Thailand for twelve months after the tsunami. It strikes me as almost adorable that he might think it's possible, in the way that fathers like to imagine their daughters remain innocent forever, against all evidence to the contrary. I'm reminded of an earlier conversation about a what-does-your-daddy-do day at kindergarten when the same child proudly announced to her classmates that he was 'the tooth fairy'. He beamed proudly as he retold the story too. Fathers and their daughters, eh?

'So I dropped the kids off at their mum's house and I went straight to work,' he continues. 'They rented me an apartment in one of those giant buildings across the road and I just stayed there for three months.'

I want to know if Richard can explain the feelings he experienced as he drove back to work that day, knowing something of what lay ahead. He says he remembers thinking a lot about logistics. He thought about the other odontologists around Australia and the world whom he could call in if he needed, and what equipment he'd have to stock up on and that sort of thing. But then his eyes drift upwards and he remembers a feeling.

'I remember feeling good that, once again like Thailand, I was about to be doing what I'm meant to be doing. This is what I'm meant to do.'

As significant life markers go, the 2004 Boxing Day tsunami and the 2009 Black Saturday bushfires are notable in anyone's language. Coming as they did just over four years apart, they represent some clear turning points in

Dr Bassed's life, and they cast long shadows over his philosophical perspective, both professionally and personally. When he got the call-up to assist with victim identification after the Boxing Day tsunami it was his first big overseas forensic job, a career milestone. It also came at a personal low point, as he was newly divorced.

'I was staying with my parents. I had no money and nowhere else to stay so I was back on the farm. When the tsunami call came through and I said yes, I really wanted to go.'

On the morning of 26 December 2004, a massive earthquake shook the ocean floor off the west coast of northern Sumatra, Indonesia, at 7.58 am local time. Measuring 9.1 on the seismic magnitude scale, it was a 'megathrust earthquake', meaning it was caused by one tectonic plate sliding underneath another one and was one of the most powerful earthquakes possible on Earth. Millions of people who lived along the shoreline of the Indian Ocean – in countries like Thailand, Sri Lanka, Indonesia, India, Malaysia and the Maldives to name a few – were affected. And due to the timing of the earthquake, just after Christmas, those countries were also hosting millions of holiday-makers from around the world.

Along with the Indonesian island of Bali, the island of Phuket off the west coast of Thailand is popular as the first overseas adventure for many Australians. It has accommodation options for everyone, from the once-in-a-lifetime honeymoon, to the family-friendly fortnight and the cheap and nasty end-of-season trip with the boys. The entertainment options are equally broad, with Bangla Road in Patong being the road to either avoid or direct the taxi straight to from the airport, depending on the purpose of your trip. Some things never seem to change.

But things have changed a lot since 2004. Consider how long it takes now for a silly celebrity social media post to be heard around the world. Then try to imagine how two hours after the tsunami had levelled massive areas of the city of Banda Aceh in Indonesia, a city that's just 200 kilometres away as the crow flies over the Gulf of Thailand, millions of people in Thailand still didn't know about the tsunami at all.

The tsunami swept through Banda Aceh in three massive waves just twenty minutes after the earthquake, killing tens of thousands of people. Yet somehow the major international resort island of Phuket wasn't warned. The quake itself was felt by many people on Phuket. As if that wasn't bad enough, an hour after the tsunami hit Phuket, it hit Chennai in India, which was similarly unprepared. Ten thousand people, mostly women and children, died in the Chennai area that day.

The first iPhone didn't hit the market until 2007. In 2004, we were still years away from spending our beach days scrolling through our phones, which I would suggest is how the tsunami sneaked up on so many people that day.

There were many handicams at the beach, though. In the days and weeks after Boxing Day, innumerable home videos played out on the news, in which puzzled holiday-makers watched on from busy beaches while the water beneath them slipped away. Out, out, out, all the way out it went in the eeriest manner, leaving the ocean bed bare. Parents can be heard in every language of the world attempting to explain the phenomenon to their children as a slightly darker blue line appears on the horizon. Ominously, small sunburnt children with beaded hair frolic carelessly on the wet sand right out the front. Their parents squint and shade their eyes as they try to make out what's happening out there.

As it draws closer, the blue line turns white at the top and then breaks on the fishing boats, tossing them like bathtub toys. The voices on the videos often marvel delight-edly at first. What a wonder! And to think I actually have it on film!

But the wave doesn't subside like normal waves do, this one surges forward and forward and still forward as if it's never going to stop coming. As it swallows up the fragile timber furniture of the local sellers it actually appears to be gaining momentum. It's like it's feeding on things in its path. The parents start to get nervous. They're not smiling anymore. They're snatching up the children and running.

Most eyes and cameras are trained inland now, confused by the water advancing through the resorts and streets, when the second wave crashes behind them. It's so much bigger and more forceful than the first one. It's the second wave that will do much of the structural damage.

The second wave will smash windows, sheer off balconies and destroy entire buildings. It will sweep it all up, along with every man, woman and child at ground level and stir them all up together. It will turn timber posts and corrugated iron roofs into deadly spears and razor blades. One survivor described it as 'like being thrown around in a washing machine full of nails'.[3]

Survivors, who, by a twist of fate, stood on balconies above the third floor of buildings built strong enough to withstand the water, watched helplessly as wave after wave surged below. The cries of the frightened and injured grew fewer in number with every subsiding swell until at last there were no more cries.

Five days later, Dr Richard Bassed arrived at Phuket Airport.

'They put us up in the fanciest hotel up at the northern end of Phuket. We walked into this fancy hotel and it was all opulent. Thai people in traditional costumes handing us cocktails, "sah-wah-dee", bowing and everything. Porters carrying our bags to the room with a giant king-sized bed and a big balcony with a view over the ocean. I'm sitting there and then all of a sudden I think, "What's that smell?"

'The mortuary, or the temple, was only three or four kilometres away . . . and you could smell it. So, it was a really strange juxtaposition of being treated like we're on a holiday but the constant reminder through this smell that we were at work.

'We left for work at 6 am every morning and got back at about eight o'clock every night. Probably twenty or thirty bodies a day. One rest day a week and we did three-week rotations. That first time was really hard work. That's when all the bodies were all disorganised, they were still bringing them in, they were still collecting them, they were all swelling up in the sun. We were building dry-ice igloos to try and keep the bodies cold because they had no shipping containers there yet.'

In Phuket the average daily maximum temperature in December is 33 degrees Celsius. The average daily minimum temperature is 25 degree Celsius, for that matter, and the humidity hovers around 80 per cent. Before the 'igloos' were invented by building a small wall of dry ice around a group of bodies and then covering the group with a tent or tarpaulin, lumps of dry ice were simply sat on top of the blackening corpses, which were laid out in rows around the temple. Lying the ice on top of the bodies was not only visually horrifying but most ineffectual. The dry ice damaged the top area of the body upon which it sat, while having virtually no chilling effect whatsoever on the underside.

After a full two weeks where Richard and others tried to keep the remains cool, refrigerated shipping containers finally arrived and thousands of bodies were carefully moved into them, with Richard mucking in as usual. But just as some kind of order appeared to be descending on the scene a rather disruptive directive came down from the

Thai government. It demanded that the remains of Thai locals be separated from foreigners, immediately.

Most of us, like the members of the Thai Government, probably have no idea why the international team of forensic clinicians in Phuket found the order so preposterous three weeks after the tsunami. I can tell you it had nothing to do with political correctness or everyone being equal in death.

'We sent them a photo,' says Richard, 'of this giant temple area full of black, bloated bodies, all looking identical. You wouldn't know if one was Thai or German or African. I mean, if they could tell the locals from the foreigners by then, they were doing better than us!'

For many reasons, this particular DVI job would be one of the longest ever undertaken.

'The biggest problem with the tsunami was that they recovered all these bodies and brought them to the temple because that's what they do in Thailand. That's their custom. When you die they bring you to the temple. Wat Yan Yao, it was. But they didn't record where they got the body from. Half these bodies were found in their hotel rooms, so they could've been so easily identified but once they were removed from their rooms we just had no context and no idea. So we had to fully examine every single deceased person and we had to examine them over and over and over again because they kept stuffing up the numbering system. They get the numbering wrong and all of a sudden, you've got to start again because you don't know which body's which anymore. You don't know which bit of paper relates to which body.

'You'd open a body bag with a number on it, and there'd be another body bag inside it with a different number on it. You'd open it and there's a tag with a different number.

'We'd do a full dental chart, X-rays of everybody, we'd take a DNA sample, which involved taking one of their teeth, a back tooth that had no fillings, and we'd also take a section of their femur.

'They couldn't find a DNA lab that would test the specimens because DNA was very expensive back then. They eventually found a lab in China that would do it. Seven hundred samples were sent over to China and they got back one positive result. The lab just couldn't do it. Too many contamination issues. People were using the same saw to cut the femur out of fifty different bodies . . .

'It was just very poor quality control. There were people there not to do any work. Just there for the fun of it.'

Listening to him speak about the work identifying people after the tsunami, it dawns on me just how different it was from the work of the MH17 victim identification team. I'd already started researching that set-up in anticipation of speaking with one of Richard's colleagues who'd attended the scene of the plane crash. I knew that after Malaysian Airlines flight MH17 was shot down over Eastern Ukraine in 2014, the recovery mission was fraught but the forensic work itself was swift and dignified. It took place at a pristine, state-of-the-art temporary laboratory in Hilversum Airfield in the Netherlands.

As I realise I've allowed myself to drift off, imagining the Hilversum space, I have to hold my hands up to interrupt Richard because I can't quite find any words to explain my confusion about the difference between that and what he's describing in Thailand. All I can manage is a stupefied 'But why?'

'Why what?' he asks patiently.

'Why was this so different to Hilversum?' I ask, as though he's somehow ruined something for me.

Even though Richard wasn't part of the MH17 victim identification team he needs no further clarification. He knows exactly what I'm asking.

'Just the numbers,' he says. 'The number of people that died and the fact that two-and-a-half thousand people who died on Phuket were from multiple different countries.

'There were lots of arguments about who was going to be in charge. It ended up that the Australians were in charge for the first six months because we'd done the Bali bombings. The Americans weren't interested. They didn't come because there were only one or two Americans that died.'

It's at this point I realise how political these recovery missions are.

Quite simply, after the downing of MH17 the Dutch government was dealing with 283 victims, most of whom were Dutch. Therefore the Dutch assembled the best equipment and the thirty best pathologists in the world, to get the job done in the most dignified fashion possible. The Dutch, and many others, believed and still do that Putin's Russia is to blame for the incident and the matter continues to be prosecuted at both diplomatic and legal levels.

The Boxing Day tsunami, a cataclysmic natural disaster, is estimated to have killed in excess of 230,000 people across a multilingual, multi-faith, ethnically diverse and politically contentious diaspora of developing nations taking in Indonesia, Sri Lanka, Thailand, India, the Maldives, Burma, Somalia, South Africa and Malaysia. Add to that, as Richard mentioned, the region is a holiday destination for people from all over the world. There simply was no government well placed, financially or otherwise, to assume leadership in the aftermath of the tsunami as the Dutch had done post MH17. And a recovery effort of this magnitude required the same thirty best people in the world who were called up to Hilversum, plus around three hundred more, which explains how some less-than-stellar applicants were working on the tsunami identification.

'It was the largest DVI ever done and the first time this many pathologists, from this many countries, had got together to do something. So it was weird. It was a weird thing to do and I know it sounds like . . . why would anyone want to do that? But the closest I can describe it is like the way you read in books and see in movies the camaraderie between soldiers who've been in battle together. You build up this really close relationship really quickly with people that you've never seen before and never met before – coppers, doctors, there were Thai army guys – and you're all experiencing this terrible thing together. You build an incredible camaraderie. And who'd want to be a dentist?'

'You could've been an orthodontist,' I remind him as he laughs. 'You could be making millions straightening children's teeth and playing golf.'

'What a boring life!'

I remind him of his earlier, more noble response and he begrudgingly acquiesces. 'And yes, I do feel like it's what I was put here to do. It's the thing I can do, for a number of reasons, that most people can't and so it's my opportunity to contribute to the greater good, I suppose.'

He continues, 'But because I was there intermittently over the course of a year, I got to see when it became more organised and when it became more rational. After that first episode at the temple, the Norwegians flew in a sort of prefab hospital. It was these giant, long tunnels of put-together buildings that they flew in with helicopters. Then we had to re-examine everybody again.'

Richard laughs at this, although it's a laugh of exhaustion rather than amusement, even after all these years. It's a laugh-or-you'll-cry laugh. He fixes me with his wounded, challenging look and adds, 'By then they were really decomposing.'

It turns out those shipping containers weren't exactly consistent in their refrigeration capabilities.

'The shipping containers were stacked up on top of each other, three high, all around us. Hundreds of shipping containers with probably forty bodies in each one. You've been to Thailand, you've seen the wiring. They'd bring these containers in and they'd have blokes on the roof with sticks, pushing the power lines out of the way so the containers could get through.'

Evidently, some of those low-hanging wires carrying electricity to the shipping containers were damaged during that process.

'Some bodies are frozen, some are not frozen and every now and then a container breaks down. There was one that no one noticed for about a month. The only way we found out about it was because of the chickens who started congregating underneath it and pecking at the sand the fluids were leaking onto. They were christened the "cadaver chickens". The doors were bulging on it. I was one of the people who had to go in and clean that out.'

Even a farm boy has his limits. Surely the day Richard had to nudge the cadaver chickens aside to clean out the broken-down shipping container in the heat and humidity of Thailand after months of examining and re-examining remains was a low point that left some emotional imprint. Camaraderie is only going to carry you so far.

'My mum and dad used to say, "We're all going to get eaten by worms one day."'

Mixed with the usual humidity, cooking smoke and spices and the smells of the DVI, the atmosphere was heavy with grief. Many families, local and foreign alike, waited close to the temporary mortuary for months on end, hoping every day for news. Hoping to take a loved one home.

'I found it horrifying that there were these boards of photographs of rotting, decomposing bodies, and families would walk up and down trying to pick which one belonged to them. It's horrifying for those families. Dreading, dreading that they'll find someone they recognise, and dreading not.

'And really, there's just no hope, right? They still do it now in mass disasters around the world. It's just a waste of time and it ends up with wrong identifications. Someone takes the wrong body home and then you've made two mistakes.

'In my later rotations we were actually releasing bodies. We had to do this pre-release check. Every time someone was identified by DNA or dental records or whatever, they had to check all the paperwork, check this, check that, then I had to re-check the body. Then the family would be waiting outside. If it was a Thai family, the body would be given to them, in a coffin, just outside, under, believe it or not, a tent that had a Sprite logo on it. Then they'd carry it about two hundred metres down the road to a tap and they'd open the coffin, take every bone out and wash it before putting them all back in the coffin.

123

'I was so wired for the whole three weeks every time I went over there. I'd come home and I'd be miserable. It was so confusing. There were monks wandering around . . . it was surreal, but it was also exciting. I thought, "I'm doing some real good and I'm helping people get their families back," so it really felt like the defining point of my career . . . up until that point.'

Thousands of children were killed just in Phuket during the Boxing Day tsunami. Without mentioning that fact specifically, I ask if Richard found it harder to keep in regular touch with his own young children while he was in Thailand, or if it made him need to hear their voices more.

'Definitely more,' he says without hesitation. 'I talked to them on the phone a lot. Actually, I did have terrible nightmares about them after that, though, for a long time.'

He looks me straight in the eyes. 'They were dead and I had to wash their hair in a sink. One by one.'

'Do you still have that nightmare?' I ask him after a long pause.

'No, I haven't had it in years. I'd forgotten about it, actually.'

He switches tone, clearly swapping the shaky memory for a stronger one. 'They actually came and stayed in the apartment with me a bit during the Black Saturday period,' he says jauntily.

I'm shocked by the thought that, after a day of identifying the remains of bushfire victims, a slumber party with three teenage girls would seem relaxing but he assures me they were great nights, even if he did smell like a bonfire no matter how hard he scrubbed in the shower.

Clearly, by the time the calls started coming through about the bushfires, Dr Richard Bassed was in a more confident place in his life. He held a much more senior position at VIFM and was asked to attend some of the scenes with police on the Monday and Tuesday after the fires, to help recover remains.

'There were one hundred and forty-five death scenes, but they called us to some of the ones where they thought they might have trouble separating one individual from another. We had to try and work out which body part belonged to which person because often they were all huddled together. You know? When the fires came over, they huddled together.

'The scene that really got me, there was three people – Mum, Dad and the kid – who had an underground bunker that was about ten feet from the back door of their kitchen. They were found in between the back door of their house, which was gone, burnt to the ground, but where it would've been, and the door of the bunker, which was perfectly safe.

'I said to the firey, "How come they didn't make it?" The house was on a hill, and then there was a valley below it and then another hill facing the house. And he said, "The fire came over that hill opposite. They mustn't have known it was coming until they saw it pop up over the hill and it would've been rocketing along at forty kilometres an hour. By the time they ran out the back door, it's got to the top of that hill and then here at this house it would've been a thousand degrees. They didn't even have time."

'The heat, that far in front of the fire would have just killed them. Breathing in super-heated air.

'The thing that was difficult was that there were lots of scenes that we should've gone to but we didn't, just because we couldn't get there. There were fires still burning in some places. Like, there was one scene where there were nine people from five different families in the same house. All these people went round to this house because it was the only brick house in the street and they were aged from three to eighty-something. That was difficult because the police recovered that scene and there were nine people and they came back with something like twenty-six body bags.

'It took weeks and weeks and weeks to actually physically sort it out, whereas if we had've gone up to the scene in the first place it would've been a little bit easier. A burnt tooth to a policeman just looks like a burnt rock or something, but I can tell the difference immediately. I can tell the difference between a human tooth and a dog's tooth. We ended up with a lot of those.

'Some people were identified relatively quickly. Intact bodies, who were found at an address, you ring up their family and find out who their dentist was, get their dental records in the next day, then you can identify them relatively quickly. But then you've got people found in a car or in the forest, then you've got no idea. Then you've got to compare them to all the dental records you've got of all the people who've been reported missing. And when you've got really tiny, fragmentary remains, then you've got to reconstruct them first.

'There was a lot of teaching police and ambos about fragile body retrieval. A lot of bubble wrap and hairspray,' he says, uncrossing and recrossing his legs.

Naturally I'm interested to know where and how people unwind after long days of this work, whenever slumber parties with daughters aren't on the cards. Again, Richard's personal growth during the four-year gap between the two disasters reveals itself.

'There's a little café down the road, it was called Blondies then, and I booked it out for the three months we worked through the Black Saturday DVI. So we could just go there for breaks and to download. We'd all go there at the end of every day for a few drinks and then I'd go to the IGA and buy a box of noodles for dinner. I'd put the telly on and watch anything but the news. I didn't watch the news for months.

'You can't get rid of the smell. It was the same in Thailand. Different smell, but the same in that it got in everywhere and you couldn't escape it. Nothing gets rid of it. Sticking stuff up your nose and all that, none of it works. You've just got to get used to it.

'In Thailand we used to go to a bar every night but it was very different. It was called the Timber Hut and it rocked. It was packed every night with people working on the tsunami: medical people, police, army guys, everyone just blowing off steam. It had this balcony that used to shake under the weight of the party and we'd joke about when it was going to come crashing down.

'You know, I actually went back there a few years later and it was really weird. I was on holiday with my girl-friend, who is now my wife, and some friends and the guys behind the bar remembered me and it was all exactly the same but for some reason I got really angry and upset. It's never happened before or since. It was really weird. The guys we were with were saying it was boring and they wanted to go somewhere else and it made me really angry. They just didn't get it.'

Richard doesn't do as much 'on the tools', as he puts it, these days.

'I feel like I've done that. I feel like I've kind of outgrown that. My main focus now is on researching better ways to do stuff. I spend my whole life on developing research projects that will help us be more efficient. For instance, one project I've got going now is developing a facial rec-ognition algorithm for the dead. So if you ever get five thousand dead people in one place again like after the tsunami, before they decompose, someone will just take a photo of every single face with their iPhone. Then we can use facial recognition software to compare them to all the driver's licence photos, identity photos and passport photos. So families won't be walking around trying to find people anymore.

'The research is much more interesting for me now, but I'm sure if another big thing happened, I'd be the first one trying to get on the plane!'

Oddly, of all the things we talked about, there was one old case Richard mentioned that niggled me and I found myself searching for more details about it days later.

It was what he'd said about the Ramage case as he was preparing himself for our conversation. The one where Richard had to recover the wife's body from the forest after the husband had murdered her. I didn't remember that case at all, which was strange because, frankly, I usually have some recollection of cases when other people ask if I remember them for one reason or another. I wondered why I didn't remember a case that sounded so terrible, tragic and recent.

A quick Google search delivered all the details of the case but left me with many more questions than answers, and I emailed Richard immediately to ask if he could spare me another quick Zoom session for a follow-up question. The next afternoon I reminded him of the way he'd described the Ramage case to me, just to be sure it was how he still imagined it.

'I remember being called by the coppers and them saying we need someone to come and help us recover a body. We know where it is, and everyone else was busy so I went out. I didn't know what state it was going to be in or anything. It was in Kinglake.'

Kinglake, you may recall, was also one of the epicentres of the Black Saturday bushfires. That seemingly invisible stream of consciousness that connected this case in Richard's mind to the place he needed to get to in our first conversation glimmered for a moment like a spider web in a streetlight.

'We came to this area of disturbed earth, with police tape around it, you know? She's in there somewhere. They gave me a trowel and in I went. I started scraping the dirt away and eventually I uncovered what was a completely intact, visibly identifiable, looked like she was asleep, tiny woman, dressed in riding boots, jodhpurs and a Laura Ashley shirt.

'I guess it stuck with me because normally the only people I recover are burnt, smashed, decomposed, beyond recognition. To recover a completely intact person was kind of a weird experience for me. It's the only time it's ever happened to me. I remember she was sort of in a foetal position, on her side with virtually no signs of injury. But I remember the facial expression. It was . . . like . . . surprised.'

The detail he remembers from that afternoon is aston-ishing for a number of reasons. Firstly, he's shocked to learn it wasn't a 'few years ago', but 2003. Before the tsunami, before Black Saturday. He's seen so many things since then and yet he remembers so many details about this perfectly intact lady. What he'd forgotten was that, far from nobody knowing why her husband got up one day and killed her, the case created a media storm and led to legislative changes in several Australian states.

Yes, the Ramages were indeed a rich family from Canterbury; their home was said to be valued at around $1.5 million back in 2003. They were, however, anything but a 'perfectly happy couple', and within days of Richard lifting Julie from the soil of Kinglake, an hour north of Melbourne, her husband James's years of violence towards her was public knowledge. By the time he was sentenced for manslaughter a year later, the case was a media sensation, due to the legal loophole his defence team used in court.

Married for twenty-three years, evidence of the terrifying ordeal Julie was living inside their multimillion-dollar mansion had long been on display. She arrived more than once with bruises and black eyes to collect her young children from kindergarten. She once confided in another mum, Gilda Pekin, who became a lifelong friend, that her husband James had headbutted her. Julie told colleague Joanne Mclean that James demanded sex every morning whether she wanted it or not. 'She hated it,' remembered Joanne. 'She couldn't stand it.'[4]

Julie was frightened to leave James, according to her friends, and clearly she was right to be. We now accept that women in abusive relationships are at the greatest danger during the period just after they leave their abusers. The loss of control seems to be a tipping point for some abusers, who take their irrational aggrievement and entitlement to terrifying new levels in an attempt to regain it somehow. This phenomenon wasn't fully understood in 2003 and rarely if ever spoken about, but instinctively Julie's friend Joanne felt afraid for her. 'I felt if she left Jamie she'd be in a lot of danger,' she said later. She admitted, 'I would tell her that he would kill her. I don't know why I felt this way.'[5]

Julie waited for James to leave the country on a business trip in May 2003 and made her move. She transferred $100,000 from their joint account into one in her own name and moved into a rental property. Surprisingly, upon his return, James embarked on a charm offensive in an attempt to woo her back. He also called in tradesmen and commenced renovations on the house that Julie had been asking for. On 18 July, just two months after her escape, Julie and James sat together watching their son play football. Julie took the opportunity of the football game to deliver some news to James. She had started seeing another man.

Whatever he felt upon hearing the news, James Ramage managed to conceal it. Julie made a passing mention of the conversation to her mother the following day but was much more interested in talking about a 'blissful' outing she'd had with her new partner. James wasn't really on her radar anymore, although she had agreed to meet him at the house the following day, Monday, to lend her designer's eye to some plans he was working on with the builder. When she arrived just after midday, there was no builder; only James, and he beat and strangled her to death.

He then dragged her body to the boot of his Jaguar, which he'd prepared by reversing it into the garage and laying a drop sheet inside. He mopped up her blood with some tea towels and soapy water before changing his clothes. He collected all the contaminated clothes and towels in a plastic bag, put them in the boot with his dead wife and drove an hour north to the dense bushland of Kinglake, where he buried everything in two shallow holes. At sentencing, Justice Robert Osborne accepted the prosecution's evidence that James had to have dug the holes previously in preparation to murder Julie, because he attended an appointment to choose granite for a kitchen benchtop later in the afternoon and wouldn't have had time to dig them during that trip.

In the police interview, James claimed from the outset that Julie had 'provoked' him by telling him that she was repulsed by having sex with him, and that her new lover was so much better than he ever was. As he was probably aware, the accusation of provocation by Julie was significant and very handy to mention as early as possible because in the jurisdiction of Victoria in 2003, it was still considered a mitigating factor.

Ironically, when the defence of provocation was introduced into the Victorian Crimes Act in 1958 it was envisaged that it would be used by female victims of long-term domestic violence who killed their abusers. In reality, though, more than one long-term domestic abuser who killed his victim successfully used the provocation defence to obtain a manslaughter conviction rather than a murder conviction.

It was the successful use of the defence of provocation by the team representing James Ramage that led to the abolition of the law in Victoria in 2005. Cold comfort for her family as he served just eight years for killing her and returned to his life and his fortune.

Ramage surfaced in 2012 when the *Sunday Herald Sun* revealed that the then 53-year-old was out of jail, living with a new partner and working as the General Manager of Dimmeys, the venerable Richmond department store, under the alias James Stuart.[6] The General Manager of the Victorian Parole Board at the time, David Provan, confirmed for the newspaper that Ramage did not have permission to use an alias and that doing so without the board's permission was a breach of his parole conditions. The board, however, chose not to sanction Ramage.

He was last seen in 2015, being stalked in the street outside his house by a *60 Minutes* crew. They were asking him if he thought it was fair that he was a free man, with a new million-dollar mansion and a new partner after he'd bashed and strangled Julie to death. I'm sure he found that disturbing, but I have to wonder if James Ramage is as disturbed generally by what happened to Julie as Richard Bassed is. I wonder if he thinks about her as often as Richard does.

We talk a lot about the ripple effect of violent crime and about the uniqueness of the grief and trauma associated with death by homicide, but have you ever considered including the forensic pathologist in the list of people who might still be thinking about the victim on a daily basis seventeen years later? I have to say I hadn't. The fact that Richard remembers none of the sensational details of the case but recalls every detail of Julie Ramage as she lay covered in dirt and leaves that afternoon in 2003 astounds me. Just sit for a moment, if you can bear it, and meditate on the different ways Julie's earthly remains were treated by the two men in that same place. The definition of 'intimacy' within a relationship springs to my mind again.

5

THE AMAZING
MASLINS

Marite 'Rin' Norris and Anthony 'Maz' Maslin don't exactly finish each other's sentences but they do finish most sentences by looking at each other, no matter who else is taking part in the conversation. There's no sense they're seeking approval, they just seem to be locked in one fascinating, funny, flirtatious conversation without end. A conversation the rest of us wander in and out of occasionally. It's hard not to walk away feeling envious.

It's equally hard, though, to imagine envying a couple who've experienced a loss they refer to quite reasonably as 'the cataclysm' and 'when the world ended', but that's the enigma of Rin and Maz.

It's typical of their self-awareness and candour that the couple openly admit to asking themselves sometimes,

'How is it that people who've been through so much less than us struggle to cope?'

'You know, I see people walking the streets, barking at stop signs, overwhelmed with grief, and I just think, "I'm pretty sure they haven't been through something as bad as what we have,"' says Maz, the last part directed to Rin.

'Yeah,' she says enthusiastically back to him. 'I mean, obviously, we don't know for sure, but, let's face it, most people haven't.'

'And yet, we're still going, "Why is that?" We always say it's because it's not the size that counts.' He smiles. 'I've been trying to tell her that for years!'

'I wrote that joke! I wrote that!' Rin roars, as we all laugh.

That happens when you're with Rin and Maz. Laughter frames profound observations drawn from the depths of grief. They've learned a lot since 17 July 2014, no doubt much of it they never wished to know. That was the day the world ended. The day that Rin's dad, Nick Norris, and Maz and Rin's three children, Mo (twelve), Evie (ten) and Otis (eight), were killed when flight MH17 was shot down over Ukraine.

The faces of the three Maslin children remain the images of the cataclysm in the minds of most Australians. Their smiling, tanned little faces and shining eyes beaming from photographs evoking the relaxed childhood we all strive to give our kids. Beautiful, simple, innocent Aussie kids who'd somehow been caught up in a horror unimaginable to us.

Surviving the sudden and senseless loss of Mo, Evie and Otis seems like the biggest thing imaginable.

'It's not the size of the thing that happened that determines how hard a person is going to take it, or how they're going to recover, that's what we're saying,' says Rin later. It's important to her and to Maz that this point is understood.

As we speak, the couple's fourth child, Violet, born three years after her siblings died, is sitting happily in another room watching *Bluey*, the cartoon show ubiquitous to every family with a child her age. I have a niece called Edie who's around Violet's age, so I know a little about Bluey's family. It strikes me that (apart from being a blue heeler pup,) Bluey has a bit in common with the Maslin children.

She's a child being raised by fun, down-to-earth parents in an unmistakably Australian way of life, which is to say that lots of her adventures involve tooling around outside in the fresh air and sunshine with lots of friends. Her dad makes everyone laugh, but it's her mum who has to ensure they've all topped up their sunscreen.

I remember reading in a newspaper that Rin and Maz were expecting Violet. My eyes filled with tears and my heart heaved with pain and worry for them. I'm embarrassed now by the memory of my assumptions about who they were and what they could handle.

I realise that when something truly terrible happens to people, it tends to reduce them in our imagination to nothing more than shadows beneath that terrible thing.

While we accept that before the trauma they probably were complex individuals, capable of lots of interesting and conflicting ideas, decisions and achievements, afterwards we think of them only as reactions to unbearable pain. We question the wisdom of their ideas and decisions, as though that terrible thing has rendered them suddenly and forever completely unsophisticated. We don't see them as individuals anymore, but as lists of PTSD symptoms to look out for and manage. They're 'sufferers' who need protection from themselves.

To hear them tell it, Maz and Rin are examples of the one-foot-in-front-of-the-other endurance of the human spirit. While there's no doubt there are ups and downs, and they're different people now than they were before, they are much more than sufferers, and more than survivors even. They're not only alive, but they are living.

Anthony Maslin and Marite Norris have always been full of surprises. They are the kind of people who make living a nomadic, international lifestyle with young children look not only achievable but fun. By contrast, I'm the kind of person who makes a nonstop business-class flight from Melbourne to Bali with my children look like a terrible mistake.

Otis, Evie and Mo Maslin were seasoned travellers who'd learned to pack light and settle in quick wherever their family's adventures took them. They spent time living in a remote Muslim community in the Maldives, and were equally relaxed strolling the canals of Amsterdam as they were navigating the local fish and chip shop in Perth seaside suburb Scarborough. Somehow the kids still managed to forge strong bonds in their hometown. Mo Maslin, for example, was a valued member of the Scarborough Junior Football Club.

It wasn't a stretch for the children to board a plane back to Australia without their parents on 17 July 2014, accompanied instead by Rin's dad, known to the children as Grandad Nick. They'd conquered the long-haul journey so many times during their young lives that they fell into their individual habits and rituals. Movies, computer games, books and snacks.

They were heading back to their friends in Perth and their parents were staying on for just a few extra days alone together in Amsterdam.

After farewelling their children and Grandad Nick and spending a relaxing afternoon cycling through the park, the couple sat together on a balcony overlooking a lake, enjoying a quiet drink. 'You know it just doesn't get any better than this,' Maz said to Rin as they enjoyed the view and the wine. 'The last couple of weeks have been phenomenal.'

He was awoken several hours later by the endless ringing of his phone.

'Tell me your kids weren't on that plane! Tell me your kids weren't on that plane!' Maz's assistant Jodie was calling from Perth, where it was early morning, and she was hysterical. 'MH17!'

Moments later, Rin woke to the screams of her husband. Having checked the booking information and confirmed that his children and their grandfather were on flight MH17, Maz had googled what had happened. Already, the images that would become synonymous with the lawlessness and chaos of the crash site were streaming over the internet. There, in the living room the children had noisily inhabited just hours before, Rin and Maz stood helplessly looking at a computer screen.

Like most Australians on the morning of Friday, 18 July 2014, David Ranson awoke to news of the downing of a passenger jet over Europe.

From the outset, it was a lot to process. It wasn't the first Malaysian Airlines flight that year to meet the kind of misfortune of which nightmares are made. In March, MH370 had disappeared en route from Kuala Lumpur to Beijing. At the time of writing, despite the most costly search in aviation history, how and why that plane vanished remains a mystery, as does its final resting place and that of its 277 passengers and twelve crew members.

The terrible coincidence of a second Malaysian Airlines tragedy in one year barely had time to register, though, before the macabre scene unfolding at the crash site began beaming around the world, almost in real time.

The fact that we were looking at a volatile situation was abundantly clear from the outset. If sifting through the still-smouldering wreckage of downed passenger planes like scavenging birds is common human behaviour, perhaps we've simply been spared knowing about it before. *Time* magazine asked Dr Michael Baden, the former Chief Medical Examiner and Chief Forensic Pathologist of New York City, to review photographs from the scene. Among his observations, none of the victims appeared to be wearing watches or jewellery. He also noted that some of the bodies appeared to have been moved around based on patterns of lividity – the dark discolouration that occurs in the lowest parts of the body as blood settles due to gravity. The discolouration remains after the body is moved, leaving a very clear marker as to the original position it lay in.

In his opinion, all signs pointed to widespread looting of the scene.

Our breakfast television shows scrambled to educate us on the region we were looking at in the shaky phone footage they played endlessly. It was Eastern Ukraine, they said haltingly. 'We're just hearing it's outside of a city called Donetsk.'[1]

Hastily prepped experts attempted in three-minute windows to explain the complicated conflict raging between Ukraine and Eastern Ukraine. Presenters battled to remember whether it was most likely the separatists or the loyalists who were seen strutting menacingly around the debris in the videos. Whomever they were, in their camouflage uniforms, with their automatic weapons and cigarettes, they didn't seem perturbed by the prevalence of looters. One of the soldiers squatted in front of a pile of passports. He picked them up with the same dirty fingers that loosely cradled his cigarette and flicked through them for the camera.

It didn't bode well for the recovery mission.

The television hosts fixated on finding out if any Australians were among the dead and promised to share any such news the minute it came to hand. It began trickling out by the early afternoon. The following morning, the passenger manifest listing the names of everyone onboard was on the internet.

As the diplomatic staff of the Australian High Commission to the Netherlands organised Maz and Rin's return to Perth, Australian Foreign Minister Julie Bishop confirmed that thirty-eight Australian citizens had lost their lives aboard MH17. By the time Maz and Rin arrived back in Australia, their children's faces were on the front page of every Australian newspaper, and many others around the world.

From the outset, David Ranson suspected he'd be travelling to Europe to assist in the identification of the victims whether there were Australians among them or not. His experience in such matters means that he's generally called upon in these circumstances.

From the mass graves of Kosovo to the aftermath of the Bali bombings, David has attended some of the world's worst scenes with the purpose of enabling the families of the dead to lay their loved ones to rest.

'It's fascinating what status people have in a situation,' says David, when asked about how the circumstances of a disaster can affect his ability to play his part. 'In Thailand after the tsunami they filled in the spaces between the pillars around the Buddhist temple and converted it into a mortuary. We had all kinds of police around, technical people and military people and so on, but the monks could go wherever they liked.

'You could turn around and there'd be somebody in the orange garb, you know. I mean, they were perfectly charming and supportive and so on, and we probably did all the things that they would have absolutely hated from their religious perspective. It was all okay, because the monks took care of all the funerals anyway.'

He's beaming and chuckling at the memory of the mortuary monks in Thailand, because David Ranson is fundamentally a cheerful, upbeat guy. The mention of his name in the presence of anyone who knows him is generally enough to bring a smile to their face too. The word 'eccentric' comes to mind, but that might be my own cultural bias, because David is British and although he's lived and worked in Australia for decades he retains not just the accent and phrases like 'and so on', but also the jaunty sense of fun that I both expect from and adore in British men.

David is not only a world leader in the field of forensic pathology, the Deputy Director of VIFM and an adjunct clinical associate professor in the Department of Forensic

Medicine at Monash University, but he's also a devoted member of a men's choir and the organiser of the annual VIFM staff Christmas show, where he performs his signature parody songs.

'And that,' I always think to myself after speaking with him, 'is how you do work–life balance!'

What all of this means is that his knowledge and professionalism are exceptional, and it's entirely possible to have a conversation about very difficult topics with David but also to have covered off the finer points of the works of Peter Sellers and leave with a suggested reading list on the topic of *The Goon Show*.

Dr Ranson is definitely at the cooler end of the scale in terms of temperament. He's a scientist through and through, and tells me in passing one day that he once recognised a man he knew among the victims he was identifying after a major disaster. Horrified, I attempted to draw more emotional memories from that moment out of him but in the end he had to tell me straight, there really were none.

'I didn't know him all that well,' he said, sensibly, raising his eyebrows and shoulders in unison. 'It was just a coincidence more than anything.'

I got the impression he rather regretted bringing it up.

It would be a mistake to consider David lacking in compassion, though. His emotional steadfastness allows him to perform extraordinary feats of compassion, such as regularly leading DVI missions.

I've found the tenderness with which the staff at VIFM treat their post-mortem work quite moving. I expected an impersonal, robotic approach but I've never seen it. There's a reverence there, which isn't religious, but something else. It feels like a profound respect for each human body, for all it has survived and for what it finally hasn't. Acknowledgement of the secrets it has given up or, in some cases, respect for the secrets it's keeping forever.

With all that said, I was still feeling no small amount of trepidation when I first sat down with David to talk about his experience in the Netherlands in 2014. The size of what happened to the Maslin family was so daunting, I found it difficult to know where to start when it came to asking about his incredibly intimate part in their story.

As if sensing precisely what was holding me back, David started talking, but in a particularly pragmatic fashion, which made it easier to bear.

'There were quite a large number of remains that were collected early on in the process, although access to the site was very difficult. "You can't go here, you can't go there, we've got snipers on the hill and they will shoot you!"'

He's not being flippant. Rather, David speaks of things like 'snipers on the hill' interfering with the proper procedures of victim identification as though they are so thoroughly ridiculous they simply don't deserve any dignity or gravitas. Try as I might, he just doesn't care to engage in any conversation about the scene at the crash site.

The recovery operation was the source of almost two weeks of increasing international tension and United Nations storm-outs.

I want David to be angry, like I am. I want him to express outrage and fury, but he refuses to. It's not his thing and, upon reflection, I consider it may actually hinder his work if it was. David is very clear about his place in the big picture and about what keeps him there. He can actually achieve something for victims and their families that none of us, with all of our anger, can ever get close to.

The strutting soldiers at the scene turned out to be pro-Russian separatists who were at war with Ukrainian government forces. The conflict had started over Russia's annexation of Crimea in March 2014, and the separatists were then, and are still, believed to be supported by Vladimir Putin's Russian government. The conflict in Eastern Ukraine is ongoing and tens of thousands of people have been killed since Rin and Maz lost their children.

While most of us reeled in revulsion and confusion at why on earth anyone would impede the clean-up of a plane crash site, investigators took to social media and were immediately rewarded. Images and videos of a Russian Buk missile launcher being transported around Donetsk and the surrounding villages and countryside on the morning of 17 July were clear and prolific. Many of the images had been uploaded by the separatists themselves.

The last video was time-stamped at 2.30 pm and showed the launcher moving south towards the exact location it would have needed to be to shoot down MH17 at 4.30 pm. Investigators even found a photograph uploaded to Twitter that appears to show the white smoke trail from the missile travelling towards the plane.

It's not as though the risks associated with the flight path were completely unknown. Two Ukrainian military planes had been shot down during the previous week and the Ukrainian government had closed the airspace to civilian passenger planes travelling below 32,000 feet. It must be noted, though, that MH17 was well above that level, and 160 other passenger planes had flown through that space already that day without incident. That means roughly 45,000 people slipped through that window in the twelve hours or so before MH17 was shot down.

Ukrainian intelligence released cell phone intercepts in which panicked rebels appear to admit to shooting down the plane, having mistaken it for a military jet.

It's been alleged that the reason for the delays at the crash site is that the priority was removing as much evidence of the missile as possible from the wreckage before international investigators got anywhere near it. That's the subject of ongoing legal and civil action and the Russian government continues to deny any knowledge of or involvement in the incident whatsoever.

What is indisputable is that for days after the crash the separatists jealously guarded the site, while international recovery experts waited to gain access. The remains of the passengers of MH17 lay in the hot sun, in cornfields, in people's gardens and in the smouldering wreckage, their horrified families waiting helplessly all over the world, and that shaky video continued to beam out intermittently from soldiers' phones in real time. Irina Tipunova, a 65-year-old woman, said later that she'd heard a howling noise before everything in her house began to rattle and she observed objects falling from the sky. Then the body of a woman crashed through the ceiling of her kitchen. The body remained there for days.[2]

Eventually the local people said, 'Enough.'

It was the elderly women who led the rebellion. One by one they crept out in their headscarves and housecoats from the low stone houses and cornfields. Some of them carried small shreds of colourful fabric, others held blankets, and purposefully they made their way to where they'd watched the people fall. When they found the people they were looking for, they tied those shreds of fabric to long sticks and stuck them in the ground nearby so as to help the men find them when they did eventually come. Evidently they were worried some of the people would end up lost to the cornfields if nothing was done.

Sometimes they covered the people up to protect their dignity. There's no doubt bad things happened at the MH17 crash site, but it's worth remembering that humanity and decency were there too.

Perhaps the old women managed to shame the soldiers, because the Ukranian SES were allowed to access the site soon after. They were joined by local miners and factory workers who arrived by the truckload to volunteer their help.

The Ukrainians doused the remains in formalin, a diluted formaldehyde solution, as disinfectant. It was most likely the only thing they had at hand but it created significant problems for medical teams down the track, as it emits a highly toxic vapour that can cause pneumonia when inhaled even in very small quantities.

They transported the remains to the nearby town of Torez because both the railway station and airport in Donetsk were under heavy bombardment and Torez was to the west, in the opposite direction of the front. Once there, they loaded them into refrigerated train carriages where they remained for days.

While Russian diplomats huffed around the UN, denying any ability to assist or intervene, world leaders, including the Italian, Dutch, British and Australian prime ministers and American President Barack Obama were determined to hold Russia responsible, not only for the downing of the plane, but also for the delay in the bodies being recovered.

On 21 July, four days after the crash, a spokeswoman for the British Prime Minister, David Cameron, had a message for Vladimir Putin. She said that the shooting down of MH17 was 'totally unacceptable' and Russia's failure to cease support for the separatists had 'contributed to an appalling tragedy'. She quoted the prime minister as saying that the 'world was now watching' and Putin 'must change course and work to bring stability to Eastern Ukraine'. She then went on to say:

> The evidence suggested that pro-Russian separatists were responsible and the prime minister made clear that if Russia wanted to put the blame elsewhere they would need to present compelling and credible evidence. The PM made clear that our priority is to get experts to the crash site so they can recover and repatriate the victims and collect any evidence necessary for the investigation.[3]

At the United Nations headquarters in New York, Australian Foreign Minister Julie Bishop managed to convince the Russian Ambassador, Vitaly Churkin, to meet with her privately to discuss the stand-off. When he entered the room he was confronted not only by Bishop's famous steely gaze, but also by a table covered in newspapers, each featuring large colour photographs of Mo, Evie and Otis Maslin.

'You're a father,' she said to the ambassador. 'How could you possibly deny these children and their family justice?'

'He began to cry,' she said later, 'which surprised me.'[4]

The following day, 22 July, the stalemate lifted. The train was permitted to leave Torez for Kharkiv, a city controlled by the Ukrainian government, and members of Interpol's incident response team were allowed to examine the remains and prepare them for transport to the

Netherlands. On the same day, another team of international observers was allowed access to the crash site for the first time.

Among their observations: 'There still has not been a systematic attempt to comb the scene for all human remains.'[5] In fact, remains were still being removed from the site up to two years after the crash.

David Ranson is not interested in talking about the political part of the story. I guess that's reasonable because he wasn't involved in it, but I also suspect it's because of the disorganised nature of it. I attempt to chat through it a little as a way of establishing the timeline of his travels to the Netherlands, but he starts to twitch a little and squirm in his seat. There's no mistaking the fact that he wants to pick up the story in the ordered environment of the Hilversum Airfield. Specifically, David wants us to focus on the old World War II hangar known as Corporal Van Oudheusden Barracks.

'It was really very well organised by the time we got there,' he says, more than once. 'I think there was a lot of difficulty in the early stages and once they got to the stage of going on a plane and being brought to Hilversum it was all very, very organised from that point onwards; I mean, the European interval-based system training . . . everyone knows what they're doing in that space.'

I nod in agreement as though I concur wholeheartedly that everyone knows what they're doing once the European interval-based system training kicks in, and David visibly

The Flinders Street Extension. (Image supplied courtesy of David Stevens)

The Victorian Institute of Forensic Medicine (VIFM) today. (VIFM)

'Prof': Professor Stephen Cordner. (VIFM)

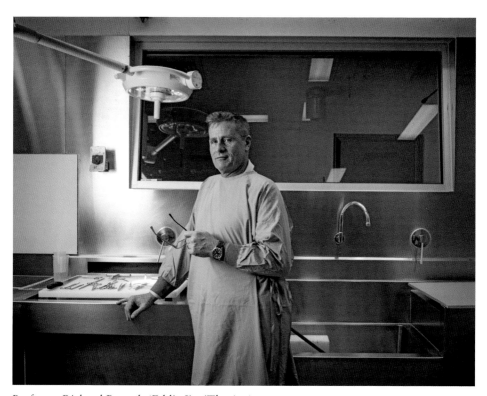

Professor Richard Bassed. (Eddie Jim/*The Age*)

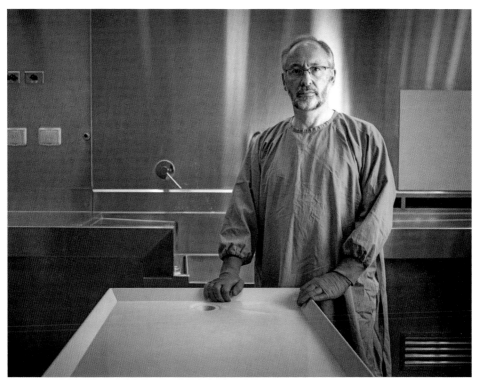

Professor David Ranson. (Eddie Jim/*The Age*)

David Ranson with colleagues Susan Dickie and Ben Stewart in the Homicide Room at VIFM. (Eddie Jim/*The Age*)

Dr Joanna Glengarry. (VIFM)

The author (left) pictured with Professor Soren Blau. (VIFM)

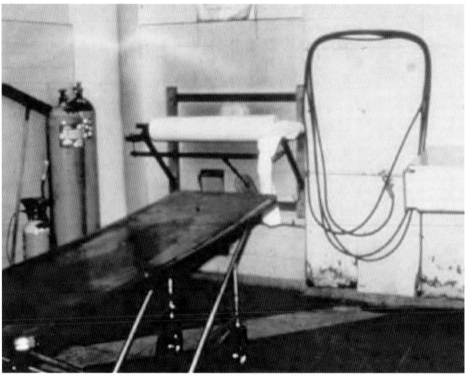

The set-up at the mortuary inside the Flinders Street Extension. (VIFM)

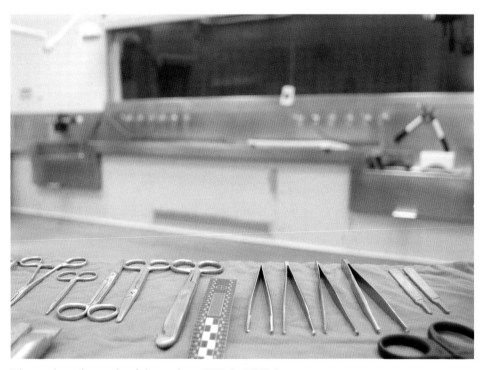

The modern-day tools of the trade at VIFM. (VIFM)

David Hookes wearing the baggy green in 1977. (Bob Thomas/Getty Images)

Bouncer Zdravko Mićević outside the Supreme Court of Victoria on 23 August 2005. He was charged (and later acquitted) with manslaughter over the death of David Hookes.
(William West/Getty Images)

Flowers and tributes to David Hookes left outside the Beaconsfield Hotel in the days after his death. (Nathan Edwards/Newspix)

Forensic specialists standing next to blocks of dry ice that were used to cool bodies at the Yan Yao Temple mortuary in Phuket following the 2004 Boxing Day tsunami. 'We were building dry-ice igloos to try to keep the bodies cold,' remembers Professor Richard Bassed, who travelled to Thailand to assist with Disaster Victim Identification (DVI). (James Croucher/Newspix)

Another shot of the Yan Yao mortuary, which shows the enormity of the task that Richard faced when he arrived in Thailand. (Andrew Wong/Getty Images)

Marite 'Rin' Norris and Anthony 'Maz' Maslin, the parents of Mo, Evie and Otis Maslin. They are pictured here with their fourth child, Violet, who was born on 10 May 2016. (Marcus Alborn/ABC)

Pathologists in PPE at Hilversum Airfield in the Netherlands during the DVI effort following the crash of MH17. They had to perform post-mortem examinations in this protective gear because the bodies had been doused in formalin before leaving Ukraine. This photograph was taken by an unknown person, possibly a member of the Malaysian delegation, and widely circulated among the international DVI team.

SATURDAY, JULY 19, 2014 $2 (inc GST)   HERALDSUN.COM.AU

SPECIAL EDITION **Herald Sun**

MURDER IN THE SKY

Aussie siblings Mo, 12, Evie, 10 and Otis Maslin, 8, are among the victims of MH17. In Amsterdam, their holidaying parents farewelled their beloved kids, who were flying home with their grandfather when a missile shot their plane down

21 PAGES OF REPORTS, PICTURES

Mo, Evie and Otis Maslin on the front page of a special edition of the *Herald Sun* from Saturday 19 July 2014, just two days after the plane they were travelling on with their grandfather, Nick Norris, was shot down over Ukraine. This was on every newsstand in Australia when their parents arrived back in the country. (News Ltd/Newspix)

Professor Soren Blau with unidentified human remains that were donated to a Melbourne op shop. (Eddie Jim/*The Age*)

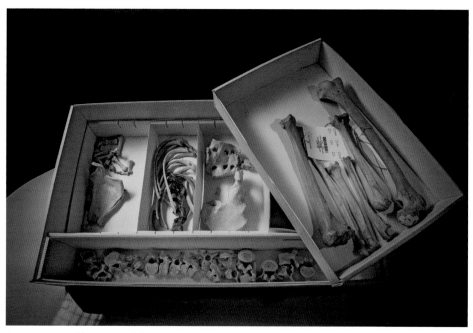

Soren's special bones. (Eddie Jim/*The Age*)

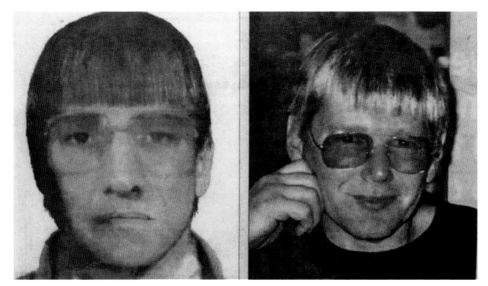

Left: A photofit image created by police based on a woman's description of a man she encountered lurking around the Greek Orthodox section of Fawkner Cemetery on the morning of 1 November 1997, the day Mersina Halvagis was murdered. Right: A photograph of Peter Dupas from the same period. (Supplied via *Herald Sun*)

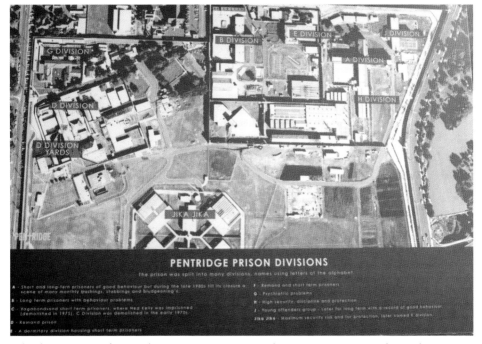

A bird's-eye view of Pentridge Prison. G Divison, where Peter Dupas was housed, is located in the top left corner. (Author's collection)

The Halvagis family in 1976. Mersina, aged four, is holding her father George's hand while her mother Christina, sister Dimitria and brother Nick look on. (Supplied via *Herald Sun*)

The Halvagis family on 1 February 2005, asking witnesses to Mersina's murder to come forward. Only a few months later, on 25 July 2005, Justice Philip Cummins found Peter Dupas guilty of the crime, after a fellow inmate reported Dupas's confession in prison. (Glenn Hunt/AAP)

This is just about the only photo that seems to exist of Margaret Maher, who was murdered by Peter Dupas in October 1997. (Supplied via *Herald Sun*)

Nicole Patterson. This photo was taken the night before she died. (Image supplied courtesy of Kylie Nicholas)

Geoff Downes with a photo of his mother Kathleen, who was murdered in her nursing home in 1997. In July 2020, Coroner Ian Gray's 2015 findings into her death were made public after the lifting of a suppression order. Peter Dupas was named in his report as the likely murderer. (Manuela Cifra/Newspix)

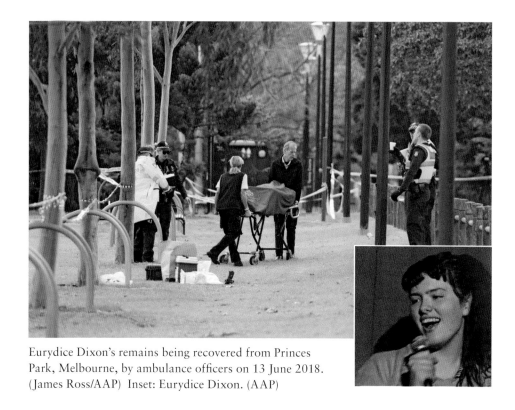

Eurydice Dixon's remains being recovered from Princes Park, Melbourne, by ambulance officers on 13 June 2018. (James Ross/AAP) Inset: Eurydice Dixon. (AAP)

Thousands of strangers huddle together on a bitterly cold Melbourne night in Princes Park at a vigil held for Eurydice. (Michael Dodge/Getty Images)

The Maasarwe family. From left: sisters Ruba and Lena, Aya, mother Kitam, father Saeed and sister Noor. (Supplied via *Daily Mail*)

Aya Maasarwe's phone at the crime scene, as seen on the news by her sister Noor. 'I saw the shoes and the phone,' she said, 'and I was sure it was her.' (Supreme Court of Victoria/AAP)

Saeed Maasarwe (second from left) at the site outside the Polaris shopping centre, Bundoora, where his daughter Aya's remains were discovered. (Stuart McEvoy/Newspix)

Former Detective Senior Sergeant Charlie Bezzina of the Victorian Homicide Squad, pictured here in 2019. (James Ross/AAP)

Brian and Carmel Russell holding a photograph of their daughter Natalie. Natalie was taking a shortcut home from school when she was ambushed and murdered by Frankston serial killer Paul Denyer in 1993. (Andrew Brownbill/Newspix)

relaxes as he begins describing the working conditions at Hilversum. There's no doubting he's in his comfort zone.

Unlike David, several members of the Australian Federal Police did visit the crash site before arriving at Hilversum. The two environments were so starkly opposed in every single way, from the darkness and the fire, to the order and the light. One of them described it as 'awesome, in the truest meaning of the word'.

The Hilversum airfield is normally quite a low-key place. From above there's little to distinguish it from the patchwork of paddocks around it. It doesn't have a tarmac runway and its tower is just two storeys high, but its neat, unassuming sheds and hangars are home to a sizeable fraternity of aviation hobbyists.

In the summer months it's usually a hive of adventurous activity, hosting gliders, skydivers and all kinds of amateur aeroplane enthusiasts. The small café allows spectators to sit at outside tables under bright red umbrellas enjoying the classic Dutch combination of beer and bitterballen (deep-fried breadcrumbed meatballs) in the sunshine.

The summer of 2014 was not a usual one, though, because Hilversum's lovingly maintained World War II aircraft hangar was hastily transformed into a state-of-the-art laboratory. By 23 July, David Ranson was inside, preparing his station and his team.

That morning, King Willem-Alexander and Queen Máxima of the Netherlands held hands as they silently watched two military aircraft, one Dutch and one

Australian, approach Eindhoven Airport from the cloudless blue sky to the east. Behind them sat Australian Foreign Minister Julie Bishop and around forty other people, also silently looking skyward, no doubt in deep contemplation of the events of the previous six days.

It had been six days since MH17 had left Amsterdam's Schiphol International Airport, bound for Kuala Lumpur with 298 people on board. As David's Australian team continued their preparations alongside teams from the Netherlands, Germany, New Zealand, Indonesia, Belgium, the UK and Malaysia, the military planes brought the first of those passengers back to the Netherlands for identification.

A bugler played the Last Post as the planes' engines droned to a stop. It was followed by a minute's silence, punctuated only by the defiant flapping of the crisp, colourful flags flying at half-mast, representing the nations of every passenger on the doomed flight.

Then, the mournful wails of relatives as coffin after coffin was carried carefully to waiting black hearses. Queen Máxima cried too when the last black car was sealed and they rolled gently out into the street, one by one, for the sad procession to Hilversum. It was a 40-kilometre journey and Dutch citizens formed a protective guard of honour along the entire route.

At the gates of Hilversum, people threw roses on the hearses as they made their way through. It was an extraordinary outpouring of grief.

Inside, hundreds of men and women waited to take their place in a chain that started with the miners and factory workers of Donetsk and wouldn't end until every last passenger had made it home. Alongside David Ranson, and his fellow pathologists and clinical staff, were countless diplomatic and security people. This was, of course, a political operation as much as a forensic one.

As we learned from the tsunami experience, an Australian forensic pathologist isn't expected to travel to an international disaster location for the sole purpose of identifying and bringing home Australian victims.

'Sometimes politicians have this expectation,' Ranson says. '"We're sending our team, to bring our people back." Well, you can send them, but unless they're prepared to work with everybody else, we don't want them. To be quite honest, you need people to be part of the broader team all working the same way. If some group comes and says, "We're working our way," then we don't want them there. It's as simple as that.'

So what is the way the broader team works? It's methodical, of course. It's ordered, and it's broken down into many singular processes, each performed in an equally methodical and ordered fashion.

'It's a broken-up process. There's what I call the ante-mortem group that are trying to collect as much information about the missing people or people believed to be in the plane. There's the mortuary phase, which is all about collecting the data from deceased persons just for the matching, and then it's the third group, which is sitting there doing the connecting. We in the mortuary always started with a sort of catch-up briefing and then we got all the clothing and gear on.'

Everyone inside the hangar had to work in very cumbersome protective equipment, including oxygen masks, because of the toxic formaldehyde gas emanating from the remains. This was due to the formalin used by the inexperienced and under-resourced volunteers in Donetsk.

'I couldn't get my glasses inside the mask. I could work as much as I liked close up but I could never see anything at a distance. Had I known it was going to be an issue I would have taken my mask from home. My poor colleague Jeremy, who is very bald, was wearing one and of course it was scraping his head because he hasn't got any hair. All sorts of little things like that you have to sort of cope with along the way.'

Once they were fully dressed, everyone moved inside, where they were greeted by five neat, long rows of shiny steel tables running the length of the hangar. The rows were divided again into separate, perfectly equidistant stations and upon each station was a satisfyingly set-out selection of shiny new laboratory utensils supplied by the Dutch Ministry of Health. Each station would vary to some degree from the next, because each had a different purpose and, of course, every team quickly rearranged and reset their space to their own personal standards and preferences.

'It's very different from the work you do normally where you have an end-to-end process,' David tells me. 'Here you've gotta grind away at getting your bit right, get the best information you can and the most value you can, make sure it's recorded properly so that others can do their jobs. I worked at the pathology station.'

Ordinarily at VIFM David would conduct an entire post-mortem examination on an individual from beginning to end. In this kind of DVI context, a different team is responsible for each part of the post-mortem, and particularly the data gathering process as it pertains to identification.

At Hilversum, it went like this.

Each coffin was submitted to a series of X-rays before it was opened (for safety and security reasons as much as anything else). From there, the coffin was taken to the triage station, which was run by a Belgian team. They opened each coffin and very carefully recorded its contents.

'They made sure there was only one body because sometimes more than one body was put into a coffin, or body parts if it was fragmented, so they would just look at it and say, "Can I be sure that this relates to the same body?" If he can't be sure, it's separated. You give it a separate number and it's treated as a separate individual, and later on maybe put back together if it's found to belong together. There were four operating lines and then there was the body fragment line, which was run by the Malaysians.

'So then you had the German line, the Dutch line, the Australian line, the British line . . . You'd start with fingerprints if possible, because you don't want to interfere with fingerprints by taking clothing off and stuff like that.'

There was a station just for the removal, photographing and cataloguing of clothes and other personal effects, and another for prosthetics. There was one station assigned to tattoos and scars, and another to dentistry. David's pathology team collected DNA and other samples. That's what they did all day long for five weeks. One body after another was placed before them, and all they did was collect the same samples every time.

'Doing every single thing in the same way with the same attention to detail all the time consistently for five weeks becomes routine very quickly. And that's really important because once you start breaking away from routines you've got risks of people making mistakes or errors.'

Eventually, every set of remains was seen by most if not all stations.

The data from every station was then sent to the 'connection' phase of the operation. The people there joined all the pieces of the puzzle together and established the identity of the person whose remains had produced all of that information. It's a way of ensuring the correct result, by way of dozens of checks and balances. No one is identified by one or two methods, and no one is identified by one or two people. It's a very thorough system.

On a professional note, it enables people to work together and learn from each other, which has significant advantages in a field as specialised and starkly populated as DVI.

The reason David Ranson pulls his suitcase down from the top of the wardrobe when he sees something like MH17 on the news is that there are precious few people in the world who can and will do what he does, and literally all of them were in the hangar at Hilversum in July 2014.

'The work on the pathology station took a little less time than some of the other stations, depending on, you know, if someone had lots of clothing, lots of property or what have you, it would take a lot longer to photograph it all and record it all. If we were still waiting for something we'd just go help wash some clothing in the clothing line. You just kept generally busy and there was a sort of flow-on effect . . .

'Occasionally we'd be asked to go down and have a look at the fingerprinting area to help them with something, or to help reveal tattoos or something like that. At one point there was a trainee pathologist in the Belgian area and she'd only just started working as a pathologist and she was helping them. And so we said, "Do you want to come and learn how to do X, Y and Z?", so she came and joined us for a while and we taught her how to take samples because she'd never done that sort of thing before. So, it was good general discussions between different groups.'

*

Back in Perth, the vacuum left by the absence of the basic business that accompanies three young kids threatened to suck the life right out of Maz and Rin, so their tight circle of friends invented the 'web of love', a roster that ensured they were never left alone. It wasn't the noise they yearned for, but it was the noise of love and care and they were wise and kind enough to accept it.

They tried to get outside, to go for walks and go to cafés but even those simple things were complicated by the fact that people recognised them as 'those parents . . . of those three children . . . from the plane'.

Rin and Maz have adapted to some degree to the awkwardness their presence sometimes inspires in people but if there's one thing that really grinds their gears it's pity. The slightest hint that anyone might be thinking of them as 'those poor Maslins' sets their teeth on edge.

It was far worse in the early days, of course. 'Strangers would be flipping over newspapers in cafés so we wouldn't see them,' says Rin, through her noticeably tightening jaw. 'And sunflowers! Yes, we did give out a packet of sunflower seeds at the memorial service and Maz planted some around the place, but I've gotta, say, sunflower emojis? Constantly? For years? Like, enough with the sunflowers now, people. That was a reminder of where they died. The sunflowers will always be about their death. No more sunflowers!'

'It was interesting for me,' says Maz, 'because I went on a sunflower-planting campaign. I was basically planting sunflowers all through the Scarborough beachfront, the car parks and all around the clocktower. There are sunflowers popping up everywhere. That was cool for a little while. I went to our old house and planted them and they grew eight foot tall and blah, blah, blah. Then I started catching on to what Rin was talking about . . .'

Rin laughs heartily at this and Maz joins in immediately. 'I'm not the sharpest tool in the shed with this emotional stuff—'

'But you really liked planting them.' Rin laughs by way of supporting him.

Of course, well-meaning missteps are to be expected, even at the highest levels. In October 2014, when all the Australian victims had been identified, the Australian government insisted that their remains be flown to Melbourne from the Netherlands. At Melbourne Airport they were met by a lone piper, and then transported to VIFM to be checked a final time. They were then officially certified by the Victorian coroner before being released to their families, some for the onward journeys to their home states.

From the perspective of the government this was no doubt a dignified and respectful course of action. For Rin and Maz, though, it was so much added agony. They had flown to Amsterdam to bring their children home, an ordeal in itself, of course, and on the way back, 'we had to fly past Perth to get to Melbourne.'

'And it wasn't just flying past Perth to get to Melbourne,' adds Maz.

'The worldwide Jehovah's Witness Conference!' interjects Rin.

They both look straight down the barrel of the laptop camera at me, mouths agape, as though they've just delivered the punchline to one of their favourite old routines.

Maz picks up his line. 'They'd booked out every hotel room in Melbourne—'

Over to Rin. 'So they put us in an airport hotel. Can you believe it? With planes!' She makes planes with her hands. 'Just planes.'

'Yeah, constant planes.'

'Move the Jehovahs! I'm sorry. Move. The. Jehovahs! They'll be cool with it!' Rin laughs.

How did they cope with flying, I wonder, as they confirm that, yes, it was their first trip since making it back to Australia after the world ended. I know they've continued to travel since then and I ask if they ever developed any kind of phobia of flying.

'The first flight was not great,' says Maz. 'It's like anything. My cliché is you can't be a slave to your scars. You basically have to front up and do it and then it lessens the power.'

'It's just your brain, isn't it?' says Rin. 'It's just your mind. The trauma, and the massive PTSD, I would describe it as massive anxiety the whole entire time. Like every minute of the day.

'So you would find that you'd have these tiny moments

that were, like, "It's not so bad now, this moment, this is actually, this moment's fine, this moment's fine." And then it was all starting again.'

'Even on the plane there were some moments . . . I think I watched Angelina Jolie with the big horns?' says Rin as she mimes to Maz.

'*Maleficent.*'

'*Maleficent!* And I remember there was a moment in that movie when I was having a glass of wine and I was watching that and I was like, "The kids would like me to be watching that", you know? You just sort of have to calm your mind and deal with it. But there was a poem going through my head from school, and it was Alfred, Lord Tennyson, 'The Charge of the Light Brigade'. Do you know it?'

I know of it, but never mind, because in a heartbeat Rin is reciting it with her customary vigour.

'Cannon to right of them,
Cannon to left of them,
Cannon in front of them
Volleyed and thundered;
Stormed at with shot and shell,
Boldly they rode and well,
Into the jaws of Death,
Into the mouth of hell
Rode the six hundred.'

'She's a bit fucking dramatic, isn't she?' Maz laughs down the barrel.

'That was going through my head,' exclaims Rin without missing a beat. 'I was going back into the jaws of death to get the kids.'

Maz smiles. 'The thing about it is, you said, "Were you ever afraid of flying?" The answer is no, because that might mean dying.'

He laughs and Rin nods.

'We might die, yay!' she chirps.

'It was more about, "This is just taking you to places you don't want to go." Taking your mind to places . . . and that's what's hard.'

Upon their return to Australia with the bodies of their three children in October 2014, Rin and Maz released the following statement to the media.

We have brought home the bodies of our children, Mo, Evie and Otis Maslin (aged twelve, ten and eight) from the Netherlands, along with their grandfather, Nick Norris. For the last three months, they have been lying in a cold room on the other side of the world. Reconciling this fact with the knowledge that our children are here with us, spiritually, every moment, is one of the most relentless and agonising difficulties of our current life.

Our love and respect for our children remains unlimited and unconditional. It will never weaken – our children have been our entire world.

We have been two of the luckiest and happiest people

on the planet. What remains for us now is to honour our children.

We honour Mo – his wisdom, his compassionate heart, and his total selflessness. Mo is peaceful and inclusive. Mo can accept people of all ages and backgrounds, make them feel special, and have them know they are with someone extraordinary.

We honour Evie and her boundless, unlimited love. She is empathetic, beautiful, funny, artistic and creative. Her gentle spirit, warmth and absolute kindness are recognised by all who know her.

We honour Otis and his complete and humbling fascination with all things outdoors, big and small, near and far. Oti provides all of us with carefree joy and laughter – perhaps the most powerful gift of all.

Our children were taken from us by a war in which we, and our country had no part. It is impossible to understand the reason they were blown out of the sky.

Our lives are an ongoing hell. The pain we are enduring is unfathomable, and we grieve alongside families in the Ukraine, the Netherlands, Russia, Malaysia, Australia and elsewhere.

Please respect our children's memory, and stop this pointless war.

No hate in the world is as strong as the love we have for our children – for Mo, for Evie, for Otis.

No hate in the world is as strong as the love we have for Grandad Nick.

No hate in the world is as strong as the love we have for each other.

Thanks to DFAT and their international support team. Thanks also to our friends and our family for their support and love. Love, only love, it is all we have left.

6

SOREN'S SPECIAL BONES

Around 38,000 people are reported missing in Australia every year. Most of them are found alive within a couple of days, but there is a small percentage that remain missing long-term or are never found at all. There are currently around two thousand people listed as long-term missing in Australia.[1]

Advocates have embraced the phrase 'ambiguous loss' to describe living with the heavy burden of not knowing where a loved one is, why they left, what happened to them, or if they are ever coming back. It's impossible to get on with grieving, because hope stubbornly remains, but it's an altogether different kind of hope. It's like some kind of cruel, mutated strain that tortures rather than comforts, and mocks the absence of bad news.

For some, just functioning in the world becomes impossible but for others, the only way to cope is to fill the hours, days, weeks and years with campaigning to keep the missing person's face in other people's faces. Often the two approaches cling to opposing sides of one family. One sibling will quit their job to run a Facebook page and chase leads while another will largely disengage, citing a person's 'right to disappear if they want to'. Perhaps a third sibling will move overseas and tell none of their new acquaintances about the missing family member. One parent might take to their bed to slowly die with tranquilisers as the other lovingly enables them to.

Part of the trauma comes from the feeling that no one is helping to look for the missing person. Most families are shocked to discover that, unless there is compelling evidence that a crime has been committed, the police are powerless to commit resources to searching for a missing adult beyond a couple of days. 'It's not a crime to go missing,' is a phrase the family will be told time and time again when they beg for more help – for a broader search, for a lead to be chased up.

Someone says they saw him in some town? It's not a crime. We can't dispatch a squad car every time someone sends a Facebook message saying the missing person might've been in their bakery six months ago, sorry.

I remember once speaking to someone who worked on a TV show that tracked down missing persons. I loved the show and I asked why they stopped making it. She said it was a really tough gig because, more often than not, they'd put a lot of time and effort into finding someone, only to be told they'd disappeared for a reason and they had no interest in a reunion, let alone a filmed one. Sometimes people disappear for a reason their family has no idea about – or most of their family, at least.

Sometimes, sadly, the long-term missing are long-deceased.

Helping police to identify unknown remains is just one of the many jobs that falls under the remit of VIFM's Senior Forensic Anthropologist Soren Blau.

'There really is no average day. Once I get here in the morning it could be anything from a conversation with Victoria Police around going out to look for a missing person or they might have information about bodies being dumped or buried somewhere . . . maybe they've just got a photograph of something they believe is the skeleton. I can usually tell immediately if it is and if it's human and how long it might've been there, so I can potentially save them a lot of time just with a photograph. It might be, you know, "Please, we've found a body, can you come and help with recovery."'

Forensic anthropology is essentially the application of anthropological and archaeological methods in legal and other investigative contexts. I know it doesn't sound glamorous when I put it like that, but in a lot of ways, this is the stuff the TV shows are all about. Soren is the brilliant young woman called out to baffling and macabre crime scenes by world-weary detectives. She's the one they look to for answers. Male or female? How old? What ethnicity? How long's he been there? Could it be this bloke? In a movie Soren would be played by Cate Blanchett. In fact, I think she was, in *Hot Fuzz*.

Forensic anthropology has enjoyed increased interest from university applicants over the past decade, no doubt due in some part to its pop culture moment, but it's worth remembering that, in its heart of hearts, it's for hardcore science people only. The discipline hinges on a very thorough understanding of forensic osteology, forensic archaeology and forensic taphonomy, which amounts to the facts of how environmental factors affect the decomposition of the human body.

Apart from domestic crime scenes, forensic anthropologists are called upon with depressing regularity to assist in cases of crimes against humanity, war crimes, massacres and mass-grave excavations. For Soren Blau, Timor-Leste was the first such trip.

Having been colonised by various European superpowers over centuries, the tiny island province of Timor-Leste declared itself independent on 28 November 1975. Nine days later it was invaded by nearby Indonesia and the 25-year occupation that followed was characterised by brutal suppression of the East Timorese population. It's estimated up to 200,000 local people perished as a result of the occupation. The average population of the province hovers around 800,000.

Of all the violent events recorded in Timor-Leste, the one known as the Santa Cruz massacre, in which many young protesters lost their lives in the central cemetery of the capital, Dili, in 1991, holds particular significance. It has been seen in retrospect as a turning point in the revolution, despite – or perhaps because of – the fact that so many of the dead were never accounted for.

Several unverified lists of names of victims exist but two sites have been consistently rumoured to be the locations of mass graves associated with the massacre: Tibar and Hera.

After mounting international pressure and a concerted campaign by the UN, Indonesia finally withdrew from Timor-Leste in 1999 and control was handed over to the first fully independent government of Timor-Leste in 2002.

In 2003, VIFM and the Argentine Forensic Anthropology Team (EAAF) began discussions with government ministers of Timor-Leste about supporting an investigation into the Santa Cruz massacre. In 2007, all three parties signed a memorandum of understanding, agreeing to undertake the work, specifically to recover and identify those killed during the Santa Cruz massacre.

Along with the altruistic element, there's a practical benefit to these trips for all concerned. Local police receive training enabling them to continue the work when the visitors are gone and young technicians like Soren get valuable field experience.

While Soren and the other technicians were no doubt completely ready for the technical rigours of their trip after months of classroom and field training, they possibly found, as I have tended to in similar situations, that the all-important 'cultural sensitivities' component needs to be soaked up in situ.

If I were to ask you to prepare yourself for full immersion into a society that's deeply religious, and the religion in question is a rather theatrical mix of Catholicism, supernatural animism, herbal healing and witchcraft, how confident are you that you'd be an expert upon arrival? Best to arrive ready for anything, but mostly for listening and saying a lot of, 'Okay, we'll make it work.'

The souls of the dead are very much part of the lives of the living in Timor-Leste, and as such, the many rituals the dead demand for co-operative behaviour were always going to be a big part of the Santa Cruz recovery operation. Another factor that needed to be respected was that spiritual communication with the living was deemed by many locals unquestionably more reliable than the investigations of the visitors.

For example, as Soren wrote in 'We Need the Truth', an academic report into enforced disappearances in Asia:

While the International Forensics Team had shown there was no evidence of a grave in the areas of interest at Tibar, the families needed to follow their own line of enquiry. This involved using a medium to facilitate the finding process by calling the spirits of the dead to guide them to potential locations of graves. With information about possible grave locations the families obtained mechanical excavators and paid for the fuel to dig (even at night) numerous enormous holes without positive results. While respect for the needs of the families is necessary, the above scenario highlights the requirement for the forensic specialists to have an open mind, and to make an effort to explain to the relatives as clearly as possible why, for example, an excavation stops at the point when sterile soil is found, resulting in no need to excavate any deeper.[2]

'There was one particularly challenging case,' Soren told me later, with palpable sadness seemingly shifting the axis of her brown eyes, 'where we actually had a DNA match for a man's son. We could one hundred per cent positively identify him but he wouldn't believe it because he said his son had come to him in a dream and told him he was still alive.'

After giving up on Tibar, the official search moved to Hera, a location forty minutes' drive east of Dili. Former members of the Indonesian military had confessed to burying victims of the Santa Cruz massacre in Hera and their evidence was deemed credible by UN observers. An eyewitness who'd escaped Timor-Leste soon after the event claimed to know of thirty-six bodies that were buried at the site.

All forces were summoned in hopes of success.

Before any exhumations occurred, typically there would be a church service or an animal sacrifice near the area to call the spirits of the dead forward to make themselves found. Initially, when we were failing to locate graves, a so-called spiritual man worked with another man to put him in a trance, to let the spirits of the dead talk through him. This resulted in the families locating what they were convinced was an area containing graves. Our forensic team found no evidence of a grave or human remains in that spot but based on the information of another witness and standard archaeological excavation techniques, the team opened a total of twenty graves at Hera.[3]

Of the twenty graves excavated, sixteen contained the remains of single individuals. Analysis showed that all of the individuals were young men ranging in age from fifteen to thirty-five.

Of the sixteen individuals, six had at least one gunshot wound to the head or the back. The ballistic evidence was consistent with weapons known to have been used by the Indonesian military.

Eleven of the victims exhumed at Hera were identified. To this day the names of the other five are unknown, and to their families, they remain missing.

The idea that unknown remains exist is insufferably sad. That a person's life could end without a careful collection. It makes me think about the drive home from the hospital with a newborn; the almost idiotic attentiveness that goes into that journey. To think that someone's final drive could be so lonesome. That a person's very body, their face that smiled for people, that sang nursery rhymes and learned to whistle, their hands that once reached for comfort and to give it, are just . . . uncollected. Unknown.

It's a very sad thing.

Within the context of the Indonesian occupation of Timor-Leste it makes sense inasmuch as it's a crime, committed intentionally and concealed maliciously. But how can a person become unknown remains in modern-day Australia?

It's not as uncommon as you might think. There are currently somewhere between five hundred and eight hundred sets of unidentified remains stored around Australia.[4] For me, that estimate raises another big question: how is it possible that we don't even know exactly how many unidentified bodies we have?

The answer is actually very sensible.

'It kind of depends on how you define it,' says Soren. 'Active unidentified human remains in our mortuary? We've got about forty cases but that's everything from tiny fragments through to reference material.'

The 'reference material' Soren refers to includes very old human bones.

'You can imagine there are cases of ancestral remains, pre-contact.' In other words, skeletal remains of Aboriginal people that predate white settlement. It never occurred to me before but naturally these remains must be accidentally uncovered from time to time.

'Once I've determined that those remains are pre-contact Aboriginal and of no interest to the coroner – in that they're not related to a crime, for example – we work with Aboriginal Victoria to return those remains. Then you've got long-term cases where, for example, at the time they were admitted the DNA technology perhaps was poor. These individuals might have been buried but are still on our books as unidentified.

'If an investigator gets additional information, or say, DNA technology advances, an investigator can apply to the coroner for an exhumation, but exhumation is very, very expensive and labour-intensive so we do tend to keep individuals in our mortuary. I can't remember the last time we buried remains.'

I hope she doesn't mind my saying so, but there are a couple of these individuals that Soren seems particularly attached to. Without exception, every clinician at VIFM says that certain cases stay with them for whatever reason. Some say it tends to be the children, some say it's the cases that remind them of someone they love. For whatever reason, there are two unknown individuals under Dr Blau's care at VIFM that extract an unmistakably maternal defensiveness in her.

For example, when I ask her if we can talk about the box of op shop bones, and I add, probably far too blithely, that it's a really fascinating story, her kind face rearranges itself again. In an instant she has a fierce quality. She asks me, unblinkingly, 'Really? Why does it fascinate you?'

We've spoken about this case before, several times, but on this occasion, she's caught me without my manners. I snap to attention and remember what – or indeed *whom* – we're talking about and the kindness returns to her eyes.

In August 2018, the volunteers in the sorting room of the Sacred Heart Mission op shop in Prahran encountered a handmade wooden box among the day's trash and treasures. Upon opening the box, they discovered it contained bones, slightly yellowed, in all shapes and sizes. While none among the sorters were experts, they agreed the accompanying handwritten documentation appeared to confirm their suspicions. There were several pages of notes detailing what muscles would have originally glued the bones together, all written in very neat cursive writing.

'Everyone was very curious about the donation,' Sacred Heart op shop area co-ordinator Trish Williams said on the news that night. 'It caused a bit of excitement for us and our customers, especially when the police came!'

Soren also appeared in the news story. 'It was clear as day to me that the bones were of no forensic significance,' she said. The reporter added soberly that experts believed the bones were likely from India, exported for use by medical professionals as a learning tool.

This brings me to the answer to Soren's question. 'Why does it fascinate you?'

I accept that 'fascinating' is not the right word, but I do think it's worth highlighting the fact that if you ever saw a skeleton hanging in a doctor's surgery or a dentist's office right up until the late 1980s at the earliest, it was probably real and probably came from India as a 'bone box', bought, along with their med school textbooks, for around one hundred dollars.

I for one had no idea about the so-called 'Indian Bone Market' that furnished the international medical profession, completely legally, for over one hundred and fifty years. In theory, the primary source of the skeletons was unclaimed bodies. Bodies left in hospitals or found in rivers or by the roadside, for example. These were collected and processed in very professional operations known as 'bone factories', with those in Kolkata becoming the most famous.

Naturally, with demand and prices high, some unscrupulous dealers chose not to wait for unclaimed bodies but, rather, to steal them from cemeteries and cremation pyres. Interestingly, it was Westerners' distaste for this business model that created the market for the Indian bone trade.

Edinburgh was the centre of anatomical study in the early nineteenth century and its students had an insatiable appetite for fresh cadavers to dissect. Scottish law required that cadavers for medical research could only be sourced from prisoners, suicide victims or foundlings and orphans, a pool that was quickly exhausted.

Edinburgh's most ambitious anatomist, Dr Robert Knox, let it be known that he would pay for fresh bodies, which led to grave robbing on an industrial scale.

Families were forced to camp out atop their loved ones' graves for weeks on end to ensure the deceased's body remained safely buried. Eventually, two enterprising men by the names of William Burke and William Hare realised that bypassing the graves altogether made things a lot easier and they murdered sixteen people so as to deliver their corpses to Dr Knox.

They were found out, and the grisly case drew attention to the need for regulation around the study of medical science. The Anatomy Act of 1832 severely restricted the use of human remains (from the United Kingdom) for scientific dissection. It offered no provision, however, for the importation of human remains for educational purposes, and thus the Indian bone trade was born.

India finally banned the trafficking of human bones in 1985, which coincided with the accessibility of cheap plastics. You'd think that would be the end of the story, right? You'd think the cheaper, less creepy plastic skeletons were probably killing the bone box market anyway but, actually, in 1984, the year before the industry was outlawed, India legally exported sixty thousand skeletons. That was pretty consistent with the previous twenty years.

There's evidence to suggest India's bone trade continues to this day. Smuggler Sanjay Prasad was arrested in December 2018 with fifty human skulls in his possession, which he confessed he was trying to move into Bhutan. Amazingly, he was travelling by train.

The op shop bone box wasn't the first nor was it the last identified by the VIFM team.

'We get quite a lot of these handed in,' says Soren, 'because, you know, the dental surgeries had the model or a reference individual hanging in there and it's suddenly dawned on them. Then they actually really don't want that hanging in their dental surgery anymore.

'So they can give it to us for safe-keeping. There's deceased estates . . . people will be cleaning out their father's cupboards or their grandfather's things and they'll find some terrible trophy he's hidden away. They're not coronial, but of course they were real people. We've had trophy skulls from PNG brought in, for example, that people brought back from the war. They've been hidden away, and their families didn't know anything about them until they discovered them in a shoebox at the back of a wardrobe.

'We have an international licence that legally allows us to retain individuals where the coroner is satisfied that they're not of coronial interest and they can never be identified. We can keep them and care for them here.

'I mean, it's a whole other complex discussion as, you know, this poor person ended up in the op shop, which is nuts. The fact that someone, with the number of public resources available, would just kind of go, "Old clothes, old books . . . oh yeah, and a skeleton." I mean . . . I guess

I'm a bit conflicted, too, because these individuals were an incredibly valuable learning resource, and we should be grateful for that. But he – he was a man, I know that much – and he was a little baby once, who looked up at his mother like the rest of us. So, to think of all that, and then someone just threw him away . . .' Soren's face changes again. I think we're both imagining a long-forgotten baby's eyes. She shrugs, speechless, and sighs a big sigh.

I need to ask about her other special bones. Soren's purple-scarf man, who in a melancholic way is a yin to the Indian man's yang.

Unlike the man in the bone box, condemned to remain anonymous forever, Soren's purple-scarf man's identity seems frustratingly close. Like an important detail skipping just ahead of a tired mind. Since 2006 he's been one of VIFM's unidentified individuals.

This man isn't a tiny bone fragment. His complete skeleton was discovered near a tree during a controlled burn-off in bushland in the Dandenong Ranges. He isn't from a bygone era. He pulled on Country Road pants and a Thinsulate jumper on the day he died. He also had a distinctive purple scarf. The kind of scarf people notice. The kind of scarf people remember.

The scarf was wrapped around the noose he'd used to end his life.

Dr Blau has established he was a Caucasian man in his twenties, but police still have no reports of missing persons to match him.

'I think this case speaks of the nature of the society we live in, and there are many things that are deeply sad about that. And yes, the nature of long-term missing persons is that either the person wanted to go missing, and on the other side of that, the family, wherever they are, the possibility is that they may not have reported that person missing or that they don't know.

'It's amazing that we live in a world like that. Probably our grandmothers were far more connected in some ways than we are. We can see what we want and work where we want and that's full of fabulous things, but I guess at the human level it has ramifications. This young man is very identifiable from our forensic, medical perspective. It really is a situation where we need to connect with the family somewhere, a relative somewhere. It really depends on somebody wanting answers.

'I've had experiences where a person has disappeared, not been heard of, and for whatever reason, it might be years and years later, for whatever reason one of the relatives decides to come forward. They might've had a niggling question, or perhaps there'd been a discussion about the person seeking a new life or whatever . . . there's no protocol for this.

'There's so many different scenarios and that's what makes this process, where we work with coroners and police, so complicated. Humans like nice boxes. These cases are not so perfect. We often talk about "the families" as though they're all the same but everyone is so different . . .

one response for everyone isn't going to cut it. There is no typical response to this scenario. There was no working hypothesis as to who this person was. Often, we'll get remains but the police might say, "We think this is John Smith," and we work along those lines, but there was no hypothesis with this scenario.

'We then do an analysis of the completeness of the remains, and in this case the individual was really very complete. The preservation and completeness then dictate how far you can go, so if we didn't have the skull that would be very limiting in terms of the dentition [the arrangement and condition of the teeth].

'We were able to develop a biological profile, which is basically a person's ancestry, their sex, age and stature. We know that that doesn't identify the person as John Smith, but it narrows it down. So, in this case we could say the individual was a young Caucasoid male of average stature.

'Now, what does that say? Obviously lots of young men go missing or suicide, sadly, for various reasons. He had dentistry so at some point he has visited the dentist and that, as you know, can be very helpful but, again, in this scenario, without a working hypothesis of who this person might be and with nowhere to start, we can't go searching for dental records.

'What's next? He had no evidence of trauma. That setting with the context with the noose was highly suggestive that he had hanged himself but there was no other apparent evidence of trauma, so no hope of retrieving evidence that might lead to another individual.

'Next we took a sample to try to get DNA, which we did. That DNA was then uploaded with a post-mortem profile onto the Victorian missing persons database and it's compared with anyone who has provided a reference sample. So, again, this young man needs someone from his family to be looking for him, to be working with us from the opposite direction.

'So, it's still a work in progress but unless and until someone from the community comes to us, with this particular case, there's just not much more we can do.'

'Surely someone knows this young man with the bright purple scarf,' I say. 'I mean, he was also wearing socks and Maseur sandals, so he seems like a pretty memorable young man.'

'He was found with a bottle as well, actually,' says Soren, allowing herself a wistful drift back to the early days with the purple-scarf man.

'We were looking at trying to use the barcode on the bottle, just to see whether we could get any kind of data from that about where he might have bought it or his last movements. It didn't come to anything, but you try all sorts of ideas,' she says, wearily.

For now, the purple-scarf man remains tucked up safely in his neatly catalogued, climate-controlled cocoon. He, too, was once somebody's baby. He, too, looked up at a mother. Where is she now? Is she looking for him? How has this sad thing happened to them both?

For him and his family at least, a hope of sorts remains. For Soren Blau, the purple-scarf man is hope, too, because she may yet give all that was valuable about his life back to him in a way she never can for the bone box man nearby.

7

NICOLE PATTERSON

I started working as a brothel receptionist in 1998. It's a long story, and not a terribly interesting one to be honest, but the facts are that I was twenty-five, brothels are legal in Victoria and it was cash-in-hand.

In 1999 I was firmly entrenched in a busy little place in Caulfield by the name of 'Club 857'. It was a very peachy affair inside, with low lighting, thick shagpile carpet and lots of mirrors on the walls. On any given Friday or Saturday night, ringing the doorbell out the front would summon me, blonde hair piled up for the gods, face made up to perfection and full of youthful confidence.

Behind me was the tantalisingly low-lit brothel, all pink and soft and warm, but the men had to get past me first, which was part of the fun and the ritual of the brothel visit but also a genuine weeding-out process. I was responsible for the safety of the women inside. There were no burly men employed to hang around all night in case anything kicked off. It was just me, my acid tongue and the phone.

Guessing whether or not a man might kill us is a calculation women make all the time. We mostly don't even know we're doing it. You know you're doing it in the doorway of a brothel, though, because every girl behind you has a horrifying story about when it went wrong. About when someone let a bad one in and he got her. It's a massive responsibility, and you know they're not going to announce themselves at the door. It's the ones you don't see coming who ruin you in the end, everyone knows that.

Ice-T said that pimpin' ain't easy, and I couldn't agree more.

I don't know how many drunk real estate agents and junior bankers you've had to be polite to for fourteen hours at a time beginning at 7 pm on a Friday, but let me tell you, I needed a performance enhancer. For me, that was amphetamines. Roughly half the girls were also on amphetamines and the other half were on heroin. You'd need to speak to them about their reasons for that.

Obviously hard drugs are generally frowned upon in any workplace, but in a brothel they could be catastrophic. In an attempt to prevent them from becoming full-on dens of depravity, the Victorian government legislated that if any drugs or even alcohol were found in a brothel, it would be immediately shut down and the licensee's permit to operate would be terminated.

Our drug use was a genuinely heavy burden because our boss, 'Miss Vick', was one of the best people I've ever met in my life and we were risking her livelihood every night. If we'd been raided, she'd have been finished. Mind you, inflated confidence is sort of part of the reason you take amphetamines, and drug addicts are manipulative, selfish liars so the truth is it didn't really trouble us at the time. If it had, we wouldn't have done it.

Miss Vick had been a sex worker herself before moving into owning a place and she encouraged us younger women to look to our futures too. She instituted a monthly staff meeting, which, I must admit, we all thought was dumb and hilarious. She laid on free food and drinks at a bar two doors down from the brothel one Friday evening a month and even offered bonuses to everyone who showed up. There were two or three older women who worked in the brothel during the day, and when I say older, I mean in their forties. While they didn't catch many bookings, they never missed the free food at the staff meeting or an opportunity to lecture the rest of us about the nature of time, and its tendency to take flight and dump unprepared young women on frightening and inhospitable shores in middle age. As a middle-aged woman myself now, I think of them often and I miss them. They were right about many things.

Miss Vick organised a guest speaker every month to

come and talk to us about everything from getting bank loans and buying houses to family law and custody issues. One month, Miss Vick invited a very nice lady to remind us about the importance of checking every client for STIs before every booking. Spare a thought for sex workers now that you know most of them inspect the genitals of every prospective client as soon as they get them into the room, before they've showered, for the presence of various symptoms of sexually transmitted infections.

The trouble started when the presenter revealed an overhead projector and started yelling. She seemed either unaware of or untroubled by the fact that the bar we used for our meetings was still open to the public. There was no warning for the dozen civilians who'd popped in for a casual Friday night drink that they'd also be treated to a high-volume pageant of pustules, blisters, rashes, discharges and fungal infections, as the smell of deep-fried spring rolls wafted up their nostrils.

The month after the debacle of the giant infected cocks on the back wall, which very nearly saw us banned from the bar, Miss Vick truly outdid herself. A pretty young blonde woman was setting up a little pamphlet table when we arrived. She looked like she was roughly the same age as me and most of the girls, which was a good start. She was resplendent in the socially conscious, downplayed grunge fashion of the day – a long, A-line washed-out blue floral skirt over tights and Doc Marten boots, with a cute, tight-ish sky-blue pullover. She wore no make-up (and didn't need to) and her short blonde hair was pulled back over each ear. I had on a bucket of make-up (I needed to), heels and a massive blonde bun piled on top of my head. I thought she was fabulous.

She was very softly spoken but it was fine because we all sat silently and leaned in to listen. Her name was Nicky, she was a counsellor, and she was there to talk about mental health and self-esteem. She didn't really talk that much, though. She asked questions, and the girls started talking back to her, raising their hands and nodding along with each other. They asked her questions about how she thought they could approach certain scenarios in their lives and she answered them cautiously because they were very complicated issues.

There was one girl whose working name was Dani. She was Greek, only nineteen years old and already the mother of a little boy. Her father had insisted on taking her to Greece when he discovered she was pregnant at fifteen. He insisted on keeping her baby and raising the child as his own. He made the rules about when she could go and see her son and when she had to leave. And when she was in Melbourne she lived with her heartbroken mother, the two of them grieving together.

Dani had the worst heroin habit of anyone I've ever known in my life, and I've known a lot of heroin addicts. On one occasion, the man from the service station across the road came into the brothel at 3.30 in the morning and asked me to come and get her from the floor of his public toilet. She'd left work at 2 am, gone over there, asked for the key to his toilet and been there ever since.

On another occasion she left at 2 am, went around to the back of the building where she'd left a window open for herself and climbed back in. Then she stood behind a curtain in a freezing dressing room for three hours until the rest of us packed up and went home. Then she tried to break into the safe. I know because it was all caught on CCTV cameras.

She passed out on clients many times. The good ones came downstairs to complain.

We never sacked Dani because we all felt so very sorry for her. She was such a beautiful child, and she was in so much pain. If we had sacked her, she would've gone straight to St Kilda to work the streets. She already went there on the nights when she hadn't made enough money with us. At least when she was with us, we could keep an eye on her, try to feed her, tell her she was smart, funny, wonderful, and that we loved her.

At this staff meeting, Dani opened up to Nicky. She had a tough shell, callused by disappointment, but there was something about this softly spoken lady that made her feel safe. She asked questions about standing up to her father and about getting on some kind of path to self-worth, and at the end she asked Nicky for a card with her details.

I'm not making this up. It was the first, and as far as I can remember the only, time the staff meeting ran over time. Miss Vick was trying to get us out of there and back to work, and Nicky ran out of cards! I wanted one too because I thought maybe I'd make an appointment with her sometime, and as she wrote her number down on a piece of paper for me, she explained that she was just in the process of setting up her own practice. She was going to start seeing patients from home, which was why she didn't have many cards yet, and I noticed she'd hand-written her number on the ones she did have.

We went back to work and talked intermittently that night and the night after about how cool she was. The topic came up a few times over the next week and we all kept saying we had to get around to making that phone call and getting an appointment. About a week later one of the girls, Ricki, a busty 28-year-old size-eight brunette, complained that she'd left two messages for Nicky and hadn't heard back. We just put it down to being busy and assumed Nicky would get back to her.

How could we have guessed what had happened to Nicky? We were so busy going about our business, which included protecting ourselves from predatory men, it never occurred to us that one of the most sadistic predators Australia has ever produced had managed to get his hands on Nicky.

Already well known to authorities as a prolific and violent rapist, Peter Dupas had also become a serial killer and Nicky Paterson was his last known victim.

The fact that Dupas was living in the community in 1999 after having already committed so many brutal crimes against women is a testament to the judicial system's view of our worthlessness. Frankly, it can be seen as nothing else. I've chosen to use the past tense in 'viewed' as a mark of goodwill and of hope that it's no longer the case because, trust me, by the time you reach the end of this chapter, you too will be grasping for hope.

Peter Dupas was a quiet, bespectacled, overweight boy, eking out an unremarkable existence in Glen Waverley, in Melbourne's deep eastern suburbs in the 1960s. It was a very conservative time and place. Dupas was the son of elderly parents, Norris and Merle, who were often mistaken for his grandparents. He later said they spoiled him, although he added that his father was a perfectionist who made him feel inadequate. This description was transcribed by a prison psychiatrist, so make of it what you will, given that it was delivered by a self-serving master manipulator and reported by an all-too-often-ignored expert.

Glen Waverley is the kind of place where lots of Peter's old neighbours still lived years later when journalists came knocking. They remembered his close relationship with his parents, and one lady said, 'He was the light of his mother's life.'[1] They also started remembering the sorts of things that tend to come back to people when they realise they've been living inside a puzzle. They remembered underwear going missing from clotheslines – only women's underwear, though. There had also been a 'prowler', as they used to call them in those days, or a 'peeping Tom' having a squiz through the windows at night-time.

'There'd been a lot of chat about it around the neigh-bourhood and everyone had become very vigilant.'

Dupas didn't have any friends at school to speak of. He was a poor student who repeated Form One at Waverley High and was nicknamed 'Pugsley' by his peers for his uncanny resemblance to the character from *The Addams Family*.

One afternoon after school in October 1968, fifteen-year-old Dupas arrived at the back door of a neighbour's house, still in his school uniform, asking to borrow a sharp knife to peel some vegetables. He knew very well the neighbour would be home alone and had only recently returned from hospital with a newborn. As she went to the kitchen drawer, she remarked on what a good boy he was, peeling vegetables for his mother. Then she handed him the knife and, without saying a word, he used it to slash her face, her neck, her fingers and her arms.

'He knocked me down on to the floor and he fell on top of me. He kept on stabbing me with the knife and I kept trying to ward him off,' she told police. 'I felt the knife cut into my hands, mainly the right hand, my face and my neck. I was holding onto the knife at one stage, trying to break the blade. I was lying on my back and he was sitting on top of me. He said, "It's too late, I can't stop now, they'll lock me up."'[2]

Dupas then banged her head on the floor and covered her nose and mouth with his hand before he suddenly stopped the attack and broke down in tears. She fought hard for her life, and, no doubt, for her baby's, and he gave up eventually and ran away.

It didn't take long for the police to catch up with young Peter, of course, and when they did, he said simply that he 'didn't know why' he attacked his neighbour. He just couldn't help himself, he told them.

'I can remember having the knife in my hand . . . I must have been trying to kill her or something,' he said.[3]

He was placed on eighteen months' probation and admitted to Larundel Psychiatric Hospital for evaluation. A supervising psychiatrist noted Peter appeared to have been overprotected by his mother. He was released after two weeks and treated as an outpatient. As he was a minor, no permanent criminal conviction was recorded.

His mother, Merle, described the incident to a friend as 'just a brain-storm that he's had'. Presumably she meant she didn't believe it was a true insight into his character or that it would be repeated.

Noticing he was living back next door just two weeks after trying to murder her with her own kitchen knife, the victim of the attack asked police, 'How do we know what he's going to do next?'

According to her, they answered, 'We don't. We don't know.'

She packed up her family and moved out.[4]

From that point on, whenever Peter Dupas wasn't incarcerated, there was a certain radius around wherever he lived, inside which terrible things happened to women.

In October 1969, almost a year to the day after his visit to the back door of his neighbour, there was a break-in at the mortuary at the Austin Hospital, which was roughly a thirty-minute drive from the Dupas family home, where he was again living with his parents. The bodies of two elderly women were mutilated with pathologist's implements. Flesh was removed from the upper thigh of one of the bodies, which would become of great interest to detectives some thirty years later, when they were investigating the crimes of the adult Peter Dupas.

Peter's family rallied around him and he left school to work for his older brother as a fitter and turner. He hung around a bit with the other blokes from work and even got himself a girlfriend, but when Peter's girlfriend turned up to a party with two black eyes, one of his workmates decided to have a quiet word with him. Peter flew into a rage and belted the other man.

In 1972 Dupas was apprehended by an Oakleigh man who caught him peeping at his wife through a bathroom window. In 1973 police were called by a man who reported Dupas for following the family car so as to stare and smile through the window at his twelve-year-old daughter. Later in 1973, Dupas was arrested on his first charge of rape.

In an escalation of the circumstances of his teenage attack, the victim was not only home alone but was also the mother of a newborn whom Dupas threatened to harm if she resisted his attack. He received a nine-year sentence with a five-year minimum.

Police discovered that, in the two weeks between the rape and his arrest, Dupas had attempted two very similar but ultimately unsuccessful home invasions involving women who were home alone. Women he'd obviously stalked for some time previously.

One of the most upsetting aspects of the crimes of Peter Dupas is their predictability. Senior Detective Ian Armstrong, who had the displeasure of interviewing him on 30 November 1973 at the Nunawading police station, had this to say about the encounter.

'He stood out. To me the guy was just pure evil . . . His attacks were all carefully planned, and he showed no remorse. We could see where he was going. I remember thinking, "This guy could go all the way." He is an unmitigated liar . . . he is a very dangerous young person who will continue to offend where females are concerned and will possibly cause the death of one of his victims if he is not straightened out.'[5] The senior detective doesn't specify how he'd have 'straightened out' Dupas, given the chance.

Remarkably, while waiting to face a judge for the knife-point rape of that young mother, Dupas was remanded to Mont Park Psychiatric Hospital instead of a prison. As a patient rather than a prisoner he was allowed to take leave from the hospital and at least three times during this period, Dupas travelled to the Rosebud foreshore, a quiet, family-friendly beachside retreat near Melbourne, where he entered the women's toilet and shower block. Eventually he was arrested and delivered back to Larundel

Psychiatric Hospital (from which he'd been discharged at fifteen) and admitted as a voluntary patient. He was convicted of loitering with intent over the Rosebud offences and fined $140, all while still awaiting the rape trial.

When Dupas was finally convicted of that rape, County Court Judge John Leckie was suitably scandalised in his sentencing remarks.

'You raped a young married woman who was previously unknown to you in her own home and on her own bed,' he told Dupas. 'You invaded the sanctity of her home by a false story about your car breaking down . . . You threatened her with a knife, you tied her up with cord, you struck her when she tried to resist and, worst of all, you threatened to harm her baby when she tried to resist . . . while accepting that you are psychologically disturbed, I believe you were fully responsible for your actions.'[6]

That His Honour felt the victim's marital status was significant enough to mention in sentencing remarks is perplexing, to say the least. Sadly, though, his decision to protect more women, married or otherwise, from such a calculated and vicious serial offender by sending him to prison for a minimum of just five years is all too predictable. It wasn't to be the last time Judge Leckie underperformed in matters concerning Peter Dupas either. Stay tuned.

During his first stint in prison, Dupas was described as being cold, unemotional, dangerous, depressed, in denial of his guilt and unable to discuss his crimes. Prison psychiatrist Dr Allen Bartholomew, who worked extensively with Dupas during that time, wrote notes on the young inmate that were as chillingly accurate as they were summarily disregarded.

'I am reasonably certain that this youth has a serious psychosexual problem, that he is using the technique of denial as a coping device and that he is to be seen as potentially dangerous. The denial technique makes for huge difficulty in treatment.'[7]

Dupas served his minimum five years and then joined his parents in their new home in Frankston, a seaside suburb in south-east Melbourne.

Approximately two months after he was released from his first prison sentence, Dupas embarked on a ten-day molestation frenzy in which he sexually assaulted at least four separate women. During each of these attacks he was outfitted with a balaclava and a knife, as was his new routine. The first victim was raped in a public toilet block in Frankston; the worst (physical) injury was sustained by an elderly woman whom he stabbed while he raped her.

As a result, he was back in the dock in February 1980. Judge Leo Lazarus did the honours on this occasion, issuing a six-and-a-half-year sentence with another five-year minimum to Peter Dupas, whose attacks against women had escalated from stalking to slashing to rape to stabbing while raping.

He was twenty-six.

If you're outraged by the pathetic five-year-minimum sentence now, just wait until you read the psych report tended before Justice Lazarus during the sentencing hearing.

'There is little that can be said in Dupas's favour. He remains an extremely disturbed, immature, and dangerous man. His release on parole was a mistake.'

Not only did Dupas receive another five-year minimum for this series of attacks, but he was also deemed eligible for temporary leave from prison months before that minimum sentence had been served. How do we know this? Because on 13 February 1985 Helen McMahon was beaten to death while sunbaking at Rye beach in Victoria. It didn't take long for homicide detectives to discover that Peter Dupas was living in the Rye area, thanks to a prison pre-release program designed to assist inmates in re-assimilating into society.

He was never charged in relation to the Helen McMahon matter, which remains unsolved, but police make no secret of the fact that they believe Peter Dupas was responsible. Although he was already out of jail, he was formally released from his custodial sentence ten days after her murder. Just four days after that, Peter Dupas stalked a 21-year-old woman in his car along the road leading to the beach at Blairgowrie (an eight-minute drive from Rye Beach). When she left the walkway and made her way onto the sand, he left his car, followed her and raped her at knifepoint. He later told police, 'I'm sorry for what happened. Everyone was telling me I'm okay now.

I never thought it was going to happen again. I only wanted to live a normal life.'

Dupas stood before Justice Leckie again for this attack. Fascinatingly, at sentencing, His Honour acknowledged that Justice Lazarus's attempt to rehabilitate Dupas with his last five-year minimum prison sentence had 'failed miserably'. He didn't mention how successful he believed he'd been in doling out the same sentence to Dupas the time before, though.

Leckie didn't hold Lazarus responsible, however. He said it was clear the judge had only accepted what he'd been told by forensic psychiatrist Robert 'Bob' Myers, who was a proponent of a controversial approach to dealing with inveterate sex offenders.

Dr Myers remains an internationally revered expert in the study of the intersection of sexuality and criminology, even decades after his death. He was the founder of the Australian and New Zealand Association of Psychiatry, Psychology and Law (ANZAPPL). The association's academic periodical, the *Psychiatry, Psychology and Law Journal*, is still a highly respected resource for professionals in all three fields today.

So now that we've established his credentials, let's have a look at the advice he gave in 1980 that, according to Judge Leckie, led poor Judge Lazarus to inadequately sentence Peter Dupas.

By 1980, Dr Bob Myers was advocating the use of Depo-Provera in the treatment of sex offenders.[8] While many of us know of it as a contraceptive option administered to women as an injection, when administered to men Depo-Provera lowers testosterone levels and suppresses their sex drive. Studies have shown it has the potential to lower the risk of sex offending by 500 per cent, but it doesn't take an international expert to tell you that there seems to be an awful lot riding on the word 'potential'. Dare I say any woman who knew she'd be living within a thousand-kilometre radius of an uncaged Peter Dupas could have told Judge Lazarus and Dr Myers that the potential was still too high.

As it happened, all the studies and potential were irrelevant anyway because, despite the recommendations of Dr Myers, which were so heavily relied upon by Justice Lazarus, someone further down the chain decided not to take them up. Dupas wasn't treated with Depo-Provera or any other hormone medication during that particular stint inside or during his subsequent parole. So much for Dr Myers being the fall guy.

Dupas was treated with Depo-Provera during a later stint inside, incidentally, and it was observed to have had little to no success. So much for the potential.

In 1985 Judge Leckie upped the ante and sentenced Dupas to twelve years for the rape at Blairgowrie Beach, with a minimum of ten. Dupas was shipped off to G Division of Pentridge Prison, which was the psychiatric unit.

G Division was tucked up tight in the prison's western corner, where the high wall ran along Pentridge Boulevard, and in the shadow of a guard tower. It was where Chopper Read was trying to escape to when he sliced his ears off in 1978. He miscalculated the blood loss and ended up in the infirmary, but he didn't end up dead, which he would have done had he stayed in H Division, as there was a contract on his life.

The other wall making up the G Division corner ran alongside Holy Trinity Anglican Church and St Paul's Catholic School, a co-educational primary school, with a large oval that was doubtless filled with the sounds of children several times every day. Sounds that must have been clearly audible next door in G Division.

Dupas attempted suicide twice in G Division, which brought him to the attention of one of the nurses. Her name was Claire and she was sixteen years older than him. Dupas believed she cured him of the need to rape women. Thanks to her, he was able to better understand himself, to become more assertive and this, he believed, was the key to his being able to live a normal life with her on the outside. They were married in Castlemaine Prison and settled together not far from there in the picturesque town of Woodend when he'd completed his minimum sentence in 1992.

As it so often does, though, married life outside prison walls proved rather anti-climactic for Peter's wife. She later admitted to feeling regretful about the marriage quite soon after he came to live with her. She found him selfish and lazy and uninterested in any conversation that didn't revolve around him. On the topic of sex, she complained it was 'very basic, almost non-existent . . . it got to the stage where I could not bear him touching me.'

Claire later said that it felt more like a 'mother and son relationship' than anything else. 'He was very possessive of me, like if any of my family came, he had to be right there. He had to be number one.'

Claire wasn't happy in the marriage, but she was convinced Peter was finally cured of his sexual offending. So much so that she never even suspected him when 31-year-old Renita Brunton was found stabbed to death in the kitchen behind her second-hand shop in Sunbury, a thirty-minute drive from their home, in November 1993. If Claire was given pause for thought when she learned the victim actually lived in Woodend, just like them, she's never mentioned it publicly.

People who worked in other shops in the same arcade as Renita Brunton's store told police they didn't hear a scream or any commotion at all during the time they now know she was killed. A witness did come forward to say they'd seen her involved in a heated argument with a man in her shop the day before. That man has never been identified. A close friend of Renita's told police she had been giving what she called 'informal counselling sessions' in the back of her shop and on the day of her murder would have been counselling a man with a violent sexual history.

Almost two months after Renita's murder, sometime around Christmas 1993, Claire was preparing to leave for a night shift at her new job at an aged care facility closer to home. Peter had a panic attack at the thought of being without her all night and demanded to come with her.

'He was standing between me and the door and I said, "Will you just please get out from under my feet and do something, anything",' she remembered later. '"Just do something, anything, but please just get out from under my feet, you're driving me crazy!" He had gone down to the shed and said he'd prepared everything he needed to go fishing.'

The next day Dupas followed a woman into a public toilet block at Lake Eppalock, an hour's drive from Woodend. He was armed with a knife and the victim sustained serious injuries as she fought him off, but he suddenly ceased the attack and walked away.

The victim ran from the toilet block and raised the alarm, at which point her boyfriend and his friends spotted Dupas leaving the scene in his car and chased him. He panicked, crashed the car and was dragged out by the men, who held on to him until police arrived. The police uncovered a horrifying kit inside the vehicle, including knives, a balaclava, condoms and a shovel.

Any delusions Claire had of her husband being cured of his deviancy were shattered by his arrest.

'I– I just can't tell you how bad I felt,' she said later. 'I just couldn't stop crying.'

Judge Leo Hart sentenced Dupas to three years with a minimum of nine months. Naturally, he was released after nine months.

Upon his release, Dupas visited his estranged wife in the aged care facility in which she worked. During that visit she told him their marriage was over for good. His parents had finally been driven interstate by the shame of his actions and he was very much on his own.

As he did every time he was released from prison, Peter moved to a new part of Melbourne to start again. This time it was Brunswick, bisected by the throbbing thoroughfare of Sydney Road. He was employed in a Salvation Army workshop for former prison inmates in the area and began a new relationship with another mother figure.

To drive the length of Sydney Road, from Melbourne's CBD until it turns into the Hume Highway, which leads all the way north to, indeed, Sydney, is to experience Melbourne in all its many moods and flavours. From the cultural melting pot of Brunswick and Coburg, the home of Pentridge Prison, up through the old-school working-class suburbs of Coburg North with Preston, Reservoir and Thomastown swinging off to the east, you eventually arrive at the newer outer suburbs of Somerton, Roxburgh Park, Broadmeadows and Campbellfield.

In the 1990s, those outer suburbs were rough as guts and they were the stomping ground of forty-year-old Margaret Maher. She was a fixture of the local shops in Gaffney Street, where everyone figured out what 'kind' of person she was. They traded theories about her among themselves but she was no trouble at all and always polite, so they let her be. The man at the newsagency pretended not to notice her standing quietly behind the calendar rack reading all the magazines. The lady in the clothes shop let her lay-by things for ages, paying off two and five dollars every couple of weeks when she clearly had hundreds of dollars in her busted coin purse. The supermarket staff at Broadmeadows Safeway greeted her warmly on those nights when she'd come in and wander around aimlessly for hours before leaving with something pointless, such as a notebook or a festive candle, but never any food.

Margaret's neighbours knew what was going on too. They saw men come and go at all hours, and they saw the bruises up and down her arms and legs, but, again, she was no trouble. It's tempting to describe Margaret as taking care of herself in her own way, but the state of her health at this relatively young age tells a different story.

Margaret's sex work generally precedes her. What I mean is, she's usually introduced right out of the gate as 'Sex worker Margaret Maher' or 'Prostitute Margaret Maher' or even 'Street prostitute Margaret Maher'. Margaret's sex work is about as relevant as the previous victim's marital status.

Margaret was known to work from her own flat in Campbellfield, but she was also known to work outside, standing and walking up and down the area where Sydney Road becomes the Hume Highway, waiting for clients. She was well known at truck stops in the area too. As a long-term heroin user, Margaret was on the methadone program, but to keep up with the long nights, she used amphetamines and sedatives on a daily basis. Margaret had a chronic coronary condition and a terrible cold she could never seem to shake.

Peter Dupas's new girlfriend left Melbourne for an extended overseas trip in September 1997. The night of 4 October 1997 was one of those nights that Margaret Maher was wandering around Broadmeadows Safeway. She left at 12.20 am. A woman driving along nearby Somerton Road, sometime between 1 am and 2.30 am, saw a woman emerge from the bushes on her right-hand side. The woman appeared to be naked from the waist down.

Although she couldn't definitively identify the woman as Margaret, Margaret's body was found in the area about eleven hours later. It was hidden under a pile of cardboard boxes; her left breast had been cut off and placed in her mouth, and her lower garments had been pulled all the way down.

Shortly before the attack, Peter Dupas had moved from Brunswick to Coane Street, Pascoe Vale, which was about a six-minute drive from the Gaffney Street shops. It was also close to the Austin Hospital, the site of the unsolved mortuary mutilations almost thirty years earlier.

About six minutes north of the Gaffney Street shops, just up Sydney Road, is Fawkner Cemetery. It's one of those places that seems to have an atmosphere completely independent of the world around it. I'm not particularly superstitious about cemeteries in general; I've been known to spend hours wandering among damp old gravestones, running my fingers over forgotten names, dates and dedications as a holiday activity. But there is no Gothic romance about Fawkner Cemetery.

There is an endless, swirling, grey wind there, every day, no matter what the weather is like elsewhere in Melbourne. Perhaps it's created by the interplay between the cemetery's geometry and that of the vast industrial park opposite. Maybe it's an illusion brought on by the particularly desolate stretch of Sydney Road the cemetery sits on. The great road, so famous for its vibrancy, becomes an eight-lane symphony of despair in D minor as it approaches the memorial park. Existential dread sucks the air from my lungs every time I crest the hill out of Coburg.

In October 1997, young women visiting Fawkner Cemetery alone started encountering a strange man there. The cemetery reflects the community around it and is broken up into many orthodox sections, visited often and tended with care, mostly by women. It's grotesquely ingenious, isn't it? As young women, who'd made time during lunch breaks from work or while small children were at school, quietly bent down to place flowers, sometimes kneeling and perhaps even closing their eyes to pray, several were startled to realise a blond man with glasses had been making his way towards them, walking very quickly. One of them said later that she felt like he was looking around to see if anyone was watching. She was so afraid, she leapt up and ran to her car, locking the door behind her. A moment later, the man actually stood at the driver's door and looked through the window at her for several moments. It was terrifying. She never forgot that face, but she never spoke to the police about it until she saw him on the news years later, such was her fear of that man.

Another woman screamed as the man ran towards her and watched as he stopped and hid in some bushes. Then she turned and ran as fast as she could and never looked back, jumping over gravestones as she went.

Eight women in all would eventually report having experienced something like that at Fawkner Cemetery during October 1997. Until 25-year-old Mersina Halvagis made her usual Saturday afternoon pilgrimage to the Greek Orthodox section on 1 November to tend to the grave of her grandmother.

Mersina failed to meet her fiancé as planned later in the afternoon. He and her father began searching for her and in the early morning they found her car at the cemetery. The young man discovered her body slouched beside two nearby headstones soon after. She'd been stabbed more than fifty times from behind as she knelt.

Peter Dupas's grandfather was buried one hundred metres away.

It's a brutal truth that some homicides horrify the community more than others. The thought of such a wholesome young woman being brutally attacked in a cemetery, in broad daylight, tending to the grave of her grandmother, was just too much for Melbourne to bear and pressure mounted on the homicide squad.

Advocating on her behalf were Mersina's parents, George and Christina. With little English between them, it was George who stood before the media most often and, to this day, I've never seen anyone summon the respect and resolve of a community with more passion and fewer words than he. To speak his name in Melbourne is to invoke a silent moment of awestruck reverence. There simply are no words to describe George Halvagis. His loss, his gentility, his dignified fight – which even now lives on for others.

In April 1998, six months after the attack, there was a breakthrough. One of the eight women who encountered Dupas in Fawkner Cemetery in the lead-up to Mersina's murder contacted police. She'd realised she was there on the very day Mersina was killed. She'd been working in the Latvian section of the cemetery when a man approached her at around 9.30 am.

She'd actually sat on a bench and chatted with the man, whom she described as being of medium build, in his late thirties, with fair to light brown hair and wearing glasses. He smelt of alcohol, seemed emotional and asked her twice what was behind a nearby hedge.

Together with police, she created a computer drawing of the man. It was a start and it appears to have kept Dupas contained for almost a year.

That changed in 1999.

Nicole 'Nicky' Patterson was excited at her weekly family dinner on the night of Saturday, 17 April 1999. She had her first new patient, a man called Malcolm, booked in for Monday morning. He'd found her through an article and accompanying ad in the free local paper featuring her and two other women who were all starting their own businesses from home. She didn't love the photo, but she was chuffed the ad had worked so quickly.

Nicky's father hosted the dinners. Her brother and sister Kylie were present, along with various partners and kids.

'Nicole was the baby and always the rebel,' says Kylie now. 'She'd just come to this most beautiful place in her life; she'd done all the work on herself and, in conjunction with that, she'd always helped other people. She was just starting her own business and she was beaming with life and love and excitement. She was so excited about this new client. She was living her passion and so excited about helping other people.'

In the weeks leading up to meeting her first client, Malcolm, Nicky began experiencing a number of ominous dreams and premonitions. She dreamt about a wolf following her and she spoke of a pain in her abdomen. She said she felt like she was 'dying and being reborn'.

First thing Monday morning, Nicky prepared to receive her new client in the front room of her Northcote home, which was about a twelve-minute drive from Dupas's new flat in Preston. When he arrived, she welcomed him in and went to the kitchen to make coffee. He, no doubt, prepared while she was gone, and when she re-entered the room he attacked her.

A friend of Nicky's whom we'll call R arrived at the house around eight hours later as arranged. They had dinner plans. She was struck immediately by the fact that the house was in darkness and, as she got closer, she realised the front door was ajar. Melbourne nights in April are already cold, and Nicky always had the house cosy. R climbed the front stairs cautiously, but she was also wondering if Nicky was playing some kind of trick. What else could possibly make sense?

Naturally she looked into the front room first. As her eyes adjusted to the black, R recognised the dark mass on the floor as her friend Nicky.

'Nicky,' she thought, or possibly said, 'stop playing around.' Because what else would she say?

Was her friend playing some bizarre game? Was this a joke? What was this?

'Nicky was a creative soul who loved painting,' says Kylie, 'so [R probably wondered] was Nicky doing something weird? And then [R] thought, "Oh my gosh, Nicky's killed herself, what has she done to herself?" And then when she looked again, she thought, "Oh no, Nicky couldn't have done that to herself."'

R didn't ring the police first. She rang her boyfriend and cried, 'Something's happened to Nicky, something's happened to Nicky!' before proceeding to tell him what she'd discovered.

R, her boyfriend and Nicky were part of a tight-knit circle that included Nicky's brother and his girlfriend.

Kylie continues, 'So my brother's girlfriend Lisa called my brother and said, "Something's happened to Nicky, Nicky's dead," and my brother's called my dad, and my poor dad . . . My stepmother rang me, and I collapsed . . . and I just remember saying, "You can't ring Mum, you can't ring Mum, you can't ring Mum."'

Nicky's father and brother drove to her house in Northcote but were prevented from entering by police, who'd cordoned it off by then to begin the forensic investigation. They sat in the car and watched the comings and goings all night. One of the people they saw was Detective Senior Sergeant Jeff Maher (no relation to Margaret), who was the detective on call that night for the homicide squad.

Now an instructor at the academy, Maher recounts his memories of the night in the typically formal fashion of a copper remembering a serious chain of events. 'The uniform van from Northcote, staffed by two female members, had been called to the scene by Nicky's friend who was supposed to have dinner with her that night. They then called the local detectives, who went in to make an assessment as to whether an offence had occurred. They assessed it was a crime scene and then contacted the on-call homicide crew, which was us.'

Maher's reputation precedes him on many fronts. He's what other police call 'a very good operator', which means he's an excellent policeman with an impressive record of catching criminals. He's funny and charming in a macho kind of way, but there is an unmistakable warmth to him. I'm not sure you'd see it if you were sitting across from him in an interview room after killing someone, but he definitely showed it to me. I think the copper-speak is not only force of habit, but also a mark of respect when it comes to talking about matters such as the murder of Nicole Patterson. It definitely seems to get thicker when police are circling close to the actual details of violent crimes and other sensitive topics.

Of his assessment of the scene, Jeff had this to say, 'It looked like Nicky and the offender had been engaging in some refreshments. And then there was obviously a violent confrontation with the offender and Nicky was killed.'

As Nicky's father and brother watched Jeff and his crew arrive and enter her house, they probably wondered who they were. Most people back in 1999 didn't recognise the guys in the dark-blue suits wielding the clipboards, biros and mobile phones as the homicide squad. Maybe most people still don't.

Kylie begged her husband to take her to Nicky's house too. 'I was saying to my husband, "You've gotta take me to Nicky's, you've gotta take me to Nicky's, we've gotta sort this out, there's been some kind of mistake, we've gotta go to Northcote" . . . I was just obsessed with getting over to her house. I know now I wouldn't have been allowed to go in there anyway, but that's all you want to do. Can you imagine as a parent or as an older sibling, you feel this protective . . . even in death you want to take care of her. That's the thing about homicide, it takes away so much. We couldn't take care of her body, and by the time we could see her body, she'd been through so much.'

Jeff continues. 'It started to piece together when we spoke to the relatives, and, very, very, very lovely people,' he leans into the microphone to say, 'but Nicky said that she had her first client on that morning, in her vocation as a psychotherapist. That, connected with the doorknocking, and never underestimate doorknocking, helped us pick up a number of witnesses who heard a violent exchange between a man and a woman on that morning.'

Forensic pathologist Dr David Ranson found that Nicole Patterson had been stabbed twenty-seven times in her chest and in her back, and some of the wounds had punctured her lungs and her heart. The cause of death was determined to be multiple stab wounds to the chest. She was naked from the waist down, and her skirt was found in another room. Her skirt and her blouse had been cut off. Dr Ranson found that both of Nicole's breasts had been removed after death, and that there was breast tissue present in the mouth; however, neither breast was located at the scene and they were never recovered. There was also a portion of flesh missing from the upper thigh region of one of Nicole's legs.

Dr Ranson found that the edges of the cuts had a 'sawtooth' appearance, characteristic of skin that had been cut by means of a sawing motion with a sharp object such as a knife.

It has taken me a long time to process that a man who was a vicious predator for over thirty years and was labelled a serial rapist was never given the maximum sentence despite continually committing the most heinous crimes against women. Every time he was released he re-offended immediately while he was on parole.

Now that he's a case study in depravity we know that Dupas stalked his victims for weeks if not months before attacking them. The police said Nicole had been stalked for six weeks.

'We were told at the viewing not to cuddle her,' Kylie says. 'We weren't to touch her because she was so badly damaged she might not stay in one piece. That final time we saw her in the coffin, she just had this tiny part of her face peeking out from a . . . this sort of . . . I don't know what you'd call it, this sort of shawl thing they draped over her.

'I had some time alone with her and I pulled up a chair alongside and I started singing to her, a Tiddas song. We were mad about Tiddas. D'you remember Tiddas? We had a song we used to sing, you know, "You are my sister"? I started singing that to her. I felt like somebody came and sat on my lap, I felt a physical presence, like it was her. It was probably God comforting me at my most heart-broken time.'

Police pounced on Dupas within days, arresting him and raiding his home. They found Nicky's blood on his jacket (he claimed they planted it there). In his wheelie bin they discovered a piece of paper torn into tiny pieces, which, when reassembled, bore the word 'Malcolm' followed by Nicole Patterson's phone number. The same number she'd written on another piece of paper for me just two weeks earlier.

'Three days after Nicky was found, the detective rang me and said, "We have made an arrest,"' remembers Nicole's mum, Pam O'Donnell. '"The name is Peter Dupas, he has a history, he's a serial rapist."'

It was a good result, but there was a niggling feeling around the homicide squad to do with David Ranson's autopsy report. There was a feeling that there were distinctive similarities in the injuries Dupas had inflicted on Nicky, and injuries inflicted upon another woman whose body had been found not too far away, a sex worker called Margaret Maher, whose unsolved case was gathering dust.

The year 1999 was a hectic time for the Victorian Homicide Squad, thanks to the gang war raging between Carl Williams, Tony Mokbel and everyone else.

'Our crew was so much under the pump at that point in time,' says Jeff Maher, clearly relaxing enough to use actual human words, 'with jobs, preparing briefs of evidence, we had a lot on, so I volunteered, sight unseen, to do the brief on Margaret Maher. Now, that's a bit unusual for the homicide squad because detective senior sergeants only do the briefs for police shootings. Which I've done quite a few [of]. But I volunteered for this and it turned out, from 1999 to 2016, it followed me all the way.'

'Doing the brief' means compiling all the documents you have regarding a case, such as the witness statements, crime scene photographs, forensics reports, post-mortem results, just everything you have, and putting it together in one nice, neat package. That package is called the 'brief of evidence' and ideally it will be presented to the Office of Public Prosecutions (OPP) as the evidence the police intend to use to prosecute someone for the crime. The detectives are always striving to create a strong brief of evidence to present to the OPP.

Only when the OPP feels the brief is strong enough to gain a conviction will they commit the resources to prosecuting a case. So, figuring out who done it is actually just the beginning of a detective's job. Strengthening the brief is crucial to getting the case to court and, frustratingly, the stronger the brief, the more likely the offender will plead guilty to the charge and receive a reduced sentence as a reward. The better they are at their jobs, the lighter the sentences for the offenders. Unbelievable, isn't it? (I know, I'm starting to sound like an old copper.)

Margaret Maher's autopsy was performed at VIFM by Dr David Ranson's colleague Dr Matthew Lynch. Dr Lynch's report certainly included a number of observations that, when compared with Ranson's report regarding

Nicky Patterson's autopsy, gave rise to the theory that there was a common 'signature' present.

The earliest researchers of serial killers discovered that the killers tended to repeat some element of the process for a reason close to their own personal psychopathy. This is known as their 'signature' and it's an important part of determining whether a serial killer is at work. When the researchers worked backwards with their first subjects, they were often able to unravel the reasons why those signatures were meaningful to the individual serial killer.

Ed Kemper, for example, one of the FBI Behavioural Science Unit's earliest subjects, confessed that he buried the heads of many of his victims in his mother's garden, because 'she always wanted people to look up to her'.[9]

In reality, Kemper's mother had been abusive towards him as a child, while spoiling his sisters, which is probably the truer reason for his desire to debase young women and secretly place them around her.

Dr Lynch's autopsy report on Margaret Maher created an interesting but not uncommon challenge that illuminates the truly independent position forensic pathologists occupy in our judicial system. Despite the fact that she'd clearly been savagely attacked, Dr Lynch was unable to establish Margaret Maher's exact cause of death. The best he could do was 'combined drug toxicity in a woman with a heart condition and subtle signs of neck compression'.

Remember those health issues Margaret Maher had? Years of walking up and down the Hume Highway all night, of not eating, of existing on a diet of heroin, meth-adone, amphetamines and sedatives instead, meant that when it came to determining what actually stopped her heart from beating in that final moment, Dr Lynch was unable to say.

Subsequent testing found that Dupas's DNA was present on a black glove found near Margaret Maher's body, but Dr Lynch would've had no way of knowing that as he conducted his examination back at VIFM. Even if he had, it would have had nothing to do with his results, unless DNA was present on or inside the body itself. The forensic pathologist's job is not to figure out how the biological evidence fits in with everything else. It's to learn as much as possible from the remains and to present that evidence to the judge and the jury with as much clarity as possible. Sometimes, more often than anyone would like and certainly more often than popular culture would have us believe, the forensic specialists can't give the court all the answers.

It's often impossible to ascertain exactly what stopped a person's heart from beating (and it's virtually always impossible to know without an eyewitness exactly when a person died).

Dr Lynch told the court that some people with coronary artery disease, such as Margaret Maher, die suddenly. It was a fact. On top of that, the four types of drugs in her body could well have affected her breathing and heart rate too. Her injuries, including the neck compression, could have happened after her death. He simply had no way of determining whether she died naturally or was killed, and telling us the absolute truth of what he knows about that is what we've entrusted him to do.

Many homicide investigations have ended because the victim has had a pre-existing health condition that could just as easily have killed them as could have another person. The accused doesn't need to prove they didn't kill them, of course, they just need to prove that there is a reasonable doubt about what killed them.

Dr Lynch definitely did observe the same jagged, sawtooth cutting patterns that Dr Ranson observed, and Margaret's breast had also been removed. It had been placed in her mouth, and Dr Ranson said there was evidence of the same thing in Nicky's case although the offender had then removed it, whereas that had not happened in Margaret's case. It looked a lot like a signature to a lot of people.

'I charged Dupas with Nicky's [murder],' says Jeff Maher. 'And then what happened was there was a detective by the name of Paul Scarlett, who's now a Detective Senior Sergeant . . . and an outstanding operator.' He leans into the recorder again for that last bit. 'He, together with Mick Daly, who was at the homicide squad at the time and is now an Inspector, and also then you've got Mick Roberts, who was my boss until I retired at the arson explosive squad – excellent operators as well – they were involved in the Dupas job, Nicky Patterson in particular. Then they formed Taskforce Mikado to have a look back to see what other murders Dupas had done. I stayed back at homicide to make sure we got him on Nicole's.'

Jeff Maher did get Dupas on Nicole's murder. It took the jury less than three hours to find him guilty. That's the kind of brief of evidence you get from an excellent operator.

Dupas, who'd never served a maximum sentence in his life, no matter how hard he'd tried to destroy the life of a woman, stood before Justice Frank Vincent, who decided on that day it was over. After hearing the jury's verdict, he took the very unusual step of instructing his associate to read Dupas's entire criminal history into the record.

The court was silent as every horror was recounted.

In his sentencing remarks, Justice Vincent said, '. . . the prospects of your eventual rehabilitation must be regarded as so close to hopeless that they can be effectively discounted. There is no indication whatsoever that you have experienced any sense of remorse for what you have done, and I doubt that you are capable of any such human response. At a fundamental level, as human beings, you present for us the awful, threatening and unanswerable question: How did you come to be as you are?'

He then sentenced Peter Dupas to life imprisonment with no parole, ensuring he would never be free again.[10]

On the second anniversary of Nicole Patterson's murder, her sister Kylie was absolutely bereft and racked with agony. 'But we have to hold on to the fact that we did have her body to say goodbye to, that the perpetrator was caught and that we did get closure through the courts.

Those three things we are grateful for because we know that other families don't get that and I can't imagine what that's like.'

Taskforce Mikado went on to achieve convictions for the murders of Margaret Maher and Mersina Halvagis. In 2004, Dupas was sentenced to a second term of life imprisonment for the murder of Maher with the judge, Justice Stephen Kaye, saying, 'your offending is connected with a need by you to vindicate a perverted and sadistic hatred of women and a contempt for them and their right to live. As such the present offence must be characterised as being in one of the most serious categories of murders which come before this Court . . . you had, over almost three decades, terrorised women in this State. You have repeatedly violated a central norm of a decent civilised society . . . Based on your repeated violent offences, and on the gravity of this offence, there is no prospect of your rehabilitation. Nothing was advanced on your behalf to reflect that there is even the faintest glimmer of hope for you. Even if there were, any considerations of rehabilitation must, in this case, be subordinated to the gravity of your offending, the need for the imposition of a just punishment, and the principle of general deterrence. All those circumstances combine, in my view, not only to justify, but also to require that I do not fix a minimum term.'[11]

The Halvagis conviction was aided in no small part by the witness statement of 'disgraced' lawyer Andrew Fraser.

Fraser, who was convicted of knowingly being involved in the importation of drugs in 2001, found himself in the company of Peter Dupas in the Fulham Correctional Centre. Allow me to break that down into real terms for you. Andrew Fraser was a rich lawyer who developed a cocaine habit and ended up bunk mates with Peter Dupas, sexual sadist who's raped and murdered dozens of women over a thirty-year period. How is our sentencing system? Seriously?

Luckily Andrew Fraser the ex-drug addict had some standards, because he reported a conversation he'd had in prison with Dupas in which the rapist/killer had acted out his murder of Mersina Halvagis. Justice Philip Cummins was grateful to Fraser too, because on 25 July 2005 he found Dupas guilty of Mersina's murder on the strength of Fraser's witness statement.

Of Dupas, Justice Cummins said: 'Just as Ms Halvagis's presence at the cemetery was typical of her goodness, your presence at the cemetery was typical of your evil: cunning, predatory and homicidal.'

The knife attack was described as 'swift, savage and brutal, but directional'. Ms Halvagis tried to escape, her hands up in defence. But, as Justice Cummins said, 'she had no chance against Dupas's strength, his knife and his hatred.'[12]

In 2018, Dupas was charged with the 1997 murder of Mrs Kathleen Downes in the Brunswick Lodge Aged Care Facility. He was due to face trial in October 2019 but star witness Andrew Fraser was too ill to give evidence. It was no ruse. He was gravely ill. And perhaps in light of that fact, Supreme Court Justice Peter Almond said the decision did not constitute an acquittal and noted Dupas could be re-indicted on the murder charge at any time. He then scrapped the suppression orders that had prevented reporting of the case.

Justice Almond's statements signalled once and for all that the days of Peter Dupas's rights taking precedence over those of every woman in his vicinity were finally over.

For me, this has always been a very personal case. It began with Nicky, of course, but as the years have gone by more and more reasons have presented themselves for me to despise Dupas.

Now, as I am blessed with an overview, I can't help but see so many of his victims as kindred spirits. Margaret Maher was a woman Nicky Patterson would have been drawn to. She was a woman Nicky would have felt great affection for and seen strength in, where so many others only saw scandal and gossip. Margaret was a woman Nicky would have sought to empower.

Margaret was the potential future of our dear Dani. A young woman robbed of her baby. Our beautiful little Dani, who was accused of sinfulness by her unfaithful father, and then tried to prove it in so many ways. I'd give anything to know where she is now, or just to know she's alive, but that's not the way it goes in the sex industry, I'm afraid. The fake names and stigma make it hard to get in touch down the track.

I miss all of you, if you are reading this, and I hope you are well.

(I've kept in contact with Miss Vick, though, and she's still a stunning bombshell, I'm happy to say.)

8

NO EXCUSES

Comedian Blaise Williams was sharing one of his favourite pieces of a friend's material with another performer in
his usual animated and slightly-too-loud way. The joke
was about the public outpouring of grief after the death
of David Bowie in 2016. The crescendo was something
like '"Let's Dance" was a great track but were you at his
wedding? Did you know him? No? Well, strangers die
every day, mate. Calm down!'

With that, an elderly man approached and insisted
Blaise have some respect for the solemnity of the occasion.
It was, after all, a public vigil for a murdered woman.
And, no, none of them had known her personally, but that
wasn't the point.

But Blaise had known the woman, and she'd also

written that joke. She was comedian Eurydice Dixon, and her friends agreed she'd have enjoyed the irony of the moment immensely.

Forensic pathologist Joanna Glengarry grew up in Napier, tucked into the east coast of New Zealand's North Island. It has a population of just sixty-five thousand people today, so it was presumably much smaller when young Joanna was rattling around Tamatea High School.

'It's not known for sending people to medical school,' she said later, with a laugh.

There were no doctors in her family but she was close to her father. 'He was really handy. When I went to university, other people were getting sets of pots and pans. I got a toolbox, which was just the best going-flatting gift ever. Now I have power tools. I have a drill, and I love it.'[1]

Her father's influence can be found in Joanna's work too. Like most of her colleagues, she's added a few unconventional tools to her work kit over the years, many of which she sourced from her local hardware store.

Jo read a hell of a lot of Patricia Cornwell as a teenager. 'They sound fantastic,' she thought at the time of the forensic pathologists in the books. In a variation of the *CSI* conversation, she adds of those books, 'I can't stand them now because they're so far-fetched and ridiculous.'[2]

At least Patricia Cornwell delivered Dr Glengarry to the real profession eventually. She made a short detour first as a surgeon. I don't like to buy a ten-class yoga pass because it feels like a long way to project into the future, but I bet I'm not the only one who has no idea how long it takes to become a surgeon. Prepare yourself.

Jo studied from 1998 to 2005 to become a surgeon. That's eight years. Then, get this, she realised it wasn't her passion. Another surgeon suggested pathology might be her go, so she went back to study for another five years.

That's thirteen years of study. And that only qualified her to beg for admittance into Auckland's mortuary as a volunteer on Saturday mornings so she could finish her fellowship. That took another two years.

Joanna's story reminds me so much of my own apprenticeship in the world of stand-up comedy in the 1990s (except mine was much shorter). It hadn't changed a bit when Eurydice was working her way through it in 2018.

By then twenty-two, Eurydice spent every waking moment thinking about comedy, writing jokes and trying them out on her comedy friends. Then she'd hustle for five-minute gigs in tiny pubs around Melbourne, none of which paid a single cent. Maybe it sounds crazy, and some people do complain about it, but those people are missing the point and don't last long. This is how we learn. Most of us do this for a couple of years before we start to pick up paid gigs.

This is the process by which I learned and built a career that's sustained me half a lifetime already and diversified into areas I could never have imagined (including writing books about true crime, for goodness sake!). This is the system that started the careers of Dave Hughes, Judith Lucy, Wil Anderson, Rove McManus, Peter Helliar, Denise Scott, the list goes on. We're all cut from the same cheap cloth, stuck to a pub wall with gaffer tape. Eurydice was following a well-worn path, a path that included walking home alone through Melbourne's dark streets after gigs.

I walked home alone at least four nights a week in the early 1990s. Why? Because I had not a pot to piss in, my friends. I had a wonderful life, full of laughs and friendship and untold hope for the future, but so little money that I clearly remember walking the final stretch, along St Kilda's Acland Street, with my eyes firmly downcast, hoping to spy some spare change on the ground. I long for that time at least once a day, though, because sometimes it feels like impoverished, youthful optimism beats knowing how it all turns out.

I always felt young and strong during those walks, particularly after good gigs – invulnerable, in fact – and I'm told Eurydice was similarly physically confident. She was just over six feet tall, broad-shouldered and solidly grounded in her Doc Marten boots. She favoured the goth style that never quite goes out of fashion in Melbourne: black lipstick, a short black bob and long black dresses.

Like me and and Joanna Glengarry years earlier, Eurydice was a young woman following her passion, who felt she was finally living the life she was meant for.

'She was definitely strong-willed and independent,' says Caili Christian, another comedian who became an unlikely

231

family spokesperson in the days after Eurydice's death. 'I really annoyed her, we weren't close friends at all, because I was too mumsy and she wasn't into that at all.'

Eurydice was raised by her father Jeremy, commonly described as a 'lawyer and political activist'[3] although he would tell me later he was a 'failed lawyer, at best'. He doesn't deny they were very close. Eurydice's mother Karen died of a heroin overdose when she was just seven years old, a fact that was passed on to the tabloid press by a non-family member in the days after Eurydice's murder. It was used as part of a narrative about Eurydice's 'tragic life' by some sections of the media, which was unfair given it was the only incident cited as proof, under a headline that besmirched her grieving family.

It's repeated here only because Jeremy told me not only did he wish for Karen to be remembered but to be remembered as the 'fine woman' she was.

Although he declined to participate actively in this book, Jeremy did give me permission to tell Eurydice's story and to speak to her friends and colleagues. As the months ticked over and I chipped away, I felt compelled to check in with him a few more times, just to be sure he hadn't changed his mind, either about allowing me to write about his daughter's death or about speaking to me directly himself.

Every time I sent him a short, apologetic email Jeremy replied swiftly and kindly. He reiterated his position on both counts: yes, I still had his permission to tell his daughter's story; and no, he still had no interest in participating personally. From quite early on, though, every email was accompanied by a gift of some kind or other, such as that lovely quote about Karen. Sometimes he answered questions, sometimes he didn't. I couldn't help myself, of course, and I asked about his daughter's unusual name.

I imagined the obviously eclectic couple had named their baby girl in honour of a romantic conversation they'd once shared about gods and goddesses from obscure Greek tragedies they were charmed to discover they'd both read before meeting. He never answered my question about it, which only encouraged me. I imagined it might've become a closely guarded story now that he was the only one left that it truly belonged to.

One time, he sent me a sound file.

I'll admit I was nervous when I clicked on the link. A sound file from Eurydice's father, whom I didn't know, who was a failed lawyer and anarchist, and not yet two years adrift from her murder. I did what I do whenever unease is enveloping me. I stopped thinking and dove in.

To my astonishment, within seconds, I found myself listening to Eurydice Dixon performing stand-up comedy.

'This is the only full routine of Eurydice's known to have been recorded,' Jeremy explained in a follow-up email. 'It's an early routine, performed here at the Mad Fucking Witches' benefit for asylum seekers. My intention in sending it,' he concluded, 'is to let Eurydice speak for herself.'

'I have this weird tendency to draw unwanted attention to myself when I'm in public.'

That's the first line Eurydice says in her routine. Her voice is high-pitched with nerves and I can hear the shaking of her body in the microphone but her pace is perfect.

'I do carry a sword with me at night-time sometimes. I do acknowledge that. To some degree I'm bringing it on myself,' says Eurydice by way of explaining why she might attract unwanted attention although she goes on to say she doesn't think of it as a weapon, 'even though I believe in the right to defend yourself at night, especially if you're a woman, but not to that level. Next thing you know I'll be wanting the right to vote and it's just downhill from there, right?'

This line elicits the first encouraging sounds from the crowd, and Eurydice erupts with gratitude and youthful energy into the microphone. 'Yeah?' she yells back at the small group of people in front of her, as though she's just lifted the lid off Madison Square Garden. I've felt that combination of relief and adrenalin explode out of my own chest. I feel a little murmur in there again as it happens for her in my headphones.

I can see the room in my mind's eye, having stood in her place in so many rooms like it. The feminist benefit gig has an atmosphere all its own and I can hear it clearly. I close my eyes and I can see it and see her. It sounds like it's taking place in a café somewhere with a small but friendly audience made up mostly of distracted women and small children. The 'stage' is probably a corner of the floor, the lighting is definitely terrible and there's every chance at least one small child is standing, naked and eating a vegan muffin, next to Eurydice during most of her performance. She pushes through every line of her prepared routine without skipping a beat.

'It's not a real sword. I can't afford a real sword, and also I'm not that strong so it's a foam sword. Because I LARP.'

Eurydice explains LARPing, or live-action role-playing.

'We have large-scale, epic battles in medieval costume-slash-armour and it is the best thing in the world, and you're all objectively wrong, right? But I've got to get there and back, right? So I can wear my normal clothes . . . or my approximation of normal clothes'—a visual joke about her outfit, I guess—'but I have to carry my sword.'

As she genuinely settles into the gig and her confidence grows, Eurydice's natural charm comes to the fore and the truth behind her jokes is illuminated.

'So, there's a certain lack of context to it on public transport, right, so people tend to ask about the sword. They'll be like, "Hey, what's with the sword?" and I'll say, "Oh, I'm into LARPing," and then they'll say, "O-kay, we'll just be moving over here now . . ."

'But this one particular time, I was on the tram on the way home, it was about midnight, I was in my normal clothes, it was post-battle. It was Friday night, people's curiosity comes out a bit more when they've had a bit to drink. This dude says to me, "Excuse me, but you have the face of a warrior." I'm not sure if it's meant as a compliment or an insult, but I'll take it and I said, "Thank you."'

Eurydice feigns a frightened laugh at this point, revealing the truth of her lack of warrior spirit when it comes to an approach from a stranger on public transport. Her very sweet 'Thank you' has caught the attention of a nearby small child (I knew it!) who repeats the phrase loudly about a dozen times as Eurydice forges on with her performance.

Through the hubbub, Eurydice tells the crowd that, unlike most curious onlookers, this fellow actually seemed genuinely interested in hearing more about her LARPing hobby. That might seem preferable to the usual mocking she said, but it actually wasn't in this case because the man said he was interested in battles and he already had a knife.

At that moment, a chilling cackle (not unlike that of a mad fucking witch, appropriately enough) pierced my eardrums, like a pair of fine knitting needles had been poked brainward through each headphone.

'Oh, there's heaps more,' said Eurydice in her first confident aside. Wonderful.

'"I know how to stab people with it, too." [said the man.]

'And I went, "That's really cool, stranger on the tram, but possibly not as relevant as you think it is,"' Eurydice continues, with her fake, frightened laugh again.

She describes having to make repeated attempts at explaining the 'mock' element of LARPing to the stranger on the tram, including, '"It's twelve dollars the first time you come and you can join the militia!" But he kept finding ways to relate it back to his knife. He knew how to stab people with it.'

Eventually, through her funny, fake, frightened laugh she kind of sings to herself, 'It's a strange man, at night-time, just be polite, Eurydice, just be polite, it'll be fine.'

At some point, Eurydice skilfully departs from what I assume was a mostly true story and weaves her way into fantasy. She asks the man if he always carries the knife, to which he replies, 'Yeah, I do, just in case I need to stab anyone with it.'

Eurydice asks the man to swap weapons with her for a moment, his real knife for her foam sword. After feeling the weight of his knife in her hand, she stabs him with it.

She concludes her performance by imagining herself post-stabbing, explaining to her bleeding victim that she did it because, 'It turns out, if you have a knife, it's surprisingly easy to stab people with it.'

Nineteen-year-old Jaymes Todd was living life the only way he'd ever known how. He'd struggled through primary school, changing schools several times. Like around one in twenty Australian children, he was diagnosed with ADHD (it's more prevalent in boys).[4] He was also diagnosed as being on the lower end of the autism spectrum, which is again not uncommon among ADHD-affected children (it's estimated at a 14 per cent probability).[5] Most Australian children, however, don't live in environments like the Todd household in Broadmeadows, in Melbourne's outer-western suburbs.

Tim Marsh, who was Victoria Legal Aid's Chief Counsel when he met Jaymes Todd, described the family home thus: 'Dirty doesn't even begin to capture it. He lived in a state of squalor, which was quite honestly shocking to everybody who saw the photos of it.'

This was tendered during the plea hearing, and was something that the judge took into account. Jaymes Todd was living in that environment, sharing that house with his parents and an older and a younger brother. There was refuse from floor to ceiling in every room. It was hard in some of the photos to even see where people slept within that environment, and he was living, in a sense, a sort of bifurcated life.

Old furniture littered the front lawn outside the Todd home, but so too did some new-looking pot plants. Someone had clearly reversed into the front fence at some stage, and it was hard to know where the weeds reaching skywards from the cracks in the driveway ended and the weeds growing instead of grass began. It wasn't cata-strophic, though, or perhaps my own hillbilly heritage is showing.

The true tragedy was inside. Every morning, when Jaymes Todd woke up and put on clean clothes to attend his hospitality course at the Hester Hornbrook Academy in Prahran, he did so in a home in which the cooking was done on a portable electric single burner in the bathroom. It balanced precariously beside the sink, next to the family's single toilet, which was often blocked.

The stove in the kitchen had long since become completely unreachable. In fact, the entire kitchen was virtually inaccessible due to the rotted floor.

Tim Marsh picks up the narrative, 'Essentially, around the time of the murder of Eurydice Dixon, he was completing a hospitality training course and he would have had the extraordinary circumstance of going from that home environment into a commercial kitchen where benches were wiped down and knives put away and there was a high level of hygiene. Then he would go home to that squalor and in that circumstance it's not hard to imagine why there were times where he was preferentially homeless. He would actually go and sleep in parks rather than go and be back at home.'

When he was at home, Jaymes escaped the same way most of us do – he disassociated from reality by finding a quiet spot to climb into his iPad. For some of us it's online shopping, for some it's social media, or gaming or gambling. For Jaymes Todd, increasingly it was violent pornography.

Like Eurydice Dixon, Joanna Glengarry is unlikely to go unnoticed in a crowd. With her signature blonde hair, red lipstick and upbeat personality, Joanna was never going to make a low-key entrance into Auckland's coronial court.

It was still a decidedly male-dominated environment, as were the crime scenes she began attending regularly.

At one of her earliest crime scenes, Joanna was asked by a senior detective when the mortuary was going to send a real pathologist, instead of a nurse. In 2017 she told New Zealand's *Metro* magazine that it was still not uncommon for uniformed officers to assume she was a nosy member of the public when they noticed her on the forbidden side of the police tape. 'Miss! Miss! You can't be here!' they'd shout. 'This is a crime scene, you'll have to leave.'

'I don't know what it is about me,' she told the magazine, 'they insist on calling me "Miss", until they notice the senior detectives laughing and I gently explain that I'm Dr Glengarry, and I'm the pathologist. I can see the conflicting emotions crossing their face.'[6]

It occurs to me as we settle in for our chat that there is a first crime scene for everyone. I wonder what that experience would be like, before you're confident and before the senior detectives are on your side.

'The first times you go to crime scenes you're always a trainee pathologist,' she says of those early days, 'and you go with experienced pathologists and you just watch them. You watch and you learn. I went to dozens of scenes with respected senior colleagues in Auckland and learned from them. You learn from every crime scene.

'In Auckland I was lucky and unlucky, I suppose. Unlucky in that we had half the staff in the department that we should have had, but that was lucky in the sense that it meant I got incredibly intensive exposure. We were on call every second week. I was going to huge numbers of crime scenes. Four or five in a weekend sometimes.

'I was exhausted but the learning I got from just being thrown in and doing lots and lots was irreplaceable. The more you do the more you learn and you get your own techniques with time. It's also about building up relationships with people. You're always working with the same people at the crime scenes, it's a pretty close bunch, with the crime scene people and the homicide detectives, so you start to work out what they need from you and what you need from them.'

A small amount of time is all it takes to understand why there's a soft spot in the heart of many a homicide detective for Dr Glengarry. Detective Inspector Scott Beard of Auckland CIB described her as a 'breath of fresh air'.[7] She exudes a relaxed charm and a definite sense of fun, as much as she does capability. It doesn't surprise me to learn that one of the special additions to her post-mortem kit is a set of tree loppers. She seems like a woman who could perform an operation of nuanced precision with tree loppers.

She's also a pragmatic woman. Although she was obviously a very popular senior member of her profession, about which she was still passionate by 2017, she'd decided to leave her home town for Australia. 'In my final year in Auckland, I did twenty weeks on call. Here, we do five or six weeks on call, so since being at VIFM I've been able to get back to being a normal person again. With that extra time, we can do research as well. We have researchers coming along saying they want to do stuff but they need a pathologist – of course I'm going to say yes.

'I still like my job, but being able to help researchers and following their progress, seeing their work help us, that's win–win.'

Jaymes Todd noticed Eurydice Dixon as she waved her boyfriend off on his tram at 11.08 pm on Saturday, 12 June 2018. She'd just done a gig at the Highlander Bar in central Melbourne and the couple had walked together as far as the Flinders Street train station before going their separate ways.

Jaymes had been in classes until 3 pm that Saturday. He then caught a train into the city with friends and hung out in a park, drinking alcohol and smoking joints until about 8.30 pm when they all caught the train back towards Broadmeadows.

Jaymes didn't end up going all the way home, though. He was probably quite intoxicated by this time, having drunk vodka, cider and Jim Beam, and smoked several joints. Perhaps the encroaching reality of the home he was speeding towards in the claustrophobic clickety-clack of the overheated night train was too much for him to bear, because he left his mates and got off at Newmarket, less than a quarter of the way into the journey.

He bought tobacco and got on the next train heading

back into the city, arriving at Flinders Street station at 10.25 pm. CCTV cameras inside the station capture his restlessness as he tries to think of what to do with himself once he arrives back in the city. It's almost twenty minutes before he finally leaves the station and ventures outside onto Elizabeth Street.

Jaymes actually passes Eurydice and her boyfriend on his way to McDonald's but he doesn't seem to notice them. Perhaps the meal straightened him up and sharpened his senses, because he not only noticed Eurydice when they crossed paths again as he walked back to the intersection of Flinders and Swanston Streets, but he locked in on her, and was never more than twenty seconds behind her for the rest of her life.

Jaymes stalked Eurydice for the next hour as she headed towards home. Most of the walk they shared was through the Saturday-night bustle of Melbourne's CBD. Heavy bass thumped from creeping cars, and swarthy, track-suited passers-by walked quickly and scrolled seriously on phones, trying hard not to be recognised. They could have been famous actors, or they could have been drug dealers. That's just the Melbourne vibe.

On an average Saturday night there are incredibly talented musicians playing for change on the street corners; the smells from restaurants run by some of the world's most exciting chefs wafting around; and homeless, mentally ill people in various stages of survival, trying to make sense of the world around them.

With all that stimulus, and a good gig under her belt, it's no wonder Eurydice didn't realise she was being followed by the nothingness of Jaymes Todd. A good gig leaves a comedian, particularly a young comedian, in a state of euphoria for some time. We often don't sleep for hours afterwards. We go over it again and again, savouring it, and truth be told, marvelling a little bit at our magic. It's intoxicating. And distracting.

Eventually, Eurydice and her nefarious shadow left the city lights behind them. The noises of revelry and mistakes in the making gave way to traffic as they walked past the historic Queen Victoria Market. The stalls were covered and silent, the long, dark rows unmistakably alive with nocturnal secrets. Rats and feral cats probably, but who would dare to enquire? It's one of those places with a nightlife all its own and best left to it.

They picked up the pace and moved on to Royal Parade. It's a long, busy road, probably as old as the town itself, and in an attempt to cope with the growing city around it, over the years the council has placed garden beds between traffic lanes. Again, it's a very Melbourne vibe, but the result is that it's incredibly confusing to drive a car along this stretch.

Alongside Royal Parade are very grand old trees. They cast heavy shadows, particularly at night. The result of the shadows and the intense concentration required by drivers to navigate Royal Parade is that few would notice or remember anything happening in their peripheral vision.

There's generally a fairly constant stream of pedestrians wandering around that vicinity because the Melbourne University campus is close by, as are the residential colleges. Students stream between their accommodation and campus all day and all night. Eurydice and Jaymes Todd would both have blended right in.

Eurydice and Jaymes are captured on Melbourne University CCTV at 11.54 pm, heading towards Princes Park. It's the last time Eurydice is seen alive. At 12.02 am, she messages her boyfriend: *I'm nearly home, HBU?* [How bout you?]

At roughly 4.30 am on Sunday, 13 June, after having slept for a few hours at the nearby Royal Park train station, Jaymes Todd made his way back to where he'd left Eurydice Dixon's body lying on the grass of Princes Park. When he got there he found it had already been turned into a crime scene by police so he beat a hasty retreat. Eurydice had left several scratches on his face and neck, which he knew because he'd used her stolen phone to inspect them.

He made his way by train back into the city, ate a pie, drank a coffee and went home. Once there he climbed into his iPad to search 'Princes Park' so he could read about the discovery of Eurydice's body. He then searched 'Strangulation and rape porn', chose a website and browsed the 'Strangled and Raped', 'Brutal Rape', 'Choking til Death', 'Strangled and Forced' and 'Curvy Emo Girl' subheadings.

'I remember when I went out to the scene where Eurydice was found,' says Joanna, 'and you just know straight away these cases are going to be huge. I remember thinking, "Okay, everything I do here is going to be scrutinised. Scrutinised at the scene by the media, in court later on, by other pathologists who review my work as part of the normal review processes that go on in these big cases. Probably even twenty years down the track when some Sunday evening true crime documentary show is made. Everything has to be perfect."

'So I try to keep an open mind, because the last thing I want to do is go into a scene biased towards one outcome and miss something else. I want to go into it with a completely open mind, and form opinions based on what I'm seeing there. Then I'm thinking about all the possibilities of what could have happened there. What do I need to do to tell this person's story? That's what I'm there to do. The bad guy? He's not my job.'

'Seeing the Victoria Police homicide squad when they are really in action on these cases where there is an unknown offender still at large, when they really get the wheels of investigation going – I would not want to be a criminal on the other end of it. They are an impressive group of people, they really are.'

Around the same time Jaymes was settling in with his iPad in Broadmeadows, Victoria Police Superintendent David Clayton fronted the media at Princes Park, near the site where Eurydice was found. He said there would be

24-hour police patrols of the area, but he also called upon the community to 'take responsibility for your own safety', and to be 'situationally aware'.

By six o'clock that evening, it was widely reported (and edited to look as though) Victoria Police were repackaging old sexist slogans about women being responsible for their own sexual assaults and murders.

It was weeks before I personally saw the unedited media conference and realised the police's position had been misrepresented.

'It wasn't directed at women,' Assistant Commissioner Stephen Leane tells me later. 'We didn't know what this person was prepared to do. When he [Clayton] said "be situationally aware", make no mistake, the situation he was referring to was Melbourne that morning. The situation was that we had a murderer wandering around. It was clear to us he'd been in that park some hours before but at that stage he could've been anywhere and we didn't want another homicide on our hands. We wanted everyone in the community to be aware of the situation.'

I'm ashamed to say that I was part of a TV show that perpetuated the initial story against the police. Like Eurydice's 'tragic life' story that was circulating around the tabloids, it was just another angle to generate more news. Neither had anything to do with Eurydice, or her family or the people who sacrifice so much to actually deal with the crimes of the Jaymes Todds of the world.

Victoria Police didn't allow the noise to distract them, however. By the end of the day they'd released a CCTV image of Jaymes Todd taken at Flinders Street station the previous night. They were asking either the man in the image or anyone with any information about the man to contact them urgently.

Sometime that evening Jaymes was contacted by a female friend who told him about the image of him she'd seen on the news. She told him that if he didn't go to the police, she would, so at 7.09 pm Jaymes Todd telephoned Broadmeadows police station. He told the desk sergeant who answered the call that it was him in the image on the news, but he had nothing at all to do with the dead girl in Princes Park. The sergeant told him he'd need to come in anyway and at 8.29 pm he did indeed present himself at Broadmeadows police station, accompanied by his mother.

At 9.15, Detective Senior Constable Meade began the interview, in which Jaymes would give the first of three accounts of the night before. At 11.43, they were joined by two members of the homicide squad.

The interview was terminated at 12.55 am, and Jaymes was left alone in the interview room with Detective Sergeant Millar of the homicide squad. They chatted amiably, and Miller explained that the break was so that some paperwork could be organised. What for? Well, just to request some forensic procedures. Miller went on to explain to Jaymes that the offender had left some DNA behind during the attack on Eurydice, so they'd be asking for some samples from him to compare against that DNA.

'Don't worry about DNA,' said Jaymes immediately. 'I did it, I'll tell you everything.'[8]

The interview recommenced at 1.06 am and Jaymes confirmed everything he'd said to Detective Sergeant Millar for the benefit of the tape.

A little later Jaymes is recorded on the telephone confessing to his father. He told his dad how disappointed he was about it all. But the longer he spoke, the more he revealed how misplaced that disappointment was. He said he 'felt like shit' and that he just 'hoped it would be better next time'.

As much as anything, Jaymes's crime had exposed the disfunction in his family and the media couldn't get enough. If they were hoping for salacious pictures and quotes about Jerry Springer-style antics to come tumbling out of that chaotic house, they were sorely disappointed. They located the Todd family easily, and when they did, Jaymes's father offered only the eloquent if baffled words of another broken man.

'We are struggling, obviously – it's a huge thing we didn't think we would ever have to deal with in our lives,' he told a doorstopper from *The Age*. 'We had no inkling anything like this was possible to happen. I was in hospital, I didn't even know it happened. Me and my family offer our deepest condolences, we are sorry for what happened and ashamed our family was part of it.'[9]

*

By a twist of fate, Joanna Glengarry was on call again roughly six months after she attended the scene of Eurydice Dixon's murder, when another young woman was followed as she walked home alone into the Melbourne night. Bizarrely, Palestinian student Aya Maasarwe* had been at a comedy club with friends before jumping on the 86 tram to Bundoora on the night of 16 January 2019. As with Eurydice, the simple misfortune of Aya's crossing paths with the stranger who ended her life is unbearable.

Aya was the second of four daughters born to Palestinians Saeed and Khitam Maasarwe of Baqa al-Gharbiyye, a predominantly Arab city in the Haifa district of the West Bank. Since the early 2000s the city has been divided by the contentious Israeli West Bank barrier, the concrete-and-barbed-wire wall that stretches for more than 700 kilometres through the Occupied Palestinian Territories.

In a way that we Australians find hard to fathom, Baqa al-Gharbiyye remains a modern, prosperous and peaceful tourist mecca despite being split in two by a wall designed to antagonise age-old tensions. Its Mediterranean climate has made it a haven for kibbutzim, (that's the plural of kibbutz), the Israeli farming communes that produce around 40 per cent of the country's agricultural output.

---

*This is the Palestinian variation of the spelling of Aya's name. Its use was requested by her family. See BBC News, 'Aya Maasarwe: Murdered student's body flown home from Australia', 22 January 2019, bbc.com/news/world-australia-46954783.

The rolling hills around Baqa al-Gharbiyye are dotted with European-style guest houses boasting sparkling swimming pools and modern menus reflecting their proximity to the kibbutzim.

Saeed runs a business in the Chinese city of Guangzhou and his family has spent a lot of time there. Aya had plans to join him in his work after her studies and, along with her older sister Noor, was enrolled at China's Shanghai University. Already fluent in Arabic, Hebrew and Mandarin, Aya took up an exchange position at La Trobe University in Melbourne in 2018 to improve her English. Her family was looking forward to holidaying in Australia with her later that summer.

Codey Herrmann was a young man of profound disadvantage. In her sentencing remarks, Justice Elizabeth Hollingworth noted, 'It is necessary to consider your background in some detail, to understand how you came to be the seriously damaged young man who committed these offences. Much of your life history has been extensively documented in more than 2000 pages of welfare records, in your file kept by the Victorian Aboriginal Welfare Agency.'

Her Honour then went on to devote some significant time to the life story of 21-year-old Codey Hermann, born to an Aboriginal mother and a German father who were both 19 and had a daughter already. There was no doubt, according to the judge, that the first three years of Codey's life were characterised by 'extreme physical and emotional deprivation'.

He was removed from his parents for the first time at six months of age, left by his mother at twelve months with a relative whose own children had been removed from her care because of neglect, and at eighteen months admitted to a hospital with scabies. At three years of age, with rotten teeth, and skin and digestive problems, Codey and his sister were placed in foster care, which became a permanent placement.

While their mother was granted access to visit the children, she often forgot or arrived intoxicated. Their father was declined access to the children and played no part in Codey's life after the boy was six. When Codey was thirteen, his mother died. His behaviour and mental health both began to decline rapidly from this point and 'anger, cannabis and alcohol use . . . began to emerge as problems'.[10]

At sixteen, Codey was sometimes choosing home-lessness over his foster family. He was also using ice and had become known to local police. At eighteen, he was admitted to a psychiatric facility for the first time for assis-tance with a psychotic episode. He had ongoing paranoid thoughts and couldn't be trusted to take his anti-psychotic medication.

Codey was twenty years old in early 2019. He was properly homeless and lost. Although his sister, who still lived with their foster mum, was worried sick about him, their relationship had broken down. The only people he had any contact with were other meth users who hung around the shops – the people he'd been with on that Tuesday night.

Trundling north-east through Melbourne's sleeping suburbs, Aya was isolated from the outside world in the 86 tram. The tram's mercilessly bright interior lights meant she could see nothing but reflection in the windows surrounding her. She sat towards the front for safety, although she was the only passenger for most of the trip. She zoned out, taking in the driver's view through the windscreen most of the way. With no cars on the roads and no passengers to stop for, Aya was almost rocked to sleep by the swaying of the tram, with its steady soundtrack, and the endless tunnel of darkness punctuated by rhythmic streetlights in front of her.

She resisted her phone. She was saving the battery because she wanted to FaceTime her sister Ruba back home in Baqa al-Gharbiyye when she got off the tram. It always made her feel safer when she had to walk the short distance to her apartment alone at night.

It was 12.05am when Aya climbed down from the tram in Bundoora. She crossed Plenty Road towards the Polaris shopping centre and started dialling Ruba's number.

Codey Hermann had been hanging around the Polaris shopping centre on and off all day, doing a lot of nothing in particular. He had no money, having already spent his unemployment benefits on drugs, but he shoplifted food from supermarkets and entertained himself in various ways around the shops.

He left the shopping centre at 12.07 and made his way through the car park towards Plenty Road. As he walked out of the car park, Aya Maasarwe was walking directly towards him.

Upon answering her sister's call, Ruba heard just seven words: 'I didn't expect you to pick up—'

Over the following seconds, Aya's phone hit the ground, Ruba heard her sister scream, and say in Arabic, 'You piece of shit.' Then she heard four bangs, and that was it.[11]

Eventually Ruba gave up yelling her sister's name into the phone and called their other sister, Noor, who was studying in China. Over the following seven or eight hours, the two young women tried to contact Aya, with no luck. They feared she'd been kidnapped, or she'd fallen and was lying unconscious. Noor watched every Australian news service she could find. It was a long shot, but they were out of ideas.

Around twelve hours after that terrifying phone call, news broke of the discovery of a young woman's body in Melbourne.

A crew of workmen were about to begin maintenance on an illuminated sign at the entrance to the car park of the Polaris shopping centre on Plenty Road in Bundoora when they heard a woman screaming hysterically. They ran to her aid and realised she'd discovered a body clumsily concealed in shrubbery near the road about one hundred metres from the tram stop.

'I [saw] in the news that they found a body. They didn't say who it was, but it matches all the details. It was on the same road. Everything. I was just praying that it's not her,' said Noor later. 'But then I saw the shoes and her phone . . . and I was sure it was her.'[12]

Unreported initially was the fact that the victim was partially naked, and it appeared the offender had attempted to burn parts of her body using some kind of accelerant.

Aya's father Saeed Maasarwe arrived in Melbourne early Friday morning. It was less than twenty-four hours since he'd learned of his daughter's murder, and he was led to a small viewing room at VIFM to formally identify her. Supported by a small group of family members, he then embarked upon an extraordinary pilgrimage around the city. He wanted to be where she had been. He wanted to be where she had died.

A very Australian memorial had been created in the shrubbery near the Polaris shopping centre car park. Somewhere during our brief history we've developed our own ritual for public grieving, which revolves around handmade cards and teddy bears strapped to power poles and guard rails with sticky tape. Aya's was just such a tribute. As Saeed Maasarwe and his family approached it, blushing onlookers stepped back unsure of what his reaction might be.

'I am sad because this is the last place my daughter was,' he told the journalists who'd followed him there.[13]

If he was offended by the media presence, or by the presence of strangers adding tokens and paying their respects, Mr Maasarwe didn't show it. He wept openly, accepted condolences and prayed.

'I did find those two cases really hard particularly because they were so close together,' admits Joanna to me. 'It's the randomness. It could be any one of us walking home from a job.'

Traditionally in Islamic culture, a body must be returned to the family as soon as possible so that religious rites can be performed and burial can take place quickly. For Saeed Maasarwe, who'd travelled to Australia immediately, the fact that his daughter's remains hadn't been released to him by the coroner's office forty-eight hours after her death was baffling and devastating. By the Friday evening, he was on the steps of state parliament and surrounded by thousands of people at a candlelit vigil for his daughter. News of an arrest in the case had broken and yet Saeed still couldn't take his daughter home.

Exhausted and grief-stricken, he was nonetheless clearly bolstered by the support of the community. 'She liked everything in Australia; she had a good time here. Really, I appreciate all the people, the five months she was here. She enjoyed and had a good time here. But then this has come, the very worse. The most worse this can be,' he said to the crowd on the steps.

'When I see people here like this, huge people to support us and give us good feeling here about Australia and the community here in Australia. It's not good my feeling [about Australia]. But when I see people like this it makes me to feel, maybe change my mind.'[14]

Somehow Saeed Maasarwe found the strength to fight on and the following day, Saturday no less, he met with Prime Minister Scott Morrison.

'The words will fail me, I'm sure, as one father to another,' Mr Morrison said at an earlier press conference before he, his wife and daughters laid flowers at the scene of Aya's death in Bundoora. A spokesperson for the Prime Minister's office said later that the coroner was working as fast as possible for the family, and that the office had offered any support necessary to the Victorian government to aid a speedy repatriation.[15]

'That was quite a challenge and really hard to manage. There was a lot of background pressure going on around that which just adds to the challenge,' says Joanna looking back. 'We had to balance the needs of the investigation so as to catch the offender who was still at that stage unknown, and that's not something we can do quickly, but clearly it's competing with religious and cultural needs for early release of the body.'

For Joanna, respect for the patient remains paramount. 'I see myself as the person's last doctor. They can't speak anymore so it's up to me to tell the story of what happened. Sometimes it's to provide answers for the family, so they know, sometimes it's providing knowledge and information to the police and the courts so they can bring someone to justice. It's not up to me to arrest the person, and in court we are independent experts, so it's not up to me to avenge the deceased. But it is up to me to tell their story.'

Aya was released to her family on the Monday following her death. She was transported to a local mosque where she underwent an Islamic cleansing ritual called a Janazah before her long journey home.

Just as Eurydice and Aya were both Joanna Glengarry's cases, so too the responsibility of representing both their killers in court fell to Tim Marsh.

Codey Herrmann pleaded guilty to the rape and murder of Aya Maasarwe almost immediately. The entire attack was captured on CCTV cameras and he was well known to local police. It had only been a matter of finding him.

During the subsequent hearing in which the prosecution and the defence present what they deem to be relevant factors affecting sentencing, Codey Herrmann sat at the back of the court. For three days, the callousness with which he raped and murdered a young woman he didn't know and the devastation it had wrought upon her family was weighed up against his life of loneliness and deprivation.

Codey spent most of the time biting his lip and looking at the floor. To most people in the court, he seemed to be in a world of his own, but in retrospect it appears he may have been mulling over something else.

Tim Marsh presented a picture of Codey's life to that point, much of it given as evidence by forensic psychiatrist

Dr Andrew Carroll, who interviewed Codey in custody but who also studied the two thousand pages of material pertaining to Codey from the Victorian Aboriginal Child Care Agency.

Carroll's evidence was that Codey had a severe personality disorder with particular characteristics. His childhood neglect meant he avoided and suppressed his emotional distress. His unresolved trauma led to a 'deep well-spring of sadness and anger' that he had no skills to process. He had distorted assumptions about other people, with 'persistent expectations of being exploited, humiliated and belittled'. His ability to function normally was seriously impaired and there was 'a sense almost of dissociation, a sense that he just doesn't matter in the world, that he's not real in some way'.

Carroll further testified that Codey's personality disorder seriously affected his ability to make judgements and was, with other factors, the underlying reason for the murder. It was an 'eruption of suppressed rage' that had built for years. It erupted for some unknown reason on that night, against an innocent woman, with no known trigger.

'This is the manifestation of male rage towards a female.'[16]

At the very end of the hearing, Codey handed Marsh a handwritten note he wanted read into the record.

'It was certainly something of a dramatic moment for me,' Marsh says. 'As he was being led to the dock he just passed me the note. Sometimes these things happen but generally we try to avoid surprises because the cynical among the population might say, "I bet his lawyer said to do that." Had I coached him to write a letter I certainly wouldn't have been saying produce it on the third day of play and I'm certainly not famous for such drama. So, it was a genuinely surprising moment for me and I thought its contents were illuminating. I mean, in the ultimate wash-up I don't know that it's going to make a great difference but if that was of some small comfort to the family then that was probably a positive thing.'

The note was a letter to Aya's family. It read:

Im sorry, your daughter didnt deserve such a terrible and tragic thing to happen to her.

I don't expect any forgiveness as I will never be able to forgive myself and I will be trying to make amends for the rest of my life.

There is no excuse

I truly apologize, I will pray for you and your family everyday.

Don't give into hate like I Did. love

Goodbye.

'I'm very sensitive to the fact that people are for the most part unprepared and unready to hear people who've committed terrible crimes humanised in any way,' says Marsh. 'That the mere act of humanising them or providing any kind of context about them or their personalities is somehow seen as providing an excuse for their offending . . . there are some people that I have represented in my career, and I'm sure every criminal barrister would be able to say the same, who are out-and-out monsters but I can only think of one or two in twenty years. I can think of a lot of people who have done monstrous things, but they're not monsters.

'I think whenever we use the phrase "monster", the effect is to reduce the dialogue about offending to a really infantile level and that distracts us from some potent factors about our society . . . The thing that struck me when I was briefed to represent both Jaymes Todd and Codey Herrmann was how on earth do nineteen- and twenty-year-olds, with no prior convictions, end up doing something like that?

'In the case of Eurydice Dixon's murder at the hands of Jaymes Todd, who also pleaded guilty and was sentenced to life with a thirty-five-year non-parole period, one can't help but wonder how large a part online porn played.'

As for Codey Herrmann, Marsh reported, upon having visited him in the Melbourne Assessment Prison (MAP) some weeks after his arrest, life had undoubtedly improved from his perspective.

'I asked him how it was going, and he said something that really stuck with me. He said, "Most of the other men in the unit talk about all the things they've given up since they've been incarcerated. I've gained a safe place to sleep, I get fed three times a day, I have a shower. I've also gained a sense of hope that maybe one day if I behave myself in custody, I might get to a prison that has good programs."'

'Neither of these cases went to court where I had to give my evidence,' says Joanna. 'For the sake of their families, and for the media circus that would have accompanied my evidence, I'm really glad.

'Through all the hours that you spend documenting all the injuries and photographing and writing up the report . . . I know exactly what went on. I know how these two young women died and I'm glad their families were spared the worst of it, I'm glad they were spared cross-examination around it. I'm glad for the girls as well. That's not how we want to remember them. Not for this injury and that injury. They should be remembered for who they were when they were alive.'

Justice Elizabeth Hollingworth sentenced Codey Herrmann to thirty-six years jail with a minimum term of thirty years. In December 2019, two months after Codey Herrmann's sentencing, staff at the MAP were forced to intervene as a heated verbal exchange between Codey Herrmann and Jaymes Todd became physical. Neither inmate was seriously injured, and no further details have been released as to what their dispute was about.

After seven years, Tim Marsh left Legal Aid in late 2020 and returned to private practice, where he continues to focus on mental impairment and disability law. He's rather famous around the traps as a philosophical fellow, and I strike him at his introspective best when reflecting on his time defending the so-called indefensible, like Jaymes Todd and Codey Herrmann.

'I've certainly experienced some considerable hostility, both in and out of court from the families and people associated with the families of victims. I remember a particular case in Wangaratta where, it was a very, very troubling case but the family were very distraught, and I was pushed and spat on outside court . . .

'To be honest, what I find far more difficult to deal with is families who are gracious. There have been a couple of examples where I've been approached by the families of victims in murder cases and thanked by the family members, and I actually find that devastating. It's very hard to deal with because being brought face to face with somebody's grace in the face of such unimaginable grief is a really confronting thing.'

I send one more email to Jeremy Dixon. Just to be sure and to seek permission to share one more story about his family. 'Can I tell them it was you who thanked Tim Marsh on the steps of the Supreme Court, Jeremy, for the dignity with which he conducted himself as he defended the man who murdered your daughter?'

The reply was awaiting me when I awoke the following morning.

'Yes, it is true that I thanked Tim Marsh for properly defending her killer,' he wrote, 'but it was in the courtroom rather than on the steps. I wouldn't want any taint of injustice attached to Eurydice's name.'

And on that . . .

'To answer your direct question, Karen chose [Eurydice's name] after a Radio National presenter she liked. I also liked the name and there we were.'

9

NATALIE RUSSELL'S STRUGGLE

Brian Russell is the personification of the word 'strapping'. He's a tall man, barrel-chested and broad shouldered, with a strong jaw. One can imagine he must have been an imposing figure in his youth and very handsome, all the more so because he carries himself with such grace.

Brian's voice is soft and low and he defers at all times to his wife Carmel, who seems like a tiny sparrow by comparison. Sometimes it's as though she's whispering in his ear while perched on his shoulder, especially when there's something very painful that needs to be said. She then looks at the ground as he squares up and speaks for them both.

At seventy-six and seventy-five respectively, Brian and Carmel both show the strain of the unexpected twists and turns of the last three decades.

'We've kind of learned to live with it, which we've had to do for the other children,' says Carmel. 'As I say to Brian, "You and I are nearly there, we don't have that long to go."' With that she reaches out and holds his hand and they smile wearily at each other.

'I remember the oncologist asking if I'd had any major traumas,' says Brian. 'I was a fitness fanatic all my life, and so I couldn't believe it when I got sick. I asked him why I'd get bowel cancer. That's when he asked if I'd ever had any kind of major trauma in my life. I said, "Would you count the murder of our youngest daughter?"'

Detective Senior Sergeant Charlie Bezzina was called out to the working-class bayside suburb of Frankston on the bitterly cold and wet Melbourne morning of 11 June 1993. Frankston was certainly known as a colourful community, but also as a tight-knit and salt-of-the-earth one, in which everyone knew everyone else and people looked out for their own. It might not have been Melbourne's most genteel neighbourhood, but Frankston's residents were generally pretty confident that they knew who was who in the zoo.

Frankston's fortunes have waxed and waned over the years. Its stunning ocean views have attracted the odd superstar, such as Australian television's first golden boy, Graham Kennedy, who lived in a snazzy clifftop bachelor pad there in the 1960s. By the 1990s, however, Frankston's reputation as a hub for hoons, drugs and dole-bludgers was firmly in place. The evening peak-hour train from the city to Frankston was known to make an extended stop at Mentone station (the halfway mark), so that the many passengers who'd thrown a few drinks back before and during the hour-long trip could alight and relieve themselves against the fence. 'I could hear the mass sigh of relief all the way up the front!' reported a former train driver during an ABC radio segment about the history of the famous Frankston line.[1]

Melbourne was a nightclub and live music mecca in the 1980s and 1990s, and Frankston's contribution was the legendary 21st Century Dance Club. It had a revolving dance floor, a laser light show and a giant electricity ball hanging from the ceiling that appeared to generate lightning to the beat of the music. It was a frequent stop for bands like INXS, Hoodoo Gurus, Models, Cold Chisel and Noiseworks, who were guaranteed a sold-out and spirited show.

Roughly ten minutes inland by car from the beach and bar strip of Frankston, towards the very edge of the sprawling suburban soup that is Melbourne, lies Lloyd Park Reserve, an enormous configuration of sports ovals, netball and basketball courts, car parks and picnic grounds, surrounded by bushland. It was designed to accommodate long Saturdays and Sundays of kids' sport, and it was, when Charlie Bezzina entered it on 11 June 1993, a lonely, soggy mess.

Frankston had experienced wild storms overnight, and the squelch of each footstep drenching the socks inside his shiny black shoes told Charlie there'd be precious little evidence left at the crime scene he was attending.

He stepped carefully under the police tape to take a closer look at the body of the young woman shoved haphazardly into a stormwater drain near shrubbery. While her trousers appeared to have been undisturbed, her top was pulled up, exposing her breasts. She had what Charlie describes as 'significant cuts' to her throat and a 'tic-tac-toe' pattern carved into her chest.

As Charlie feared, next to nothing in the way of evidence was found at the crime scene. The victim had no identification with her, so Charlie had his team check the missing persons database and quickly discovered that a young woman closely fitting her description had been reported missing the night before by a local couple.

The missing woman was eighteen-year-old TAFE student Elizabeth Stevens, newly arrived from Tasmania, who'd been lodging with her aunt and uncle in Frankston. She was known to be a shy girl, who'd never had a boyfriend and rarely went out at night. On this particular day, the day before the body was found in Lloyd Park Reserve, Elizabeth Stevens had left a note for her aunt and uncle, letting them know she was heading to the library to study. By 8 pm they were already concerned about the fact that she wasn't home and informed the police. By 10 pm they were clearly quite frantic, as her uncle braved the terrible weather to go out looking for her. He kept searching until after midnight, even though the weather grew steadily worse.

'One thing led to another,' says Charlie sadly, 'and she was identified that afternoon. First thing's first, we look at the family. They've called it in, she lived with them, unfortunately it's where these things usually lead back to, so that's where we start. Well, in this case we were able to eliminate them very quickly.

'So next comes the post-mortem, which takes four or five hours. By the end of the post-mortem we know that it wasn't a sexual offence because of the clothing but we take all the swabs anyway. We realise the top was probably pulled up by the motion of the body being dragged because we find drag marks on the torso and on the back.

'The stomach contents were very valuable. All of it's valuable, but especially with nothing being yielded from the crime scene. In the stomach we found fish and chips. That told us we might be able to find a fish and chip shop in Frankston where someone remembered serving her. Was she alone? Was she with someone? Was she agitated? We canvassed every fish and chip shop in Frankston, without luck.

'At the same time, we're making enquiries at the library. Did she make it to the library that afternoon? We couldn't put her at the library that day. Nobody came forward to say they'd seen her there or spoken to her, so we did a re-enactment of her planned movements with a mannequin one evening to try and jog some memories, to no avail.

'We did a massive doorknock of the local area. It turned up some things that looked interesting at the time.

One guy opened up the door and he was covered in blood. Then, when he saw it was the coppers, he told them to "get stuffed" or words to that effect and slammed the door in their faces. Well, you don't really do that.'

Charlie pauses for effect but remains completely deadpan.

'So the uniform boys think, "This might actually be something," and they call it in. One thing led to another and we got a warrant to go inside and have a look around. It turned out he was a self-mutilator. Now, we probably lost a week on him by the time we went through the process of writing it up and getting it to a magistrate and getting the warrant because you've gotta do it right, otherwise it could jeopardise the trial years later. Anyway, we finally got back into his house, which was covered in blood, but it was all his.'

Less than a month after the murder of Elizabeth Stevens rocked Frankston, on the evening of 8 July, 41-year-old Rosza Toth left Seaford train station, the third-last stop on the Frankston line, to walk home. As she walked past a public toilet block just before 6 pm, she was grabbed from behind by a man who told her he had a gun. He dragged her into a nearby park but she managed to break free of his grasp and run into the street where a car happened to be passing and stopped for her.

That same evening, new mum Deborah 'Debbie' Fream, left her twelve-week-old baby, Jake, at home with a neighbour while she popped out to a nearby shop for some milk.

It was around 7 pm when she left and the shop was literally around the corner. When she hadn't returned by 8 pm, the concerned neighbour called her husband, the police and the local hospital.

Debbie's car was found the next day in the Frankston CBD but its discovery only heightened fears that she'd met with foul play. Well before forensic testing found traces of her blood inside the vehicle, her family noticed frightening evidence that Debbie hadn't been the last person to drive her own car. She was a petite woman, of particularly short stature, and the driver's seat had been wound all the way back to accommodate someone much larger than her.

Four days after her disappearance, on the afternoon of Monday, 12 July, a farmer driving through nearby Carrum Downs saw from a distance what he first thought to be a discarded mannequin by the road. He decided to take a closer look and soon realised it was the body of young mother Debbie Fream, whose disappearance he'd been following on the news.

'We started thinking then that we had a serial killer on our hands but we don't want to come out publicly because it's so foreign to us as Australians. The fear in the community is already growing,' says Charlie.

'Actually, the Premier gave an address to the community because it was like a bushfire or something, that was the level of distress in the community after Debbie Fream. We got another ten detectives after Debbie.

'Finding the car was the first breakthrough, because then we knew the offender lived close by.'

But why, I wanted to know.

'*Why?*' Charlie repeats my question somewhat impatiently, as though I must've had a little snooze during an important lecture. 'Because crooks are lazy, Meshel. We know that. We now know he lives within easy walking distance of central Frankston. We have a search zone. He's driven that vehicle back from the dump site and then left on foot. He wouldn't have wanted to walk far to his house, because crooks are lazy. They like to operate in their own environment. That's our first break.

'Our second break is that blood discovery in the car. That's telling us there's another crime scene. When the body is discovered we're able to ascertain that the dump site is not the crime scene, so we're starting to compile a picture now.

'At the same time, though, it's not happening fast enough for the community. We're working eighteen-hour days, we're making solid progress, but at the end of the day, the buck stops with us. The community knows it's only a matter of time before this guy strikes again unless we catch him. The pressure is just unbelievable. I mean, really, forget the media or what have you, it's the mental pressure of trying to prevent another death. That's what we have to try to put aside so we can keep level heads.'

The Russells were as rattled as any other Frankston family by the news of Debbie Fream's murder, just a month after Elizabeth Stevens. They're a blended family, 'like the

Brady Bunch', they like to say. It's the second marriage for both Brian and Carmel, and children were part of each package. 'I had two and Carmel had two when we met,' says Brian, 'then we had two together.'

'Natalie was Brian's and mine,' says Carmel, 'and Damian was the youngest.'

It's obviously a clear distinction in Carmel's mind. Natalie was theirs. All of theirs. Having met several of their other children, I believe the sentiment is shared. Natalie was the baby that bonded their two tribes. Damian was 'the youngest' and that's an identity all its own, but Natalie was 'Brian's and mine.'

'She got very close with Brian,' says Carmel. 'She started to work with Brian at Brakes Plus. What'd you used to say to her? What'd you threaten her?'

'Oh yeah.' He chuckles. 'I used to threaten her, "You'd better hit those books and get that HSC, otherwise this might become your full-time job! As a mechanic!" And she'd say, "Oh, well, that wouldn't be so bad, Dad."'

Carmel chimes in, 'She loved it, see, because all those fellas used to come in saying, "Hello, Natalie!"'

Everybody laughs.

'Then on the way home there'd always be a pair of jeans or something she liked,' says Brian, his face lighting up like a Christmas tree, 'and then it'd be, "Aw, Dad, could you advance me a few dollars?"'

'She was funny,' says Carmel. 'The week before she was taken it was my birthday and I got so many flowers she said to me, "Do you want to open a florist shop, Mum?" Well then, the next week I said to her – because I was talking to her all the time [even after she was gone], "Well, gee, Natalie, look at all this!" Even her funeral, there were over a thousand people there, and I said, "Look at this, Natalie, you're getting something like a king or queen [would] get!" I don't know what the driver must've thought.'

Everyone's smiles become forced all of a sudden, and anguish envelops Brian as he watches Carmel shrink, helpless.

After a long silence she whispers, 'The guard of honour,' to him and waves her hand in my direction, before casting her wet eyes away and down at the floor.

'And all the kids from all the schools in the area came,' he says, sitting up straighter, 'and they formed a guard of honour all the way along the road from the church to the cemetery.'

Deep sighs fill the room after that. Brian's eyes return to his hands clasped gently in his lap and Carmel shakes her head at some unspoken thought.

On Friday, 30 July 1993, three weeks after the murder of Debbie Fream had convinced the community and Charlie Bezzina that a serial killer was on the loose in Frankston, seventeen-year-old Natalie Russell received an early mark from school and left the grounds at 2.30 pm. Just ten minutes later, Carmel happened to be driving past the school on her way home. She kept an eye out for her daughter, but Natalie was already making her way towards the shortcut, known locally as 'the track'.

Cutting clean through the Peninsula Kingswood Country Golf Club, the track is a roughly 900-metre-long gravel walkway with almost perfect visibility from one end to the other. There is nothing to hide behind. Nothing but the shade of gentle golf course gums hanging lazily over the tall cyclone wire fences on either side.

Yes, the community was on edge and warnings had been issued for women to take extra safety precautions. Yes, many parents in the area had taken to driving their children to and from school every day where they'd previously let them make their own way, and yes, the principal of Natalie's school, John Paul College, had specifically warned students against using the track at a special assembly earlier that week. Many students ignored the warning. The habit was simply too ingrained and the possibility that mortal danger could lurk in broad daylight, within the familiar bubble their community had wrapped around them, was something some of these young people simply couldn't register.

In his excellent book *Stalking Claremont: Inside the hunt for a serial killer*, Western Australian journalist Bret Christian gives the most eloquent and relatable explanation I've ever encountered for this phenomenon. Considering why a young woman, who would become a rape victim of now-convicted serial killer Bradley Robert Edwards, would walk home alone from a night out at a local pub, Christian reflects that for her and others like her, 'Claremont was familiar turf, so benign during the day that even in the black of night young women felt sheltered, close to places where their mothers had taken them shopping.'[2]

I, too, have walked drunk and alone at night through the same streets I had once wandered around while holding my mother's hand. I not only felt safe, but felt a sense of ownership over them. How could those streets have also held danger for me?

Natalie Russell had walked that track thousands of times. She'd walked it alone, with her siblings, with her friends, with her boyfriend, in rain, in sunshine, in laughter, in tears, and she'd run it for fun with her beloved father. That track was part of her home. Natalie took precautions, no doubt, she was a smart girl – but on that Friday afternoon, she was simply moving through her own space as she had every right to do. There'll only ever be one person responsible for what happened to Natalie down that track.

When she wasn't home by dark and hadn't called, Carmel raised the alarm. At eight o'clock, Natalie was reported missing. No one took the report lightly. As persistent rain fell again in Frankston, police and SES members were immediately deployed to search the suburb in cars, on foot and even on horseback, while Carmel and Brian waited anxiously at home with family liaison officers for news.

At around 10.30 pm, SES volunteers Roy Stevens and David Male set off down the dark bike track in the driving rain. They were armed with torches and instructed to check the fences for holes. They did indeed find a series of holes cut into the fence almost immediately, and upon climbing through one of them, they discovered the body of a young woman, wearing black tights and a tartan skirt, lying still in the thick, wet shrubbery.

Detective Inspectors Ron Cooke and Phil Atkins were first to arrive. As the police helicopter overhead shone its powerful lights on the scene, they were able to ascertain a number of facts immediately from 2 metres away. Natalie Russell had been found, and she'd been murdered. Judging by the defence wounds on her hands and the way the ground was disturbed around her, she'd put up a hell of a fight. With a bit of luck, she might have scratched the offender, which could be helpful in a number of ways.

Of course, the other thing they knew was that the Frankston serial killer had returned. The police presence in the community could not have been any higher, yet he'd had the audacity to strike again, and not only that but in broad daylight. It was an escalation of very worrying proportions.

While everyone at the scene knew what they knew, hard procedural practices had to be adhered to and decisions had to be made. The first decision was that the body would need to stay where it was, untouched, until daylight, when a proper forensic examination of the scene could commence. As the young woman's face was obscured by plant matter, formal identification was impossible, but everyone knew who she was and that there was a family a couple of blocks away who should be told something before the media inevitably broke the story.

Inspector Cooke decided the Russells needed to be notified that a body had been discovered on the track and he made the trip to their house himself.

'I asked him, "Is it female?"' Carmel remembers.

'And he says, "Yes."

'And I said, "Well, is she wearing a school uniform?"

'And he says, "Yes, I'm sorry."

'And I said, "Well, that's all right then. It can't be Natalie because Natalie's too strong, she'd fight and fight." I said to him, "She'd never let anyone kill her."

'We had a policewoman sit with me all night, that night,' Carmel continues. 'Two policemen sitting outside the house all night in the freezing cold, which I didn't know because my mind wasn't thinking about that, but they were marvellous. Whenever we hear anyone say something about the police we always stick up for them because they were absolutely perfect, weren't they?' She turns to her husband.

'I think over a week afterward there we still had the two policemen outside and they didn't let anyone in unless they checked with us,' says Brian.

'And then, once again, John Mooney [Detective Senior Sergeant, retired], he rang up and he said, "Do you mind if I shift them? You can keep them if you like." And I said, "Oh, I think they've probably got better things to do,"' says Brian, forcing a chuckle.

At 9.30 am on Saturday, 31 July, forensic pathologist Dr Tony Landgren arrived at the crime scene to view the body in situ. He gently turned Natalie's face and saw something of her injuries for the first time. It became immediately clear that she'd suffered a substantially more violent attack than either Debbie Fream or Elizabeth Stevens.

Former Victorian Police Inspector Claude Minisini is an FBI-trained criminal profiler. He would eventually go on to advise Western Australian detectives on the case of the Claremont serial killer in 1997, but in 1993 he was busily building a profile of the offender operating in the Frankston area.

Minisini was waiting for the team when they arrived at VIFM for Natalie Russell's autopsy, and took particular note of the ferocity of her injuries.

There was an extra intensity demonstrated by these stab wounds. There was anger and far less control in this attack. If misogyny was the simple motive for all of the murders, why would the offender have hated this young woman any more than the previous two?

Minisini left policing to enter the private sector some years ago, but had this to say about profiling serial killers in a subsequent interview:

'Each serial killer acts out for his own personal motivation that's unique to him, because the activities we see as the end product, the killing, have developed through a progressive fantasy.

279

'They do have a very active fantasy life. We all have some sort of fantasy life. We don't necessarily act out those fantasies. Society has said certain things are acceptable, therefore we control elements of our behaviour that we know are going to offend.

'Serial killers' employment has been spasmodic or irregular. They lack commitment to any purposeful activity. They have little regard to behaviour outside their killing.'[3]

As Dr Landgren gently cleaned the deep wound in Natalie's neck, a tiny sliver of human skin slid away in his gloved hand.

'This goes to show how great our pathologists are here at VIFM,' says Charlie Bezzina, 'and how very fortunate we are. This piece of skin was probably 6 mils!'

Charlie Bezzina is a keen home handyman, so he's very good with measurements and happy to talk in 'mils', or millimetres. If you, like me, are a bit rusty with that stuff, I can tell you that the piece of skin Dr Landgren found measured 2.7 centimetres by 0.5 centimetres. In lots of other ways, though, it was huge!

'It was ridged skin,' explains Charlie. 'When I say ridged skin, look at your fingerprints and your feet – those are the only parts of your body that have ridges. So, he finds this piece that was lodged in her throat and straight away he knows it doesn't belong there, because it's the wrong type of skin. He picks that out, and what a find because he quickly ascertains it isn't Natalie's.'

Clutched in Natalie's right hand, Dr Landgren also found some strands of short brown hair.

Between the countless man-hours of police work, the profiling, the forensic pathology and Natalie's powerful fight for her life, the investigation is finally starting to turn. Then another piece of the puzzle unexpectedly fell into place.

'This case was solved by a member of the public,' says Charlie Bezzina dramatically. 'A member of the public was the major breakthrough for us. We did not have a clue who we were looking for. He was out there somewhere. He, she or them.

'This [witness] was a postal worker and she was delivering letters at around two-thirty on that Friday afternoon along Skye Road in Frankston.'

Some years later, the witness, Vikki Collins, agreed to recount what she'd seen for a television documentary.

'On Friday, round about three o'clock I was on my round, just about finished, it was knock-off time for school, and I saw a car without any registration plates on the back. There was a bloke in the car with his arms crossed and he slouched down to try to hide, you know, under the steering wheel?

'And I just kept going until I found a house that I knew someone was home. So, I went in there, called the police . . .'

As she parked her motorbike by the gate of that house, a schoolgirl carrying a blue bag crossed Skye Road behind

Vikki Collins and walked towards the entrance of the track. Vikki was vaguely aware of her presence, along with all the other details she was trying to remember so she could pass them on to police, and she later identified that blue bag.

Sergeant Richard Brown and Constable Joe Aiello attended the vehicle minutes later and found no one inside. They did, however, find an interim registration label on the front windscreen. These permits allow people to drive unregistered cars under certain circumstances – for example, in 1993 it wasn't uncommon for people to buy old cars that weren't exactly roadworthy and fix them up. An interim permit could be organised for a few weeks so you could drive an old bomb around while you were doing it up. Those labels had to be prominently displayed in the front window at all times and they contained a lot of infor-mation about the owner of the car. While the owner never did reappear that afternoon, the officers were able to copy the man's name and address into their police notebooks before they left.

'He was Paul Charles Denyer of Frankston,' says Charlie Bezzina with gravitas. 'That doesn't get relayed to us on the day because there's nothing untoward about it. Everything about the car is in order. Those two officers go off duty.

'Shortly after they go home, the body of Natalie Russell is discovered, not far from that location. We had no idea that this car had been checked right at the end of the laneway on Skye Road. No reason to suspect it, until the next day when the two uniform guys come and see us. They say, "Guys, ah, look, we checked a car not very far from that particular crime scene, only 50 metres or so away."

'We put two and two together. Denyer, his address is in our search zone. I go straight round there, no one's home. I leave what we call a caller's card. It says, "We did a doorknock, we're investigating a crime, can you please contact us."

'Denyer contacts us immediately. He's living with a woman. Now, with our profiler, Minisini, we're building up a picture of an offender who hates women, and Denyer is living with a woman, so he doesn't immediately put us on high alert.

'[But] he comes in, we can see clearly he's got injuries to his hands. I think, "Oh yeah," and we start the interview.'

Denyer is a tall, overweight young man with short, floppy brown hair. His hair is combed and he wears a nice navy-blue jumper for his interview. A 'good' jumper. A jumper you'd wear if you'd been asked to go to see the police and you were the kind of young man who'd comb your hair nicely before you went.

As a child, he was described by a teacher as 'bland' and 'undistinguished in every way' except that he was 'such a big kid'. He is polite and softly spoken as the homicide detectives, Senior Sergeant Rod Wilson, who conducts the interview, and Detective Darren O'Loughlin, who takes notes, settle him into their space. They ask him if he understands that anything he says or does may be given in evidence. They are men of considerable charisma and confidence. They're worldly, wise, handsome, and well groomed in their suits and shiny shoes. Watching the earliest moments of the interview play out on grainy video all these years later I imagine how intimidated I would have been in his place, but then I see the grin flash across young Denyer's face. The grin I've heard so much about from the men who were there.

Minutes later, Denyer adopts the position and posture he'll assume for much of the long interview. He sits sideways in his chair, leaning against the wall to the side of the table between him and the detective leading the interview at any given time, so he is side-on to his interrogator. He rests one elbow on the table and the other on the back of the chair. He clasps his hands gently in front of his chest. He couldn't be more relaxed. On the table before him sit his Winfield Red cigarettes and a disposable cup.

As he rattles off his date of birth, his excitement is palpable. He squirms in his seat, barely able to contain himself. He's clearly imagined this scenario many times. He's fantasised about how it would play out, and it's finally happening, for real, less than twenty-four hours after Natalie Russell's murder.

The interview lasts for about five hours. Denials, denials.

'Here's a man who's smart enough to put himself at every crime scene,' Bezzina tells me.

'"Elizabeth Stevens murdered in Lloyd Park, Cranbourne."

'"Yeah, I was down that way, I was going down to me mum's place, getting a battery for me car."

'"Debbie Fream, abducted from central Frankston."

'"Yeah, I was in that area because I had to go to the railway station to pick up my girlfriend."

'Because he was very distinctive[-looking],' Bezzina continues. 'He was a very obese guy. If we were to say, "Well, hang on, we've got you identified as being in this location," he could say, "Well, I told you I was there."

'So we said, "Okay, why was your car in Skye Road on Friday afternoon?"

'"It broke down, it overheated."

'"Where were you?"

'"I went to get water."

'He had an answer for everything. I zero in on the injuries to his fingers: "How'd you do that?"

'"I did it on a fanbelt. Repairing the car."

'So the next step then for us is to do a forensic procedure. We need to bring a doctor in to have a look at him. Could that happen from a rubber fanbelt? Is that injury a laceration? Is it an abrasion, or a cut? We need to get an interpretation on the wounds. 'Cos here's a person, the best person we've got, and we might be able to eliminate him.'

As Senior Sergeant Wilson continues the interview, Senior Sergeant Charlie Bezzina executes a search warrant on Denyer's flat and car. Among the items seized is a pair of wire-cutting pliers that were taken to the forensic laboratory for testing.

Every pair of pliers has a distinctive cutting edge. It leaves a microscopic signature on the end of every piece of wire it dissects, just like the barrel of every gun leaves a traceable pattern on every shell casing that passes through it. The laboratory was easily able to match the pliers from Denyer's flat to the holes cut in the wire fencing along the track where Natalie was murdered.

Back in the interview room, Denyer is telling Senior Sergeant Wilson that he drove past the crime scene on Saturday morning.

'I saw some police cars when I was driving up Skye Road this morning, and SES workers.'

'You saw SES workers and all that?'

'Mmm.'

'In Skye Road?'

'Yeah, and they had some white tape across the walkway, and I saw you . . .'

After hours of cat and mouse, Denyer actually ups the ante by flirting, in a way, with the detective. 'Flirting' is the only word I can use to describe the way he looks away as he suddenly mentions out of the blue that he saw the detective earlier that very day, at the scene of the murder he's being questioned about. As he says the words, 'I saw you,' he even waves his hand cheekily in the direction of the detective. It's very nearly a hair flip.

'You saw me?' says the detective, clearly taken aback.

'Yeah, I saw you . . .' drawls Denyer, turning to make eye contact again, thrilled and emboldened that his breadcrumb trail has been picked up.

'And I saw . . . aww, the other guy.' (Another almost-hair-flip.)

'And what were you doing then?'

'Aww, we were going to the wreckers.'

All things considered, Charlie and the other detective were reasonably happy with the way the interview and the searches were going. They decided to offer Denyer a toilet break, which he accepted, and Detective Darren O'Loughlin, who'd been taking notes throughout the interview, accompanied Denyer to the toilet.

Unbeknownst to him, one of the top buttons of Detective O'Loughlin's business shirt had come undone over the course of the long interview and the small crucifix he wore around his neck had become visible. When they were alone in the bathroom Denyer suddenly asked him, 'Are you a Christian?'

Stunned by the seemingly incongruous question, O'Loughlin answered honestly, in the affirmative, to which Denyer announced, 'I did the three of them.'

'Bang,' says Charlie to me. 'But problems for us. That's admission but it's not recorded anywhere. We have to think in defence mode. We're thinking, "Okay, we have to get him back into the interview room and run record and get that admission on camera."

'Just tell us in your own words, Paul,' begins the conversation as the interview resumes after the toilet break. 'What happened in relation to the death of Elizabeth Stevens in Langwarrin?'

'I saw her get off the bus,' Denyer answers. He's sitting back in the same spot, with the same posture as before. One might expect his bathroom admission of multiple murders may have impacted his demeanour, but it doesn't seem to have in the slightest.

'I walked up behind her'—suddenly, he whips his left hand up to his own mouth—'stuck my left hand around . . .' He falters here. Does he gasp? Does he snigger? '. . . My left hand around her like this. I had my other hand right here.' He gestures to the back of his head at this point, explaining how he grabbed Elizabeth Stevens with both of his big hands round the front and back of her head.

Denyer goes into great detail about the walk from the bus stop where he'd abducted Elizabeth, to Lloyd Park Reserve where he murdered her. He's very proud of the fake gun he had pointed in her back all the way there, that had her so convinced that, even when he allowed her some privacy to relieve herself behind a bush, she didn't run away. Instead, she obediently returned to him, to continue the journey he had planned.

He calmly describes her murder to the detectives in great detail. It is shocking.

'I started choking her with my hands,' he says, as casually as you or I might describe waving to her. 'She passed out after a while. Then I pulled out my knife and stabbed her many times in the throat. And she was still alive, and then she stood and we walked around and all that. Just walked around a few steps. Then I threw her on the ground and stuck my foot over her neck.'

'Why did you stick your foot over her neck?' asks Wilson.

'Oh, to finish her off,' replies Denyer.

Senior Sergeant Wilson looks incredulously at the young man opposite him. The man he and his colleagues have been hunting for months, who's consumed their every waking hour and haunted their dreams, kept them from their own families and shattered other families forever.

Wilson asks him simply, 'Can you tell me why you attacked her on that night?'

'Just – just had the feeling, that's all,' replies Denyer, sounding a little confused, as though this might have been the one question he hadn't anticipated, hadn't rehearsed an answer for.

'What sort of feeling?' urges Wilson. 'Could you possibly describe when you had this feeling?'

'Just wanted to kill.'

'I've always wanted to kill,' he said later, 'since I was about fourteen. I've been stalking women for a few years. In Frankston. Just waiting for that opportunity. Waiting for the sign.'

Denyer went on to describe in chilling detail how he'd hidden in the back seat of Debbie Fream's unlocked car while she was inside the corner store buying her milk. She didn't notice him when she got back in, and as she drove away, he sat up, threatening to 'blow her brains out' with his replica gun if she didn't do exactly what he told her. They actually drove right past her own house on their way to her murder site.

'Why did you kill her?'

'Same reason why I killed Elizabeth Stevens. I just wanted to.'

It was early Sunday morning by the time Paul Charles Denyer began explaining to detectives the circumstances of Natalie Russell's death the previous Friday afternoon. He began by explaining that he'd cut the three holes in the fence earlier in the day in preparation for dragging a woman through one of them in the afternoon or evening so as to murder her.

'I sat in the car for twenty minutes till about quarter to three and then I saw the girl coming down the road.

'I ran out through the fence again and followed her,' he said. 'She turned around once and saw me. I stuck around 10 metres behind her until I got to the second hole, and just when I got to that hole, I walked up behind her and stuck my left hand around her mouth and held the knife to her throat. And that's where it happened.

'I cut that on my own blade,' Denyer said, pointing to a wound on his thumb that appears to measure around 2.7 centimetres by 0.5 centimetres. 'I dragged her into the trees, and like, she offered, she said, "Oh, you can have sex with me if you want." She goes, "You can have all my money, have sex with me," and things.'

Shaking his head and sneering at the detective opposite, Denyer appears to seek agreement in his judgement that this desperate ploy was poor form on Natalie's part. 'Just said disgusting things like that, really.'

Was this what had made him angry at her?

Senior Sergeant Wilson didn't miss a beat. 'And did that upset you?'

'In a way,' replied Denyer, 'and I got her to kneel down in front of me and I held the knife blade over her eye, really closely.'

'Why did you hold that knife so close to her eye for?'

'Just so she could see the blade.'

Denyer prolonged Natalie's terror in a grotto he'd prepared in the morning. Inexplicably, he had little fear of being discovered, even though another person could have wandered down the track at any moment or a golfer could have stumbled upon them. He stabbed her and tormented her until finally he slashed deeply at her throat. So deeply, he boasted to the horrified detectives, holding up his hand to demonstrate how far he was able to insert his fingers into the wound when he 'grabbed her cords' and 'twisted them' until she stopped breathing. It was likely during this act that the piece of his thumb was left behind.

Understandably, Denyer's hands and arms were covered in blood by the time he was ready to climb back through the hole and walk out of the track. He plunged his hands deep into the pockets of his tracksuit pants and affected a casual stroll. As he reached the exit, though, he was confronted by the sight of the two uniformed police officers circling his car. He simply walked slowly in the opposite direction and didn't look back until he made it all the way home.

A little later that Friday evening (after showering and changing his clothes) Denyer walked back to collect his car unchallenged. All was normal on Skye Road around the entrance to the track, which meant Natalie was still lying up there undiscovered. Not realising those two constables had taken his details from the car or that Natalie had kept part of him with her up the track, he drove off thinking he was home free.

Around dawn on Sunday, as the exhausted detectives considered concluding the interview, the unexpected confession catalyst, Detective Darren O'Louglin, tried again to reframe a question that had been asked in myriad ways over the course of the interview. It had yet to yield a satisfactory answer and it was something the team clearly felt they needed to know. It was, simply, why?

'Can you explain,' he said slowly and deliberately, 'why we have women victims?'

'I just hate 'em,' answered Denyer.

'I beg your pardon?' said O'Loughlin, genuinely stunned.

'I just hate 'em.'

'Those particular girls, or women in general?' asked O'Loughlin.

'General.'

'You told Detective Senior Sergeant Wilson that you stabbed them in the throat. Is there any particular reason why there?'

'Well, it looked like the most vulnerable spot.'

Melbourne author Vikki Petraitis wrote the seminal book about the case called *The Frankston Murders*, which was released in 2011. Having worked closely with the investigators and the victims' families on the original book, she released a revised edition, *The Frankston Murders: 25 Years On*, featuring their reflections on the lingering effects of the crimes on their lives. It's from her most recent interviews that the following updates are derived, although they are merely summaries and should not prevent you from reading her book.

In late 2019, Vikki Petraitis introduced Emily Webb and me to Carmel and Brian Russell. To be honest, it was rather against their will. You see, the Russells had, for want of a better expression, fallen on hard times.

It was as simple as this: Brian and Carmel had moved house not too long after they lost Natalie. They were still in Frankston, but they felt they couldn't stay in 'Nat's house' without her. Carmel couldn't stop setting a plate for her every night for dinner, for one thing, so they had to make a break.

They bought a place a couple of streets away and settled in. Then Brian was diagnosed with bowel cancer.

As he fought the disease and Carmel cared for him, they lost their business. Another family member stepped in to buy their home and rent it back to them at that time, but that person subsequently faced a cancer fight of their own and was forced to list the home for sale again.

Carmel and Brian's grandson turned to crowd-funding, a development that distressed the struggling septuagenarians.

'Little things have happened over the past few years,' said Carmel sheepishly when we first met. 'We didn't ever think that we'd be in this situation. It's not very nice.

'I always said to my kids, "Get yourselves a house," and now look at us.

'You don't think this will happen to you, you know, in life. When we got told we had four months' notice, we thought, "What are we gonna do?"

'We're gonna have to shift our furniture and get a bond and we thought, "Oh well, we'll have to undo ourselves and just say yes [to the crowdfunding]."'

'When I was part of one of these for another group of people,' I told Carmel, struggling to catch her tear-rimmed eyes, 'they were victims of sexual assault by clergy in Ballarat. The people who donated kept thanking me for giving them a way to show how much they cared.'

'Oh right,' said Carmel, looking up and taking an interest.

'And I think you'll be surprised at how genuinely grateful people will be for the opportunity to wrap their arms around you, Carmel, and show you how much they care, because it's hard to know how to do that.'

'Mmm,' Carmel murmured.

She and Brian opened up with the rest of their story after that. We recorded an episode of *Australian True Crime* with them and many of our listeners donated to the crowdfunding initiative. The campaign really caught on in the community, and, in a wonderful turn, an investor bought the Russells' house and committed to allowing them to stay on. The money that was raised went into repairs and renovations.

If ever there was proof that victims' families handle the aftermath differently, then, surely, this is it: the track through the golf course was officially renamed 'Nat's Track' in 1999, with the proud blessing of the Russells. In fact, as Carmel says, quite often after their daughter's death, when she'd ask Brian where he'd been for a run, he'd say, 'I just went down Nat's Track.'

'We're happy she'll never be forgotten,' says Carmel. And who are the rest of us to argue with what makes Carmel Russell happy?

NOTES

Introduction

1 Liveris, Conrad, 'Alarming statistics show that violent crime in Australia is a man's game', *Sydney Morning Herald*, 26 September 2015, smh.com.au/opinion/alarming-statistics-show-that-violent-crime-in-australia-is-a-mans-game-20150926-gjvhbt.html, accessed 28 April 2021.

2 Silvester, John, 'Crooks and stats: Time for a reality check on crime in Victoria', *The Age*, 13 February 2021, theage.com.au/national/victoria/crooks-and-stats-time-for-a-reality-check-on-crime-in-victoria-20210211-p571nu.html, accessed 16 April 2021.

3 Silvester, John, 'Crime decline raises question mark over state's prison plans' *The Age*, 12 February 2021, updated 13 February 2021, theage.com.au/national/victoria/crime-decline-raises-question-mark-over-states-prison-plans-20210212-p571x6.html, accessed 16 April 2021.

4   Australian Bureau of Statistics, 'Recorded Crime –
     Victims, Australia', 9 July 2020, abs.gov.au/statistics/
     people/crime-and-justice/recorded-crime-victims/latest-
     release, accessed 7 June 2021; see also Australian Institute
     of Criminology, 'Statistical Bulletin 28: The prevalence of
     domestic violence among women during the COVID-19
     pandemic', July 2020, aic.gov.au/sites/default/files/2020-07/
     sb28_prevalence_of_domestic_violence_among_women_
     during_covid-19_pandemic.pdf, accessed 7 June 2021.

5   Pearson, Erin, Cowie, Tom and Butt, Craig, 'Record
     family violence offences and COVID fines drive crime
     rate surge', *The Age*, 24 September 2020, theage.com.
     au/national/victoria/record-family-violence-offences-and-
     covid-fines-drive-crime-rate-surge-20200924-
     p55yqz.html, accessed 7 June 2021.

6   'Quick Facts', Our Watch, www.ourwatch.org.au/quick-
     facts/, accessed 16 April 2021.

Chapter 1: Prof

1   Professor Stephen Cordner quoted in Kissane, Karen,
     'Tales from the dead', *The Age*, 7 April 2007, theage.com.
     au/technology/tales-from-the-dead-20070407-ge4lxr.html,
     accessed 15 April 2021.

2   Schweitzer, Nicholas J. and Saks, Michael J., 'The *CSI*
     Effect: Popular Fiction About Forensic Science Affects
     Public Expectations About Real Forensic Science',
     Jurimetrics, Vol. 47, Spring 2007, p. 357, https://ssrn.com/
     abstract=967706, accessed 15 April 2021.

3   Ibid.

4   Anthony Zuiker quoted in Nanji, Ayaz, 'Prosecutors feel the "CSI Effect"', CBS Evening News, 10 February 2005, cbsnews.com/news/prosecutors-feel-the-csi-effect/, accessed 15 April 2021.

5   Tom Mauriello quoted in Cole, Simon and Dioso, Rachel, 'Law and the Lab', *Wall Street Journal*, 13 May 2005, web.archive.org/web/20130928024803/http:/truthinjustice. org/law-lab.htm.

6   Bowden, Keith, *Forensic Medicine*, Jacaranda Press, Brisbane, 1965.

7   Kissane, 'Tales from the dead', *The Age*.

8   'Khashoggi's murder: One year on, here's what we know', *Al Jazeera*, 1 October 2019, aljazeera.com/news/2019/ 10/1/khashoggis-murder-one-year-on-heres-what-we-know, accessed 15 April 2021.

9   Kirkpatrick, David and Gall, Carlotta, 'Audio Offers Gruesome Details of Jamal Khashoggi Killing, Turkish Official Says', *New York Times*, 17 October 2018, nytimes.com/2018/10/17/world/europe/turkey-saudi-khashoggi-dismember.html, accessed 15 April 2021.

10 Bas, Engin and Finnegan, Conor, 'Newly released transcripts tell last, gruesome moments of columnist Jamal Khashoggi', ABC News [USA], 11 September 2019, abcnews.go.com/Politics/newly-released-transcripts-moments-saudi-columnist-killed-embassy/story?id= 65510648, accessed 15 April 2021.

11 Akerman, Tessa, 'Saudi suspect in journalist's murder trained in Melbourne', *Australian*, 18 October 2018, theaustralian.com.au/nation/nation/saudi-suspect-in-journalists-murder-trained-in-melbourne/news-story/

bfc30e3babdd0a1cbb8987347dce6e07, accessed 15 April 2021.

12 Thompson, Angus, '"Diaries aren't meant for other people": Folbigg finally delivers an explanation on her damning journals', *Sydney Morning Herald*, 3 May 2019, smh.com.au/national/nsw/diaries-aren-t-meant-for-other-people-folbigg-finally-delivers-an-explanation-on-her-damning-journals-20190502-p51jaa.html, accessed 15 April 2021.

13 Stephen Cordner quoted in McMahon, Neil, 'Ebola crisis: "I don't think people have cottoned on to the urgency of this calamity"', *Sydney Morning Herald*, 13 September 2014, smh.com.au/national/ebola-crisis--i-dont-think-people-have-cottoned-on-to-the-urgency-of-this-calamity-20140913-10geuy.html, accessed 15 April 2021.

Chapter 2: The Flinders Street Extension

1 Frankl, Viktor, *Man's Search for Meaning*, Hodder and Stoughton, London, 1964.

2 Mary Gibbs quoted in Orr, Stephen, 'The Fierce Country: The Faraday school kidnapping', *Adelaide Review*, 12 July 2018, adelaidereview.com.au/arts/books/2018/07/12/fierce-country-book-extract-faraday-school-kidnapping/, accessed 21 April 2021.

3 Butler, Mark, 'Killer gets compensation payout', *Herald Sun*, 14 September 2006.

4 Letter from Kath Pettingill, quoted in Tame, Adrian, *The Matriarch: The Story of 'Granny Evil' Kath Pettingill*, Simon & Schuster, Sydney, 2019.

5 Ibid.

Chapter 3: The David Hookes matter

1   Wisden, via ESPN Cricinfo, 'David Hookes: Obituary', espncricinfo.com/wisdenalmanack/content/story/156021. html, accessed 29 April 2021.

2   'Hookes apologises for 'hairy-backed sheila' comment', *Sydney Morning Herald*, 13 August 2003, smh.com.au/ sport/cricket/hookes-apologises-for-hairy-backed-sheila-comment-20030813-gdh8wt.html, accessed 29 April 2021.

3   Ibid.

4   Devine, Miranda, 'Making Hookes a saint was a disservice to those he loved', *Sydney Morning Herald*, 15 May 2005, smh.com.au/opinion/making-hookes-a-saint-was-a-disservice-to-those-he-loved-20050515-gdlbp3. html, accessed 29 April 2021.

5   Tippet, Gary and Gregory, Peter, 'Death of a sportsman', *Age*, 13 September 2005, theage.com.au/national/death-of-a-sportsman-20050913-ge0v07.html, accessed 29 April 2021.

6   'Hookes abused bouncer, court told', *Sydney Morning Herald*, 17 November 2004, smh.com.au/sport/cricket/ hookes-abused-bouncer-court-told-20041117-gdk4px.html, accessed 29 April 2021.

7   'Hookes "aggressive" before fatal injury', *Sydney Morning Herald*, 26 August 2005, smh.com.au/national/hookes-aggressive-before-fatal-injury-20050826-gdlyav.html, accessed 29 April 2021.

8   'Death of a sportsman', *The Age*, 13 September 2005.

9   Ebbinghaus H., 'Memory: A Contribution to Experimental Psychology', Teachers College, Columbia University, New York, 1885.

10 Mazzoni G., Scoboria A. and Harvey L., 'Nonbelieved Memories', *Psychology Science*, 2010, Vol. 21, issue 9, pp. 1334–1340, doi:10.1177/0956797610379865

11 'Witness was sure Hookes would die', *Sydney Morning Herald*, 31 August 2005, smh.com.au/national/witness-was-sure-hookes-would-die-20050831-gdlz6c.html, accessed 29 April 2021.

12 'Witness weeps recalling brawl that killed Hookes', *The Age*, 17 November 2004, theage.com.au/national/witness-weeps-recalling-brawl-that-killed-hookes-20041117-gdz0ec.html, accessed 29 April 2021.

13 'Street battle that took a cricket legend's life', *Sydney Morning Herald*, 20 January 2004, smh.com.au/sport/cricket/street-battle-that-took-a-cricket-legends-life-20040120-gdi6wh.html, accessed 29 April 2021.

14 'Death of a sportsman', *The Age*, 13 September 2005.

15 'Witness "knew Hookes was going to die"', *Sydney Morning Herald*, 31 August 2005.

16 'Hookes the ringleader in bouncer fight, court told', ABC News, 26 August 2005, abc.net.au/news/2005-08-26/hookes-the-ringleader-in-bouncer-fight-court-told/2089498, accessed 29 April 2021.

17 'Street battle that took a cricket legend's life', *Sydney Morning Herald*, 20 January 2004.

18 'Witness "knew Hookes was going to die"', *Sydney Morning Herald*, 31 August 2005.

19 'Death of a sportsman', *The Age*, 13 September 2005.

20 Ibid.

21 Ibid.

22 Ibid.

23 'Witness "knew Hookes was going to die"', *Sydney Morning Herald*, 31 August 2005.

24 Earle, Richard, 'Time doesn't dim the pain of losing best mate David Hookes for Darren Berry', *Daily Telegraph*, 18 January 2004, dailytelegraph.com.au/ time-doesnt-dim-the-pain-of-losing-best-mate-david- hookes-for-darren-berry/news-story/fc262064501cd1648 b9dbea7c6c0e43d, accessed 29 April 2021.

25 Blenkin, Max, 'Organ donation decision was tough, says David Hookes' widow', *Advertiser*, 22 May 2010, adelaidenow.com.au/news/south-australia/organ-donation- decision-was-tough-says-david-hookes-widow/news-story/ 5ea3416955fe8f06970aec6197d1f576, accessed 29 April 2021.

26 Ibid.

27 'Death of a sportsman', *The Age*, 13 September 2005.

28 'Barrage of hate: bouncer's home set alight', *Sydney Morning Herald*, 3 March 2004, smh.com.au/national/ barrage-of-hate-bouncers-home-set-alight-20040303- gdigqb.html, accessed 21 April 2021.

29 'Hookes threw punches at bouncer, says lawyer', *The Age*, 16 November 2004, theage.com.au/national/hookes-threw- punches-at-bouncer-says-lawyer-20041116-gdz04o.html, accessed 29 April 2021.

30 *Australian Story*, ABC, 'In the midnight hour', Season 10, Episode 14, aired 9 May 2005.

31 'Hookes "girlfriends" confess online', *The Age*, 12 May 2005, theage.com.au/national/hookes-girlfriends-confess- online-20050512-ge05bf.html, accessed 29 April 2021.

32 'Bouncer relieved after Hookes acquittal', *Sydney Morning Herald*, 13 September 2005, smh.com.au/national/

bouncer-relieved-after-hookes-acquittal-20050913-gdm1zz.
html, accessed 29 April 2021.

Chapter 4: Flood and flames

1   'Justice Lex Lasry's full sentencing remarks', *The Age*,
    15 October 2010, theage.com.au/national/victoria/justice-
    lex-lasrys-full-sentencing-remarks-20101015-16n8l.html,
    accessed 19 April 2021.
2   Moncrief, Mark, '"Worst day in history": Brumby warns
    of fire', *Sydney Morning Herald*, 6 February 2009, smh.
    com.au/national/worst-day-in-history-brumby-warns-of-
    fire-danger-20090206-7zf1.html, accessed 19 April 2021.
3   *Guardian* readers and Bannock, Caroline, 'Indian Ocean
    tsunami – readers' memories: "It was like being in a giant
    washing machine full of nails on a spin cycle"', *Guardian*,
    26 December 2014, theguardian.com/global-development/
    2014/dec/26/-sp-boxing-day-indian-ocean-tsunami-readers-
    memories, accessed 21 April 2021.
4   'The slow, cold taking of a wife's life', *The Age*, 12
    December 2004, theage.com.au/national/the-slow-cold-
    taking-of-a-wifes-life-20041212-gdz6fq.html, accessed 19
    April 2021.
5   Ibid.
6   Devic, Aleks, 'In 2004, James Ramage killed his wife –
    now he wants to change his name and begin life afresh',
    Herald Sun, 25 November 2012, heraldsun.com.au/news/
    victoria/in-2004-james-ramage-killed-his-wife--now-he-
    wants-to-change-his-name-and-begin-life-afresh/news-
    story/c955b5b7bbf27767e64e7b5d32edbf02, accessed
    19 April 2021.

Chapter 5: The amazing Maslins

1 'MH17 Tragedy – Seven Sunrise' via YouTube, posted 1 August 2014, accessed 7 June 2021.

2 'MH17 Victim's Body Crashed Through Roof in Ukraine Village', NBC News, 19 July 2014, nbcnews.com/storyline/ ukraine-plane-crash/mh17-victims-body-crashed-through-roof-ukraine-village-n159386, accessed 19 April 2021.

3 Johnston, Chris, 'Cameron tells Putin MH17 victims deserve proper funerals – as it happened', *Guardian*, 21 July 2014, theguardian.com/world/2014/jul/20/mh17-bodies-passengers-recovered-pressure-russia-live-updates, accessed 19 April 2021.

4 *Australian Story*, ABC, 'After the world ended', Season 24, Episode 16, aired 24 June 2019.

5 Morello, Carol, Faiola, Anthony and Birnbaum, Michael, 'MH17: Bodies missing on train carrying remains of victims, says Dutch official', *Sydney Morning Herald*, 23 July 2014, smh.com.au/world/mh17-bodies-missing-on-train-carrying-remains-of-victims-says-dutch-official-20140723-zvv7l.html, accessed 19 April 2021.

Chapter 6: Soren's special bones

1 'Australian Federal Police: Missing Persons', AFP Missing Persons, missingpersons.gov.au/about, accessed 19 April 2021.

2 Blau, Soren, Fondebrider, Luis and Saldanha, Gregorio, 2011, 'Working with families of the missing: a case study from East Timor' in Lauritsch K. and Kernjak F. (eds), *We need the truth: Enforced disappearances in Asia*, (Colonia Bran: Guatemala, Central America), pp. 136–44.

3   Ibid.

4   Murray, David, 'Forensic push to identify remains',
    Australian, 28 August 2020, theaustralian.com.au/science/
    forensic-push-to-identify-remains/news-story/13085a0d14a
    a9bf6c45e65bc0a7b228c, accessed 19 April 2021.

Chapter 7: Nicole Patterson

1   Main, Christian, *Rot In Hell: Peter Dupas: The
    Mutilating Monster*, Bas Publishing, Victoria, 2009,
    p. 13.

2   Wilkinson, Geoff and Butler, Mark, 'Vicious serial Peter
    Dupas is the beast who roamed free to rape and kill',
    Herald Sun, 21 December 2012, amp.heraldsun.com.au/
    news/law-order/vicious-serial-killer-peter-dupas-is-the-
    beast-who-roamed-free-to-rape-and-kill/news-story/014c7a
    49bf30d3f5c6faed428e9ab594, accessed 7 June 2021.

3   Ibid.

4   Ibid.

5   Silvester, John, 'Grave secrets', *The Age*, 19 November
    2005, theage.com.au/national/grave-secrets-20051119-
    ge19qz.html, accessed 29 April 2021.

6   *R v Peter Norris Dupas*, 28 June 1985, Appendix C,
    murderpedia.org/male.D/d/dupas-peter.htm

7   Bartholomew quoted here: murderpedia.org/male.
    D/d/dupas-peter.htm

8   Wilkinson and Butler, 'Vicious serial killer Peter Dupas is
    the beast who roamed free to rape and kill', *Herald Sun*.

9   Douglas, John E and Olshaker, Mark, *Mindhunter: Inside
    the FBI's Elite Serial Killer Crime Unit*, Scriber, New
    York, revised edition, 2017 p. 116.

10 *R v Dupas* [2000] VSC 356 (22 August 2000), www6.
    austlii.edu.au/cgi-bin/viewdoc/au/cases/vic/VSC/2000/356.
    html, accessed 20 April 2021.

11 *R v Dupas* [2004] VSC 281 (16 August 2004), www6.
    austlii.edu.au/cgi-bin/viewdoc/au/cases/vic/VSC/2004/281.
    html, accessed 20 April 2021.

12 Justice Cummins quoted in 'Mersina Halvagis: Serial killer
    Peter Dupas has inflicted misery on many', *Herald Sun*,
    31 October 2014, accessed 20 April 2021.

Chapter 8: No excuses

1   Zwartz, Matt, 'Working between the living and the dead',
    Metro magazine, 4 October 2017, metromag.co.nz/society/
    society-crime/working-between-the-living-and-the-dead,
    accessed 20 April 2021.

2   Ibid.

3   Palin, Megan, 'Eurydice's tragic family past', *Morning
    Bulletin*, 18 June 2018, themorningbulletin.com.au/news/
    eurydice-dixons-family-speaks-about-her-horrific-m/
    3443693/, accessed 20 April 2021.

4   Health Direct, 'Attention deficit hyperactivity disorder
    (ADHD)', healthdirect.gov.au/attention-deficit-disorder-
    add-or-adhd#:~:text=Around%201%20in%20every%20
    20,%2C%20words%2C%20actions%20and%20emotions,
    accessed 20 April 2021.

5   Autism Spectrum Australia, 'Fact sheet: Autism and
    ADHD', November 2017, autismspectrum.org.au/uploads/
    documents/Fact%20Sheets/Factsheet_Autism-and-
    ADHD_20171113.pdf, accessed 20 April 2021.

6 Zwartz, Matt, 'Working between the living and the dead', *Metro* magazine, 4 October 2017, metromag.co.nz/society/society-crime/working-between-the-living-and-the-dead, accessed 20 April 2021.

7 Ibid.

8 Pearson, Erin, 'Jaymes Todd sentenced to life in prison for rape, murder of Eurydice Dixon', *The Age*, 2 September 2019, theage.com.au/national/victoria/jaymes-todd-sentenced-to-life-in-prison-for-rape-murder-of-eurydice-dixon-20190902-p52mzk.html, accessed 21 April 2021.

9 Fox Koob, Simone, '"No inkling": Accused murderer Jaymes Todd's father speaks out', *The Age*, 15 June 2018, theage.com.au/national/victoria/no-inkling-accused-murderer-jaymes-todd-s-father-speaks-out-20180615-p4zlrp.html, accessed 21 April 2021.

10 *DPP v Herrmann* [2019] VSC 694 (29 October 2019).

11 Cooper, Adam, '"I didn't expect you to pick up": Court told of Aiia's final call', *The Age*, 1 October 2019, theage.com.au/national/victoria/i-didn-t-expect-you-to-pick-up-court-told-of-Aya-s-final-call-20191001-p52wj5.html, accessed 21 April 2021.

12 Australian Associated Press, 'Aiia Maasarwe's sister learned of Melbourne death on TV news in Israel', *Guardian*, 20 January 2021, theguardian.com/australia-news/2019/jan/20/aiia-maasarwes-sister-learned-of-death-in-melbourne-on-tv-news, accessed 21 April 2021.

13 Cunningham, Melissa and Cowie, Tom, '"I have many dreams to be with her but I cannot now": Father of Israeli student Aiia Maasarwe makes heartbreaking visit to the scene of her death', *The Age*, 18 January 2019,

theage.com.au/national/victoria/father-of-israeli-student-aiia-maasarwe-makes-heartbreaking-visit-to-the-scene-of-her-death-20190118-p50s8y.html, accessed 21 April 2021.

14 Ibid.

15 Scott Morrison quoted in 'Man charged with murder of student Aiia Maasarwe', *Australian*, 19 January 2019, theaustralian.com.au/news/man-charged-with-murder-of-student-aiia-maasarwe/news-story/5ced593caeaf82168694c65fd3fd335a, accessed 21 April 2021.

16 Cooper, Adam, 'Aiia's killer Codey Herrmann was angry at the world and wanted to kill, court told', *The Age*, 2 October 2019, theage.com.au/national/victoria/aiia-s-killer-codey-herrmann-was-angry-at-the-world-and-wanted-to-kill-court-told-20191002-p52x2v.html, accessed 21 April 2021.

Chapter 9: Natalie Russell's struggle

1 ABC Radio Melbourne, 'The unofficial history of the Frankston train line', Drive with Rafael Epstein, broadcast 28 April 2020, abc.net.au/radio/melbourne/programs/drive/the-unofficial-history-of-the-frankston-railway-line/12194982, accessed 7 June 2021.

2 Christian, Bret, *Stalking Claremont: Inside the hunt for a serial killer*, HarperCollins, Sydney, 2020, p. 5.

3 Minisini quoted in Munro, Ian, 'Denyer: The devil within', *Sunday Age*, 27 August 1994.

ACKNOWLEDGEMENTS

Thank you to Professor Stephen Cordner, Professor Noel Woodford, Professor Richard Bassed, Professor David Ranson, Professor Soren Blau, Dr Michael Burke, Dr Joanna Glengarry, Deb Withers, David Stevens, Rowland Legg, Jeff Maher, Ron Iddles, Charlie Bezzina, Marite Norris, Anthony Maslin, Violet Maslin, Miss Vick, Kylie Nicholas, Carmel Russell, Brian Russell, Tim Marsh, Vikki Petraitis, Emily Webb, Caili Christian, Jeremy Dixon, Maria Satzmary, Alison Urquhart, Genevieve Buzo, Jessica Malpass, Bella Arnott-Hoare, Suzanne Tonks, Danielle Tonks, Sam McCully and Zoe Lea.

Thank you, Louie and Dali.

Thank you, Matthew Hardy.

Discover a
new favourite

Visit **penguin.com.au/readmore**